The Headscarf Debates

The Headscarf Debates

Conflicts of National Belonging

Anna C. Korteweg and Gökçe Yurdakul

Stanford University Press

Stanford, California

Stanford University Press
Stanford, California

Printed in the United States of America on acid-free, archival-quality paper

Library of Congress Cataloging-in-Publication Data

Korteweg, Anna C., author.
  The headscarf debates : conflicts of national belonging / Anna C. Korteweg and Gökçe Yurdakul.
     pages cm
  Includes bibliographical references and index.
  ISBN 978-0-8047-7684-4 (cloth : alk. paper)—
  ISBN 978-0-8047-7685-1 (pbk. : alk. paper)
  1. Hijab (Islamic clothing)—Political aspects—Cross-cultural studies.
  2. Muslim women—Clothing—Political aspects—Cross-cultural studies.
  3. Citizenship—Cross-cultural studies. 4. National characteristics—Political aspects—Cross-cultural studies. I. Yurdakul, Gökçe, author. II. Title.
  BP190.5.H44K67 2014
  391.4'3082091767—dc23
                                                    2013047794

ISBN 978-0-8047-9116-8 (electronic)

Typeset by Bruce Lundquist in 11/13.5 Adobe Garamond

In memory of Nükhet Yurdakul and Nina Chaya Davis

Table of Contents

Acknowledgments

THE IDEA FOR THIS BOOK came out of a long-term coauthorship that has resulted in a number of writing projects on Muslim women's problems in Western Europe and North America. We first met in 2004 and immediately felt a kinship in how we understood citizenship, belonging, and participation from an intersectional gender perspective, even though at the time we were engaged in quite different research projects.

This initial meeting led to our long-term, very productive collaboration. Although many writers choose to work in isolation, we have been collaborating across the ocean since 2004, through e-mail, Skype, and occasional meetings in Berlin, Toronto, Montreal, Copenhagen, Boston, Amsterdam, and New York City, or other places we found ourselves as we participated in the travel circuit of academic production.

Our fascination with how Muslim women are challenging and reconstructing national belonging in Western European politics became the starting point for this book. In deconstructing Western and Muslim notions of womanhood, religions, cultures, and nations while being challenged in our understandings of feminism, we found ourselves working out a puzzle. This book is not only about headscarves and national belonging; it is also about understanding the politics of womanhood across nations, through the lens of Muslim women's political and social involvements. Finally, it captures our process, as minority women in Western countries, of redefining our understanding of our own belonging.

This book represents a large multilanguage and multination project, and we could not have done the work without the support of research assistants in four countries. Inder Marwah, Lars Nickolson, Paulina Garcia del Moral, Özlem Kaya, Selin Çağatay, Natalie Lohmann, Soraya Hassoun, Salina Abji, Bingül Durbaş, Angelica Rao, Agata Piękosz, and Emily Laxer helped us to collect data and formed databases for us. They also assisted in the initial analysis of the data, and Salina Abji and Emily Laxer proofread the final manuscript while Inna Michaeli and Janna Frenzel helped to prepare the bibliography. We are grateful to them for their multilanguage skills, hard work, and dedication to this project.

Our colleagues and friends—Esra Özyürek, Marc Baer, Ahmet Yükleyen, Naika Foroutan, Riem Spielhaus, Birgit zur Nieden, Pascale Fournier, Valérie Amiraux, Klaus Eder, Julia von Blumenthal, Liza Mügge, Peter O'Brien, Dilek Kurban, Ruud Koopmans, Bilgin Ayata, Serhat Karakayalı, Juliane Karakayalı, Gökhan Tuncer, Dilek Cindoğlu, Ruth Mandel, May Friedman, Phil Triandafilopoulous, Audrey Macklin, Randall Hansen, Paula Maurutto, Kelly Hannah-Moffat, Erik Schneiderhan, Hae Yeon Choo, Myra Marx Ferree, and Jennifer Selby—as well as students at the Humboldt University of Berlin and at the University of Toronto gave us important insights during our discussions. Anna particularly thanks her graduate students for reading and providing feedback on an early draft of the book.

Together we presented some parts of this book in 2011 at the Association for the Study of Nationalities conference in New York and at the Social Science History Association conference in Boston. Gökçe presented the chapter on Germany at the Islamic Feminists, Islamist Women, and the Women Between workshop at Columbia University's Global Center at Reid Hall in Paris in 2013. She is grateful for the feedback from Nilüfer Göle, Lila Abu-Lughod, and Katherine Ewing, and to workshop participants for their comments.

In spring 2013, Anna presented parts of the work at the Wissenschaftszentrum Berlin, at the Memorial University of Newfoundland in St. John's, and at the Center for German and European Studies and the Department of Sociology at the University of Wisconsin. In addition, she presented at a workshop entitled 'Illegal' Covering: Comparative Perspectives on Legal and Social Discourses on Religious Diversity, held at the International Institute for the Sociology of Law in Oñati, Spain in 2012; and at the European Union Centre of Excellence Vth Annual Secondary School Students' Workshop, at the Munk School of Global Affairs in Toronto in 2011. She is grateful for feedback from Valérie Amiraux and Pascale Fournier, Jennifer Selby, Dagmar Soennecken, Myra Marx Ferree, Ruud Koopmans, and all those who attended the talks and workshops.

The Social Sciences and Humanities Research Council in Canada and the Humboldt University of Berlin's Gender Equality Fund provided research grants to carry out the data collection. We thank both institutions for their generous funding.

We are also particularly grateful to our editor, Kate Wahl, at the Stanford University Press for taking us through the journey of writing and publishing this book.

Last but not least, we are grateful to our families. Gökçe thanks Eda and Oğuz for inspiring political conversations on Turkey, Hartmut for lively discussions on understanding German history and politics, Michal for scholarly and personal encouragement, Daphne Yudit and Tibet for asking simple but illuminating questions on the most critical topics. Anna thanks Jim for his incredible support, her children Michal and Ruben for being ongoing inspirations, her sister Carine for hosting her during fieldwork in the Netherlands, and her adopted family—May, Dan, Noah, Molly, and Isaac—for being there. Finally, we thank each other for committing to this academic partnership.

The Headscarf Debates

1

Feeling at Home in the Nation

THE MUSLIM WOMAN'S HEADSCARF seems to attract an unusually large set of interpretations in political debates. *Kopftuch, foulard, voile, başörtüsü, türban, hoofddoek, burka, niqab, hijab*[1]—rather than simply being innocuous pieces of cloth used to cover hair, neck, face, and eyes, headscarves have become a foil for a long series of debates on the conditions under which religiously identified Muslims belong in public spheres marked by secularity or Western political traditions. Debates on *where* and on *what occasions* headscarves can be worn—in schools, hospitals, and private enterprises, only at home, or on the way to but not at work—turn into conflicts, sometimes heated, about where Muslims can show their religiosity. Debates regarding *how* headscarves should be worn—tied behind the neck, showing an earlobe, obscuring all hair, falling over the shoulders, covering the face—segue into discussions of what headscarves represent politically. Do they represent fundamentalist Islam? A threat to nationhood? Or a claim to a new ethnoreligious identity that deserves recognition, perhaps even the acceptance of belonging? Finally, discussions regarding the person *underneath* the scarf show that the subjects of national belonging can be defined in multiple and conflicting ways: are "they" Muslims, Islamists, immigrants, converts, fundamentalists, French, Turks, Dutch, or Germans?

Discussions of the headscarf's meaning and representations can also turn into pronouncements on the need for greater regulation: How should the state and others respond to women wearing headscarves in public institutions? Should "we" ban them everywhere, ban them in certain institutions, protect the wearing of the headscarf entirely, or protect it only if worn in certain ways or capacities? These questions focus on the role of the state in regulating whether Muslims can belong to the nation.

Political debates about the headscarf illustrate how the headscarf has become a symbol of the diversity resulting from large-scale, post–World War II migration into European countries and, in the case of Turkey, from rural-to-urban migration in a secular Muslim-majority country. In both popular and scholarly analyses of European countries, the headscarf has come to signify an immigration-related decline of the coherent nation-state, a decline that is either embraced as bringing a desirable cosmopolitan order one step closer, or seen as a threat to the very coherence of society. In many Muslim-majority countries, the headscarf has turned into a metonym for issues associated with the participation of religious Muslims in the public sphere.[2] This can be seen in cases where the headscarf becomes symbolic of a "dangerous yearning" for a political order in which religious authority supersedes the authority of the secular nation-state of the postcolonial era.

In this book, we analyze the struggles over the inclusions and exclusions of national belonging by looking at "national narratives," the public discourses that define what it means to belong to a geographic community governed by a particular nation-state.[3] We focus our analysis on four countries—France, Turkey, the Netherlands, and Germany—and join a group of scholars who have studied the headscarf, including the hijab, and burka, and niqab, through the lens of national belonging. We add to the work of those, such as John Bowen and Joan Scott,[4] who have written what many consider the definitive books analyzing the French headscarf debates but who do not move beyond France to see how these conflicts play out in other countries' settings.[5] Here we follow in the footsteps of Christian Joppke's comparative analysis of headscarf debates in France, Germany, and Britain.[6] However, whereas Joppke focuses on the ways in which the headscarf is perceived as a threat to liberalism across these sites, we analyze the headscarf debates as productive of the particularities of national belonging, applying a critical feminist, intersectional, postcolonial lens to this project.[7] This feminist starting point is in line with that of Sieglinde Rosenberger and Birgit Sauer, who produced an edited volume that covers the headscarf debates in multiple European countries.[8] However, we generate a discursive analysis of the way in which national narratives are produced that is much more in-depth than is allowed for in their emphasis on explaining policy change. We also move beyond their focus on Western Europe to add to our cases Turkey, a Muslim-majority liberal democratic country, in order to challenge the assumption that these are solely "Western" debates.[9]

When it comes to national belonging, for many of these scholars, but also for actors engaged in the media and politics, the headscarf symbolizes a rupture. Their analyses combine attempts to understand why, where, and how Muslim women wear their headscarves, including examination of formal political-legal regulation, in order to outline how the headscarf has inspired exclusionary practices in a given country or countries. In this book, we shift the angle of vision away from the rupture in national belonging and turn instead toward the opportunities that headscarf debates provide to revisit, reaffirm, and potentially rearticulate the meaning of national belonging. In other words, we treat the headscarf debates not (solely) as disruption but also as opportunities for articulating the national narratives that delineate belonging in the contemporary era.

National Narratives and Conflicts of Belonging

This book, then, looks at the production of narratives of national belonging, wherein we define *belonging* as the subjective feeling of being at home in one's country, of easily moving through its particular places and spaces, and the sense of comfort and joy in inhabiting a particular locale.[10] Belonging, in this sense, also means being able to articulate complaint without renouncing the claim to belonging, or the freedom to complain about aspects of living somewhere without being told that you should leave, of not being trapped in a distinction between those whose home is unambiguously "here" and those who are seen as having either a primary or secondary home elsewhere. Belonging, thus conceived, is simultaneously highly personal and utterly political.

National belonging is fundamentally about demarcating difference. Indeed, analytically speaking, national belonging is always relational, constituted by creating a boundary between who is in and who is out.[11] As Benedict Anderson and other researchers have shown, the very idea of nationhood is produced in the tension between the imagined homogeneity of the nation and the realities of difference in the populations constituting the nation.[12] Difference is thus a challenge to national belonging with the potential of inspiring a fear that national belonging can fracture. At the same time, difference is central to the constitution of national belonging—because national belonging is always constituted *vis-à-vis* what or who we are not. We label contestations about the limits of acceptable difference *conflicts of belonging* and argue that they become sites in which to confront national identities by (re)enacting or (re)defining them.

The differences through which national belonging is articulated change over time, and national belonging needs to be read in its specific historical contexts.[13] In the European case, the post-World War II influx of migrants in the aftermath of the Holocaust generated conflicts of belonging that continue to haunt the national imagination across Europe's countries. The popular story about postwar migration to Europe portrays various European nations as homogeneous prior to the shock of large-scale immigrant presence. The literature easily debunks this—each European nation-state is itself marked historically by distinctions of ethnicity, class, and religion that continue to shape these nations.[14] However, the way the image of homogeneity can be constituted through its contrast with "immigrant difference" illustrates the power of immigrant presence in constructing national belonging as rooted in homogeneity. At the same time, the reality of historical difference within these nations suggests that national belonging does not by definition exclude newcomers to the nation. Rather, national belonging is constituted through the very process of figuring out what can and cannot be accommodated.

National narratives turn the real heterogeneities that mark populations into imagined homogeneity, through appellations to a common language, religion, shared history, shared political practice, and sense of shared origin. In addition, national narratives demarcate the bases of belonging to the nation through social divisions of race, ethnicity, gender, and religion.[15] Building on an ideal-typical approach to national narratives, we argue that they are "discursive formations," constructed ways of speaking that identify the contours of national belonging.[16] Such discourses have "real" effects because they shape practices—including practices of regulation.

National narratives are by definition messy—they contain contradictory discourses regarding who belongs and who does not—but their messiness is productive, generating a sense of national belonging through the tensions and contradictions contained within these narratives. When we analyze national narratives, we see that key elements repeat over decades, even centuries, exactly because they are contested rather than agreed upon. These elements of national narratives identify the social norms, values, and practices that are seen as most in need of being defended or changed in defining belonging to the nation. Overarching concepts such as republicanism, secularism, and tolerance often become the labels for such norms, values and practices. However, these key elements in a country's national narrative are by definition not stable, but the contestations over the meaning and practices they label give them longevity and structuring force. At the same time, contestations over national belonging also enable new elements, such as gender equality, to become central in national narratives of belonging.

As we analyze the key elements in national narratives, we build on approaches to discourse and sense-making practices that are closely attuned to the multiplicity of meanings that can attach to objects, ideas, and practices. However, we approach national narratives as largely singular. In other words, our starting assumption is that each nation has a national narrative—a story told about what it means to belong to that nation. Yet these national narratives are uniform neither in time nor in content. The multiplicity enters in how the narrative elements that make up the story are interpreted and strung together. These elements reference beliefs, ideas, and practices, ranging, for example, from adherence to liberal democracy and gender equality to everyday practices of eating particular foods or separating trash for recycling. These beliefs, ideas, and practices that together form a national narrative are embedded in the everyday lives of people. In this sense, Ernst Renan's statement almost a century and a half ago that the existence of a nation is based on this "daily plebiscite" continues to hold.[17]

Approached in this way, national narratives are anchored in the development of nation-states, and it might seem that such narratives will become less and less salient in our increasingly trans- and postnational world.[18] The ever-expanding reach of the European Union, in particular, would suggest a decline in the significance of the national in structuring people's experiences of belonging. Indeed, when it comes to supra- or international processes, headscarf debates show that cross-national appeals to similar concepts come into play, which some would see as confirmation of the decline of national significance. However, we show that seemingly transnational concepts are given different meanings and are mobilized toward achieving different goals in the countries under study and, as a result, these concepts have particular meanings in different national contexts.[19] Similarly, we witness how political debates in one country are reported in other countries, and how these discourses cross national public spheres. Yet, as the Dutch, Germans, and Turks discuss the French headscarf ban, they quickly turn to their "own" way of approaching this issue, again reaffirming their distinct sense of national belonging as they confront apparently transnational processes.

Moving down the spatial scale, evidence suggests that immigrant youth, in particular, frame their belonging in terms of the city, even a certain district of a city, rather than the country they live in, in order to challenge the negative connotations of national belonging.[20] This is especially prevalent in Germany, where the Nazi past, not shared by those who came to the country after 1945, is often used as a historical reference point to discuss Germanness.[21] However, we suggest that although these historical, trans-, and postnational processes are certainly in play, they do not or cannot replace the salience of national belonging altogether, as this example from our German case also suggests.

The discourses that form the resulting national narratives circulate through the media, government reports, and other sites of public debate such as the Internet, with its homemade video clips and blogs. Writing about the formation of nation-states, Anderson argues that the shared images underlying national identity are fostered, in part, through newspapers, which generate common narratives that frame definitions of national identity.[22] Newspaper consumption reinforces the territorial and linguistic unity of the nation, creating "a sense that the nation or national society has an ongoing existence" and that "nationhood is constituted over time."[23] The media both reflect and shape the discourses that constitute national narratives. As news media speak of the politics of wearing the headscarf, discussing, for example, its presence in key sites of national identity formation such as schools and state bureaucracies, headscarf debates become objects through which to analyze contemporary constructions of national belonging.[24]

Government documents and social media are sites with different roles in the discursive production of national narratives. Government reports on the headscarf, including transcripts of parliamentary debates, social policies, and laws and regulations, delineate national belonging by referring to "shared values and practices" as they shape formal regulations that govern acceptable conduct in the context of the nation-state.[25] Also, states clearly play a particular role in the formation of national narratives, with actors in public functions drawing on and developing national narratives to further their political and policy agendas or to strengthen state legitimacy, insofar as it is seen as dependent on the coherence of the idea of "the" nation. Whereas government documents tend to focus inward on the nation-state, social media can establish national orders but also transcend national boundaries to reach a global audience and potentially resist authority by being uncensored and fast developing. In so doing, such social media can create their own interpretations of national narratives even as they might shift the locus of belonging.

Studies of national identity formation also illustrate the ways in which "regular" people discuss national belonging.[26] This literature alerts us to the ways in which national narratives live not only within the news media and formal politics but also in everyday interactions. To capture some of this, we turn to targeted interviews with Muslim women who are politically active in the headscarf debate. Some of these women, by virtue of both their minority identities and their political activism, speak through the media, but only a few can be seen as key players in these public debates. In much of the public debate, newsmakers give a platform to Muslim women who can act as code breakers for their own religious communities.[27] These women often speak with a voice of experience to reinforce stereotypical portrayals of their communities and to affirm exclusionary interpretations of key elements in national narratives.

People who dominate the media and political discourses reaffirm, rearticulate, or transform these beliefs, ideas, and practices, often in contestation with other political actors who occupy similar political, social, and cultural positions. Those who become the object of these articulations—in our case, headscarf-wearing women—often articulate their own versions of the national narrative, in terms of how they belong or do not belong. In our analysis, we focus on those elements (regardless of whether they describe values, ideas, or practices) of the national narrative that come up in headscarf debates and on how these elements are used to articulate national belonging.

The Headscarf as Symbol and Enactment: Intents and Perceptions

Throughout our analysis, we pay attention to two positions from which the headscarf can be discussed—that of the wearer and that of the nonwearer. In addition, former wearers of the headscarf often occupy a special place in debates about the headscarf. For wearers, the headscarf can have a range of meanings beyond the obviously religious (though itself complex) meaning. These meanings include the headscarf as a symbol of multiple modernities,[28] a marker of ethnic identity,[29] a way of claiming dignity that is denied to an immigrant group,[30] and an enactment of the promise of liberal self-expression,[31] as well as a way to cover up one's messy hair.[32] The voices of wearers describe the experience of wearing the headscarf, the reasons why they wear it,[33] and the effects that wearing it has on their lives, often claiming that they face discrimination in the labor market and on the streets.[34] Most work on the experiences of headscarf-wearing women in the West focuses on covering hair; very little focuses on the experiences of women who wear a niqab, which covers the face and hair but leaves the eyes visible. The burka, a garment that covers the entire face, with the eyes covered by mesh fabric, is almost never worn by European Muslims; rather, it is traditionally worn in Afghanistan. Still, many newsmakers report on burka debates in Europe when they are actually referring to the niqab. The few reports on women who cover their faces suggest that they have experienced increased hostility on the street as "burka bans" have gained political and popular support.[35] The notion that the burka stands for submission is especially strong even though many women who have recounted their reasons for wearing it claim that it is a freely chosen expression of their religiosity.

For nonwearers, discussions focus on how they perceive the headscarf both objectively and subjectively.[36] In public discourses, nonwearers who speak out against the headscarf imagine it to signify a long list of rejections, including the rejection of liberal democratic values, of gender equality, and of secularism. In their accounts, the headscarf comes to stand for the embrace of Islamic political rule and the submission of women's bodies to God and men. Muslim women who do not wear the headscarf, including those who used to wear the headscarf but took it off, can play a particular role in these accounts; they are seen to speak as liberated women who can recount the "true" meaning of the headscarf to a public hungry for accounts of Muslim women's experiences of the veil.

Those who see the headscarf—including not only the hijab but also the niqab and burka—in a negative light often discuss a highly personal sense of being judged by headscarf-wearing women. On a Dutch blog, one commenter argued that having to buy alcohol from a cashier with a headscarf made him feel judged for his alcohol consumption. Indeed, Dutch anthropologist Annelies Moors has analyzed how Dutch debates on possible burka bans reflect a strong sense of discomfort and even dislike for a garment that appears to stand for a rejection of all things Dutch. She argues that a similar politics of discomfort permeates burka ban debates in the Netherlands and elsewhere.[37]

On the other end of the spectrum, both wearers and nonwearers sup-
portive of women's right to wear a headscarf argue that they are proud to
live in a country, city, or neighborhood that can incorporate this kind of
diversity. Popular media further normalize the headscarf as they discuss the
latest trends in headscarf fashion by referring to competing headscarf looks
that appeal to different budgets, from very expensive to very modest styles,
brands, and fabrics. Such media, arguably, reflect an almost glib support
for multiculturalism, emphasizing the importance of laissez-faire in liberal
democracies and happily supporting the headscarf because it adds color to
"our" drab European streets. Such understandings of diversity try to put
the fact of multiculturalism or the presence of those who are visibly from
minority groups in a positive light. Yet they do not necessarily articulate
the degree to which such diversity should lead to a multicultural politics
in which belonging becomes reflected in the development of group rights.

In countries such as Turkey, where the headscarf is not about cultural but about religious diversity, the presence of headscarves in the public
sphere is taken by some as evidence of "true" democratic freedom, and the
rise of an Islamic bourgeoisie. This group is the target audience of high-
quality Islamic "lifestyle magazines" (*yaşam tarzı dergisi*) such as *Âlâ* (a
variation on the name of the French magazine *Elle*[38]), which discusses the
recent trends in Islamic fashion, including expensive designer headscarves
created in the style of well-known fashion designers such as Vakko and
Pierre Cardin.

The headscarf's multiplicity in meaning coincides to some degree
with a variation in terminology. In our own discussions, we use *headscarf*,
the most neutral term we can find.[39] This is also the term used most often
in the Netherlands (*hoofddoek*) and Germany (*Kopftuch*). In both countries, however, the word *veil* (*sluier* in Dutch, *Schleier* in German), with
its connotations of hiding oneself, comes up as well, and we note this
and analyze the politics surrounding the term. In France, the terminology has shifted over time and between speakers, from the more neutral
foulard (headscarf) to the more loaded *voile* (veil), which we indicate in
our analysis.[40] In Turkey, we use *headscarf* as a translation for *başörtüsü*,
the neutral Turkish word for head covering, but when applicable we also
use *türban*, which politicians use to signify what they see as the politicized
wearing of the headscarf. In both France and the Netherlands, the headscarf and niqab are often debated separately, with the term *burka* often
used to label the niqab, which women actually wear.

Agency and freedom are recurring concepts in all discussions of naming and wearing the headscarf, both within and outside academia. In 1992, Arlene MacLeod analyzed Egyptian women's newly refound practice of wearing the headscarf. She argued that these women were not responding to gendered pressures to submit to modesty but rather were actively choosing to wear the headscarf, in order to make both religious and political statements against a secular, highly corrupt political regime.[41] Attempting to escape the binary of individual resistance and submission, Saba Mahmood argued that the practices of pious Egyptian women need to be understood according to an expanded definition of *agency* as expressed directly in submission rather than always being tied to individual resistance.[42] Such an understanding of agency can also be applied to practices of Turkish and European Muslim women.

In short, the objective meaning of the term *headscarf* is difficult to pin down. Not only does it have multiple signifiers, but also the signified meaning changes according to the country's political context, the actors who are using the term, and the discursive context within which the term is used. Thus, the headscarf brings together a range of discourses. At the same time, the headscarf breaks apart these unifying discourses to reflect multiple differences that inform the ongoing formation of national narratives in each country. Thus, the meaning of the headscarf constantly evolves, and its use in political debates introduces new conflicts of belonging to the nation.

Analyzing Headscarf Debates as Conflicts over Belonging

We analyze how national narratives are reaffirmed, rearticulated, or transformed when confronted with the headscarf as a visible representation of difference associated with Islam and migration. We have chosen to focus on France, Turkey, the Netherlands, and Germany, because they form two paired comparisons that allow us to take into account the forces that might impact national narratives of belonging. France and Turkey adhere to a strict form of secularism that renders religious practice largely a private affair. The Netherlands and Germany share an approach to religiosity in which state neutrality in religion means accommodation for religious behavior in the public sphere. These different approaches to religion offer a starting point from which to analyze differences and similarities in articulations of national belonging during headscarf debates.

In both France and Turkey, belonging to the nation has been predicated on being secular. France, a civic republican country where a strict form of secularism has historically inhibited personal expressions of religion in the public sphere, is similar to Turkey, which has also rooted its democracy in a strict form of secularism. And even though Muslims are seen as newcomers in France and the historical majority in the Turkish context, in both countries, perceptions of Muslims' religiosity has positioned them as problematic citizens. As we show, in France, Muslims are constructed as former colonials and current immigrants; they represent outsiders to the nation. In Turkey, where Islam is the majority religion, religious Turkish citizens have been constructed as outsiders to the Turkish nation since the foundation of the Turkish Republic. However, in recent years France and Turkey have diverged sharply. Whereas France has retained its commitment to secularism, in Turkey, religious Muslims have recently refound a powerful place in the public sphere, with the ascent to power of an Islamic political party, the Ak Party (*Adalet ve Kalkınma Partisi,* Justice and Development Party). This ascent has meant a divergence in the meaning and impact of secularism in relation to belonging.[43] In France, a law passed in 2004 prevents Muslim girls from wearing a headscarf to school, and a 2010 ban forbids all women to wear an Islamic face covering in public. By contrast, in contemporary Turkey, many women, regardless of the length and style of their coverings, are now allowed full access to the higher education institutions that formerly denied them entry. In September 2013, the Turkish government lifted the headscarf ban in all public places where the secular state is present.

Although much of the literature on headscarf debates focuses on France and Turkey as paradigmatic cases, we turn to a second paired comparison: the Netherlands and Germany. These two countries have historically allowed greater space for religious expression in the public sphere than either France or, until recently, Turkey. Both of these countries adhere to the principle of state neutrality in the expression of religion and tend to be more open than either France or Turkey have been to creating space for expressions of religiosity, including headscarves, in the public sphere.[44] Nonetheless, the Netherlands and Germany have differed in their general approaches to national belonging, with the Dutch practicing religious tolerance and pluralism over the centuries and the Germans hewing to ethnocultural understandings of nationhood since the establishment of the modern German state in 1871.[45] When it comes to Muslim immigrants, until the late 1990s the Netherlands represented pluralism and multiculturalism in the liberal democratic context. In Germany, by contrast, denial of the fact of immigration by the long-serving conservative governments of Konrad Adenauer (1949–1963) and Helmut Kohl (1982–1998)—expressed in the term *guest worker*—left only complete assimilation as a way for immigrants to belong to the nation until the beginning of this millennium.[46] The lengthy colonial history of the Dutch and the almost complete lack of a similar experience in Germany[47] is another important factor influencing the differences between the national narratives of belonging in these two countries.

Debates over the headscarf and burka have upset national narratives of belonging in both countries. In the Netherlands, politicians' repeated attempts to ban the burka from the public sphere, starting in 2005 and continuing to the present, illustrate that tolerance, multiculturalism, and pluralism have all come under pressure. Even though these attempted bans have largely failed, the conflicts generated by both head and face coverings have activated debates over national belonging. In a similarly heated debate, in Germany, a 2004 Supreme Court decision that ultimately led to a ban on the wearing of headscarves by public school teachers cemented the headscarf's position as a foil for public debate on the parameters of national belonging.

The differences between the ways in which these four countries institutionalize secularism and protect religious freedoms also suggests a gradient in the degree of the state's role in producing national narratives. The Turkish state has been particularly powerful in this domain, followed by France and then Germany and the Netherlands, with, as our analysis suggests, the latter three having progressively stronger civil society engagement when it comes to articulating national narratives. In Turkey, however, civil society has been powerfully controlled by political parties and further curbed by three military coups and one political coup in the post–World War II era. Most recently, the Ak Party government, which took power in 2002, pressed charges against many civil society actors, including academics and journalists, some of whom were subsequently sentenced and put in jail. The street protests of 2013 show that there is strong public opposition to Prime Minister Recep Tayyip Erdoğan's policies.

In analyzing the discourses that constitute national narratives, we show that actors in each country enter into conflicts over national belonging as they debate the headscarf and burka, but they activate and reenact quite different understandings of national belonging. We do not separate the actors who propagate these understandings into "Muslims" and "others." Instead, we show how both Muslim and non-Muslim politicians, government officials, and activists creatively draw from existing discourses to reaffirm, rearticulate, or transform national narratives, noting how such narratives vary by country in their degree of uniformity. This approach does not mean that being a Muslim does not matter. Rather, it shows *when* it matters, noting when actors position themselves explicitly as Muslims, acting as cultural code breakers for their own communities, translating Islamic practices for the general population in ways that validate the generalized fear of Islam and the superiority of Western constructions of interaction in the public sphere. Alternatively, Muslim-identified actors can reinforce those elements of national narratives that support accommodating or tolerating religious practices.

Although our analysis focuses largely on dominant discourses, and on people in clear positions of power, we argue, following Ruth Wodak and her collaborators, that opportunities for change often come from imaging nationhood in radically different ways.[48] When, in 1989, three French teenagers showed up wearing headscarves at their high school located in a Parisian *banlieu* (suburbs frequently referred to as ghettos because of social (public) housing and low-income residents), they probably did not realize that their actions started a fifteen-year debate that ended in the banning of headscarves from French elementary and high schools.[49] Leyla Şahin might not have imagined that her attempt to obtain a Turkish university education would result in a negative verdict by the European Court of Human Rights that reinvigorated Turkish debates on the place of secularism in the public sphere.[50] In the Netherlands, politically successful ultraright politician Geert Wilders' claims that the "headrag" should be taxed were countered by young Muslim women who created a poster campaign that showed "Real Dutch" women in Islamic dress.[51] In Germany, social-democratic politician Thilo Sarrazin's derogatory statements regarding *Kopftuchmädchen* (headscarf girls) whose children "overpopulated" formerly "German" neighborhoods led to rounds of national self-reflection on the acceptability of ethnoreligious difference in German society.[52] In the pages that follow, we show how such seemingly individual statements and actions have reverberated through national debates in ways that have enabled vigorous rearticulations of the meanings and conflicts of national belonging.

2

Rejecting the Headscarf in France

IN APRIL 2003, in his role as France's Minister of the Interior, Nicolas Sarkozy addressed the annual general meeting of the *Union des organizations islamiques de France* (Union of Islamic Organizations of France, henceforth UOIF). In his speech, he asserted that all women must remove their veils when photographed for national identity cards in accordance with existing French law. At the same time, Sarkozy stated that he was against banning religious symbols from the public sphere, including schools, for fear of stigmatizing Muslims. His comments reignited a simmering public debate about wearing headscarves in public schools, which led then-President Jacques Chirac to appoint Bernard Stasi, France's ombudsman, to head a commission of inquiry into the principle of secularism in the public sphere. Prior to issuing the final report, Stasi publicly stated that "the veil is an objective sign of women's alienation."[1] It was not surprising, then, that the Stasi Commission unanimously proposed a law banning religious symbols in public schools. On March 15, 2004, the law was passed and "the wearing of signs or clothes through which pupils ostensibly express a religious allegiance" was prohibited in public schools.[2]

For teenage sisters Alma and Lila Lévy, the 2004 ban marked the end of a lengthy fight to be allowed to wear headscarves to school in their low-income Paris suburb. To their nonreligious mother's surprise, the sisters had gradually adopted the faith she had grown up with in Algeria, even donning the headscarf as part of their newfound religious conviction. In September 2003 they started the school year wearing their headscarves to class. By midmorning the principal called both girls into her office to tell them they must take off their headscarves or go home. The girls knew from their father, an atheist Jew who worked as a lawyer for a human rights organization, that they had a right to education and they tried to argue but the principal did not give in. Alma and Lila were left with only one option: to go home. The next few months were a whirlwind of activity. The girls were expelled for wearing their headscarves; they fought the case, and spent a lot of time talking to the press, and even wrote a book about their experiences. But the sisters lost their battle when the official ban of religious garments in public schools took effect. This ban led to a brief burst of public protest during the spring and summer of 2004, but the issue largely disappeared from public view and many continue to consider the ban a success, in part because of the lack of opposition from French Muslims, 42 percent of whom agreed that the law was a good idea.[3]

Then, in June 2009, seemingly out of the blue, the burka came under fire when fifty-eight deputies in the National Assembly signed "communist MP André Gerin's (Rhône) proposal to create 'a commission of inquiry examining the burka and niqab on the national territory.'"[4] In his proposal, Gerin asserted that the burka "no longer merely concerns ostentatious religious symbols, but strikes at women's freedom and at the affirmation of femininity. Covered by the burka or niqab, a woman lives in an unbearable situation of reclusion, exclusion and humiliation. Her very existence is denied."[5] Nicolas Sarkozy, who was now France's president, accepted Gerin's proposal to initiate a commission to study the issue. Unlike in the earlier headscarf debates, the commission did not question whether the burka and niqab should be curtailed in public space; rather, it debated the extent of a ban. A year later, Sarkozy put a draft bill to parliament. The bill stated that "no one can, in the public space, wear clothing intended to hide the face" and defined "'public space' broadly, including streets, markets, and private businesses, as well as government buildings and public transportation."[6] The punishment for wearing a full-face covering was a fine of 150 euros or being required to take a citizenship course, or both. Those who forced others to wear the covering would be charged a much larger fine of 15,000 euros and possibly serve a jail term. Although the bill pertains to all "face coverings" and is overtly neutral with respect to religion, the colloquial appellation "burka ban" accurately captures the goal of the law: to eliminate Islamic face coverings from French streets. The French National Assembly passed the bill on July 13, 2010, with only one dissenter. The Senate passed it on September 14, 2010, with a vote of 246 to 1 and about 100 politicians abstaining, not necessarily because they accepted the burka and niqab but because they felt the bill went too far by banning face coverings completely rather than from specific government spaces. The French Constitutional Council (*Conseil constitutionnel*) declared the bill constitutional and it took effect on April 11, 2011.[7]

Although wearing a burka or niqab by no means represented the everyday practices of all French Muslims,[8] both garments came to signify a general threat to the principles of republicanism, *laïcité* (often translated as "secularism"), and gender equality, which are key concepts in the French national narrative. France's history of republicanism links being French with full and equal participation in the public sphere on the basis of shared values and allegiances to the larger whole, and makes no room for claims based on subnational group identification. Laïcité signifies not simply the separation of church and state, but also the right to be free from religious dogma and the right to obtain institutional support for individual religious practices. In the context of the French national narrative, gender equality refers to the equal participation of the sexes in the public sphere. In recent decades, gender equality has become a prerequisite for republicanism and is supported by it, while laïcité prevents institutional support for religiously informed gender oppression.[9] Any difference that leads to communalist, or group-based, demands threatens these key concepts in the French national narrative. The headscarf was not a stand-alone symbol of difference but served as a visible sign of the Islam that had entered French territory through immigration and, it was feared, could become a rallying point for Muslim communalist demands.

French Muslims are both a homogeneous and a diverse group whose status as members of the French nation is tenuous in a number of ways. Almost all of France's four to five million Muslims (of a total French population of almost 63 million) originated in France's former colonies: approximately 70 percent have Moroccan, Tunisian, or Algerian heritage.[10] At the beginning of the twenty-first century, approximately half of all Muslims residing in France were French citizens. Yet, from the late 1980s onward, Muslims have been portrayed in popular discussions as "immigrants."[11] The continuing use of this term to describe the Muslim population reveals the precariousness of their belonging to the French nation.[12] French Muslims' relatively weaker attachment to the labor market and their more limited access to the world of politics compared with those who are not Muslim or immigrant reinforces their outsider status.

From a North American perspective, French Muslims appear to be partially integrated into the French economy and society. Yet many have become part of the lower socioeconomic strata of society.[13] Their experiences are similar to those recounted by immigration scholars studying second-generation immigrants and segmented assimilation in the United States.[14] These scholars argue that the socioeconomic problems of immigrants are not the result of their inability to integrate into the receiving society. Rather, when they lack the networks to connect them to the labor market, immigrants tend to integrate into the lowest socioeconomic classes, living in ghettoized neighborhoods and attending inferior schools. In France, the children of immigrants from former colonies speak French and are educated in France; this does not, however, generally translate into socioeconomic mobility or achievement of a middle-class lifestyle. French commentators and social scientists do not use the language of segmented assimilation, though many agree that poverty, underemployment, and the bleak prospects associated with living in the *banlieues* (the term for French suburban ghettos) are the real problems facing immigrants and their children.[15] However, when newspapers focused on class during the debates, they did so by turning to the headscarf and burka bans as ways to solve these deep-seated socioeconomic troubles, though some analysts would argue that these bans exacerbate the kinds of socioeconomic exclusions that French Muslims face.[16]

In this chapter, we argue that, in the French context, debates over the headscarf largely reaffirmed existing understandings of the French national narrative. They built on historically rooted understandings of French nationhood to either include or exclude Muslims from being French. Whereas the French headscarf debates focused on the circumscribed space of schools and on teenagers, who are citizens-in-the-making, the more specific debates over the burka and niqab focused on the general public presence of adult women who cover not only their hair but also their face. To analyze how all these debates informed the (re)articulation of the French national narrative, we begin with a discussion of republicanism, laïcité, and gender equality as the key concepts that have historically structured the French national narrative of belonging. Next, we discuss evidence pertaining to the headscarf and burka or niqab debates, which we gathered from three main newspapers: the high-brow, politically moderate *Le Monde* and the politically right-wing *Le Figaro* for the headscarf debate, adding the high-brow, politically left-wing *Libération* to analyze the burka ban debate. We then draw on these data to analyze how politicians, newsmakers, and civil society reaffirmed the French national narrative as they argued over the extent to which religious symbols like the headscarf and burka should be allowed in different sections of the French public sphere. We conclude with an analysis of the political candidacy of Ilham Moussaïd, a young headscarf-wearing woman, to illustrate how the version of the national narrative articulated during the headscarf and burka or niqab debates left only the most marginal space for interpretations that place headscarf-wearing women within the boundaries of French belonging.

The Narrative of Belonging:
Republicanism, Laïcité, and Gender Equality

From the French Revolution (1789) onward, the French republican state has striven to create a unified nation from a diverse array of regional affiliations.[17] Over the centuries, belonging to the French nation has become predicated on a republican citizenship that prioritizes equal participation in governance.[18] As suggested by the fact that French women did not gain the right to vote until 1944, this ideal has not always been easy to practice. Nevertheless, a key republican ideal motivates these historical processes of political incorporation: the notion that one becomes a citizen through participation in the public sphere, where everyone is fundamentally assumed to be equally capable and versed in the practices of citizenship.

As Cecile Laborde argues, one of the peculiarities of French republicanism is the centrality of the state in shaping citizenship and belonging.[19] Unlike countries in which pluralism or multiculturalism informs national narratives of belonging, such as the Netherlands (see Chapter 4 in this volume) and to a lesser degree Germany (see Chapter 5), the French state has promoted an abstract individualism that rejects public expressions of group or collective identity-based particularity.[20] Belonging to the nation is thus dependent on leaving distinctive practices and ideas, quite literally, at home. People have a right to be different *in private,* but their differences should not inform demands for state recognition. They must become "public similars," as Laborde suggests, or "abstract individuals," as Scott describes them.[21]

This republican ideal has historically been articulated in relation to religion, with ongoing attempts to diminish the power of the Catholic Church over everyday life and politics. Laborde even goes so far as to argue that laïcité, the French approach to secularism, "encompasses a comprehensive theory of republican citizenship."[22] This theory centers on three ideals: "equality (religious neutrality of the public sphere or secularism *stricto sensu*), liberty (individual autonomy and emancipation from religious oppression), and fraternity (civic loyalty to the community of citizens)."[23] The specific meanings of these ideals have been contested at least since the 1880s, the decade during which secular public education was established and schools became key sites of citizenship formation.[24] Battles over the church's role in governance resulted in the passing of the Jules Ferry Laws of 1881–1882 and 1886, which made education compulsory and pushed the Catholic Church out of primary and secondary schools; a 1901 law that ensured freedom of voluntary association; and a 1905 law in which article 1 guarantees "freedom of conscience and free exercise of religion" and article 2 states that the state "neither recognizes, nor pays the salaries of, nor subsidizes any religion."[25] These laws are usually cited as institutionalizing laïcité, though they do not actually use the term.[26] The term *laïcité* first appeared in the 1946 Constitution and was retained in the Constitution of 1958, which states that "France is an indivisible, secular, democratic, and social Republic."[27] The continuing centrality of laïcité in the contemporary French national narrative might well be due to the fact that being *laïc* lacks a precise definition, which allows for the concept of laïcité to take on multiple meanings.[28]

In her analysis of the headscarf debate, Joan Scott argues that instead of recognizing difference, as happens in pluralist or multicultural states, the French state's task has become that of guaranteeing "equal protection . . . *against* the claims of religion and other group demands."[29] Others portray the debate as a battle over interpretations of laïcité, which vary in the role they attribute to Catholicism as part of France's patrimony.[30] Laborde adds a third interpretation of laïcité, one that argues for a tolerant republicanism in which "equality [means] secular impartiality, liberty [means] non-domination, and fraternity [means] trans-ethnic integration."[31]

French laws regarding laïcité leave room for such multiple interpretations. Indeed—and perhaps surprisingly given the ways in which French secularism is often discussed outside France—the laws that are considered the root of French laïcité do not preclude state support for religion. Catholic and some Protestant churches receive funding for building maintenance, and Catholic and Protestant religious schools receive public support as long as they teach the standard curriculum and do not prevent anyone from attending. By distinguishing between personal religious practices (which fall outside the purview of the state and are considered "religion") and the institutional face of a religion (*culte*), the state has interpreted the second clause of the 1905 law to mean neutral state support for the free expression of religion. The 1905 law protects institutionalized expressions of religion, but laïcité interacts with republicanism to limit individual religious expressions in the public sphere on the grounds of public order.[32] As a result of these apparent ambiguities in the boundaries of what is properly laïc, the place of religious expression in the public sphere continues to be contested in the French national narrative of belonging.

Within this context, the headscarf, and especially the burka and niqab, have come to serve as the focal points in a renewed debate on laïcité in France and Islam's place within it. These debates over how to regulate religious expression are often articulated by discussing republicanism and laïcité in terms of their opposite: communalism (*communautarisme*), or the idea that one's primary *public* sense of belonging is expressed through one's affiliation with a subset of French citizens, be they Bretons, Catalans, Muslims, or Seventh-Day Adventists, rather than with the abstract French citizenry as a whole. As republicanism's and laïcité's opposite, communalism raises the specter of the dissolution of the French state and the French nation. Insofar as the headscarf in general and the burka or niqab specifically are seen as public expressions of membership in a group different than the French, they are interpreted as signs of communalism. In the French national narrative, fighting against communalism means mobilizing the state to curtail group-based political and other expressions through law.[33]

Finally, the headscarf, especially the burka and niqab, has come to symbolize women's oppression, signifying a differential treatment of women and men not befitting the republican, laïc French citizen. In France, as in many European nation-states, second-wave feminism has transformed gender equality into a core value. In practice, however, gender equality is often fragile and incomplete. Key actors in the discourses that have dominated the headscarf and burka debates—mainly politicians focused on protecting Muslim women—have generally been men. The French political field is still predominantly male; in 2006 only 12.2 percent of parliamentarians were women.[34] Though recognition of group-based difference is generally anathema to republicanism, French politicians have passed two successive laws encouraging political parties to increase the number of women on their electoral lists.[35] Failure to do so results in a fine being levied against the political party, which the majority of parties have opted to incur. As a result, the face of France represented by the politically powerful in these debates continues to be largely male and white, an indication that the politics of abstract individualism, as opposed to identity-based politics, might not be the best route to ensuring participation by all citizens in the public sphere of politics.

This approach to gender suggests that in contemporary France gender equality is simultaneously linked to republican sameness and gender difference.[36] As Scott points out, dominant French understandings of masculinity and femininity emphasize difference, particularly when it comes to physical embodiment.[37] In public discourse, the classic image of the hyper-feminine, highly fashionable French woman is juxtaposed with that of the elegant yet masculine French man, indicating that equal treatment means the right to express this difference. Debates about the headscarf, and particularly the burka or niqab, which hide (parts of) the feminine body, reveal the emphasis on gender difference and its tense relationship with republican "sameness" in the French national narrative.[38] In this way, the headscarf and burka debates exposed contradictions within the heart of the French narrative of belonging even as they reaffirmed the centrality of republicanism, laïcité, and gender equality.

French Newspapers Involved in the Headscarf and Burka or Niqab Debates

For our analysis of the French headscarf debates we turned to *Le Monde* and *Le Figaro*. We added *Libération* for our analysis of the burka ban. Each newspaper has a different readership and a different approach to politically charged issues.

Le Monde is very much the newspaper of record; it aims to represent as wide a range of positions as possible, with a diverse set of authors and informants, including intellectuals, philosophers, public figures, and politicians. Its coverage of issues combines analysis with news and human-interest stories. The editorial board of *Le Monde* disagreed with banning the headscarf in schools but provided a platform for a wide range of arguments in the debate. The same can be said about its discussion of the complete ban of the burka or niqab.

Le Figaro is more of a lowbrow, politically right-wing newspaper. Its coverage of the headscarf and burka debates revealed how the political right tended to frame the national narrative that informed the debate. Its coverage tends to take the form of shorter articles, and it unambiguously opposed the wearing of both the headscarf and the burka.

Libération represents the left of the French political spectrum. During the niqab debates, it presented the entire issue as little other than a cynical vote-grab by the governing but embattled *L'Union pour un Mouvement Populaire* (Union for a Popular Movement, henceforth UMP), which traded on Islamophobia. *Libération*'s coverage tends to focus much more on analysis, with longer articles that include considerably more detail than either of the other two newspapers.

Banning the Headscarf in Schools

National narratives are always unstable, and the boundaries of belonging that they demarcate are constantly under negotiation. In France, for example, republican "sameness" did not extend to women until 1944, when they were granted the right to vote. Similarly, the apparently clear boundary between religion and participation in the public sphere is blurred in the case of state funding for Catholic schools, and even for church maintenance. Such tensions can be disruptive, but also productive, of national narratives. They stimulate the very debates that (re)produce the sense of belonging to the nation. The headscarf first took center stage as a source of such productive tension in 1989, when three thirteen-year-old girls attending a high school in Creil, a lower-class immigrant suburb of Paris, were ordered to remove their headscarves or be removed from school. The girls fought back, but in the end, one (Samira, a daughter of Tunisian immigrants) left school for good and the other two (Leila and Fatima, daughters of Moroccan immigrants) removed their headscarves, in part at the urging of the king of Morocco, who encouraged them to continue their education on French terms.[39] This all took place despite the fact that the *Conseil d'État* (the Council of State, which rules on the correct application of existing law) ruled that expelling the girls from school solely for wearing headscarves constituted discrimination. In other words, at this point, the Conseil d'État interpreted the boundaries of belonging to include expressions of personally held religious beliefs, indicating that French republicanism could accommodate such expressions of difference.

The Conseil d'État's decision in this case governed the wearing of headscarves in elementary and high schools until 2004, when the French parliament passed a ban on wearing headscarves in schools. Until that time, girls could not be expelled solely for wearing the headscarf, because it would violate the first clause of the 1905 law guaranteeing freedom of conscience. Schools were permitted to expel a headscarf-wearing girl if they had evidence that the girl in question had threatened public order, was proselytizing, or was endangering herself or others (for example, wore the headscarf during physical education or chemistry class).[40] Between 1992 and 1994, forty-nine headscarf cases appeared before the Conseil d'État, and forty-one cases were decided in favor of the girls.[41] In 1994, François Bayrou, then French Minister of Education, challenged the 1989 decision upholding the right of girls to wear the veil; he argued that all ostentatious signs of religious belonging constituted a form of proselytizing. In this way, Bayrou was attacking the idea that the headscarf was a private expression of religiosity and therefore protected by law and accommodated by French republicanism.[42] To Bayrou (and the school principals who tried to expel the girls), the headscarf was a public statement announcing that good Muslims should set themselves apart from the general French public or, in other words, practice communalism. The Conseil d'État rejected Bayrou's challenge.[43]

Many school principals shared Bayrou's rather than the Conseil d'État's approach to the headscarf, and Bayrou's attempt to change the regulations governing headscarves in schools did result in an increased number of expulsions. To deal with this development, Bayrou appointed Hanifa Cherifi, an immigrant from the Kabyle region of Algeria, to mediate between headscarf-wearing girls and school principals. John Bowen describes how Cherifi "would try to convince the girl to give up the scarf for the sake of her future." If that did not work, she would try to mediate by convincing the girls to wear, and the school to allow, a "'discreet' scarf" or bandana that would let their ears and the roots of their hair show.[44] Cherifi tended to look more favorably on girls who wore a headscarf because they came from a devout family than on those who chose to wear the scarf against the wishes of their family. In the former instance, the headscarf symbolized a private religious commitment, in the latter a political-identitarian one. This interpretation of the headscarf's meaning revealed that the headscarf continued to be seen as signifying the threat of communalism and the tension between public and private that lies at the core of the French national narrative.

The work of state-appointed mediator Cherifi vastly reduced the number of expulsions, often because the school and the girl in question would come to a compromise regarding the amount of coverage of her veil.

A girl who revealed her earlobes and hairline and tied her scarf behind her head was far more acceptable to school principals than a girl who wore a veil that covered her hair, ears, and part of her chin. Bandanas became a favored option for headscarf-wearing girls.[45]

Still, the issue would not disappear, in part because the headscarf did not unambiguously represent just privately held beliefs. For those who saw the headscarf as a public statement, it symbolized larger national and international political processes that destabilized French nationhood. Nationally, the headscarf stood for immigrants who did not fully integrate into the French nation. This perception of immigrants bolstered the anti-immigrant ultraright Front National party of Jean-Marie Le Pen. In response, center-right governing parties also focused increasingly on the headscarf in an attempt to draw votes away from Le Pen. Internationally, certain events reinforced the idea that the headscarf signified the threat of Islam as a global political movement: in 1989, Ayatollah Khomeini issued his fatwa against Salman Rushdie; throughout the 1990s, Algeria was rocked by upheaval resulting from the dissolution of the Islamic party that had won the 1991 elections (with various kidnappings and murders dominating the French media in 1994); 9/11 and the (second) invasion of Iraq and of Afghanistan also colored the interpretation of the headscarf during the first decade of the twenty-first century.[46] These international events bolstered the public's perception that the headscarf represented a Muslim tendency toward communalism, and that the headscarf served as a symbol of allegiance to political Islam rather than to the French nation, and thus could endanger the French republic.

Given the republican emphasis on the state's role in producing and securing boundaries of belonging, it is not surprising that the French turned to law to regulate the headscarf. When Nicolas Sarkozy, then French Interior Minister for the center-right UMP, announced in his April 19, 2003, speech at the twentieth annual meeting of the UOIF that the laws governing identity card photographs should be enforced and that a woman should remove her headscarf for her identity card picture, he opened the door for a renewed discussion of headscarves in schools. Sarkozy's speech to the UOIF's very well attended annual gathering drew considerable media attention. A number of members of the National Assembly framed the headscarf as a non-French practice, implying that a headscarf does not belong on a French identity card, which in turn created an opportunity to push for a law banning religious symbols from public schools. On April 24, French

Education Minister Luc Ferry announced that he intended to propose such a law to Parliament.[47] Within a few weeks, parliamentarians from the center-right UMP (Yves Jégo and Jacques Myard) and the center-right *Union pour la démocratie française* (Maurice Leroy), as well as from the left *Parti socialiste* (Socialist Party) (Jack Lang), had either proposed or supported similar laws.[48] Although the proposals were grounded in the legal principle of laïcité in public schools, their stated motives were far more complex, referencing all key concepts of the French national narrative.

Ironically, Nicolas Sarkozy had wanted to *avoid* the issue of wearing headscarves in schools in his speech to the UOIF and was among the parliamentarians initially opposed to such legislation. He worked to convince Prime Minister Jean-Pierre Raffarin to let the issue remain as it had been since 1989, that is, adjudicated on a case-by-case basis, in order to avoid "poisoning things by voting for a law on the subject."[49] Sarkozy and others, including Dominique Perben (Minister of Justice) and initially Luc Ferry, feared that a headscarf ban would increase the stigmatization of Muslims. These politicians did not like the headscarf, but they liked the *conflict* over the headscarf even less, fearing it would increase rather than decrease communalism among French Muslims.

The appointment of Ombudsman Bernard Stasi to head a commission to investigate how to safeguard the principle of laïcité was President Jacques Chirac's attempt to move the debate forward. The Stasi Commission took its expansive mandate seriously and made a number of other recommendations to strengthen not only laïcité but also social cohesion in the face of diversity. For example, it proposed legislation to officially recognize the Muslim holiday of Eid al-Kebir (also known as Eid al-Adha or Kurban Bayramı, the festival of sacrifice) and Yom Kippur, the most important Jewish holiday, as national holidays. However, out of all these recommendations, only one became law: the recommendation to ban all ostentatious religious symbols from public schools. Thus the attempt to expand the French national narrative to include non-Christian religious practices within the boundaries of French belonging failed. As our analysis of the newspaper debates shows, this failed attempt at inclusion did not allow for the articulation of new key concepts in the French national narrative. Rather, the debates reinforced the perception that republicanism, laïcité, and gender equality define belonging in France. The actors participating in these debates contributed to this perception by rearticulating the meanings of these concepts, albeit in sometimes contradictory ways.

Analysis of the National Narrative: Headscarves in the French Newspapers

French newspapers showed two main lines of argument during the debates about headscarves in schools that took place between April 2003 and early 2005. The first argument built on the longstanding link between the Republic and laïcité, interpreting the headscarf as a communalist threat and generating discussions about whether Islam can be French and about the stigmatization of French Muslims. Teachers played a particular role in articulating these arguments as they debated whether the presence of headscarf-wearing girls undermined their capacity to teach republican, laïc values in schools, thus reinforcing the centrality of schools in the creation of a republican, laïc sense of belonging. The second line of argument presented the headscarf as signifying women's oppression within Islam, and generated a particular understanding of gender equality within the French national narrative. These arguments largely provided support for banning headscarves in schools. The resulting debates reinforced a particular understanding of secularism as foundational to French republicanism, and of schools as sites for educating French citizens about this connection. In addition, they reinforced the perception that the contemporary understanding of gender equality was a core attribute of the French national narrative of belonging.

Republicanism and Laïcité: The Headscarf, Communalism, and Stigmatization

The headscarf debates reinforced the idea that republicanism and laïcité are unambiguously at the core of the French national narrative.[50] However, participants in these debates mobilized these concepts (and the linkages between them) in different ways. In particular, politicians disagreed about whether the headscarf created a direct or indirect communalist threat to republicanism and laïcité. Those who perceived the headscarf as a direct threat argued for a ban on headscarves in schools. Others used republicanism and laïcité to argue against a ban. These actors feared that the stigmatization attending a ban would inspire the danger of communalism. Representatives of Muslim organizations provided a third way of understanding republicanism and laïcité, arguing that there is no tension between being Muslim and acting in the public sphere.

Generally, politicians who opposed the wearing of headscarves in schools made direct references to the French laïc, republican tradition in order to argue for a ban. For example, at the start of the 2003 debate on headscarves in schools, Prime Minister Raffarin was quoted as saying, "The veil is a symbol for those who wear it. It's also a symbol for those who contest it." In making this claim, he declared himself firmly opposed to "communalism."[51] The argument mounted by Raffarin and others against the headscarf as an intentional affront to republicanism and laïcité by "those who wear it" was not simply rhetorical; it also informed the work of the Stasi Commission, which, according to Raffarin, focused on how best to protect "schools from communalistic deviations and from all forms of zealotry condemned in the name of republican *laïcité*."[52]

The notion that republicanism and laïcité required a defense was largely shared across the political spectrum. Later in the same year, former Socialist Prime Minister Laurent Fabius, now a deputy in the National Assembly, argued for a headscarf ban, stating, "Laïcité means defining the conditions for a common life where the chosen community supersedes communities of origin, and enacting the public policies that secure each person's standing in the Republic."[53] Such arguments, however, did not generate calls for a general ban on headscarves in the public sphere but rather focused specifically on the school as one of the primary state institutions through which to instill the meanings and practices of belonging to the French nation-state.

Despite the fact that fewer than 10 percent of French teachers had any direct engagement with headscarf-wearing girls,[54] teachers and their unions were very active in the fight against the headscarf in schools. Two teachers involved in a highly contested expulsion case in Lyon that unfolded during the 2003 debates argued that "for extremist groups, who elevate religious law above the Republic's, the veil is a political flag to hoist in schools. Their religious project is political. We must therefore reaffirm the separation of politics and religion today."[55] For these teachers, the headscarf needed to be eliminated from the classroom in order for schools to reinforce the centrality of republican laïcité. Thus teachers brought together the defense of republicanism and laïcité with a perception of the headscarf as a political rather than religious sign in order to argue that there was no place for headscarves in schools.

Not everyone shared this logic. Some argued that the stigmatization attending a headscarf ban would inspire Muslims as a group to respond by turning to communalist group demands. One journalist for *Le Monde* wrote, "The socialists will have to begin listening to Loubna Méliane, a feminist and activist with SOS-*Racisme* who has joined the Socialist Party's national council. 'We have to stop lying to ourselves. Whether we like it or not, such a law [banning headscarves] would stigmatize Muslims.' In her opinion, 'communalists' thrive on 'social injustice. That's where we need to act.'"[56] In making this argument, Méliane rejected the headscarf ban. However, by using the term *communalists,* she also invoked that particular opposite of republicanism. By situating arguments against the ban firmly within the common elements of the French national narrative, Méliane and others arguing against the ban affirmed rather than reframed the centrality of republicanism as the opposite of communalism in the French national narrative.

Center-right politicians made similar arguments regarding the threat, not of the headscarf itself but of the communalist demands that a ban of the headscarf might inspire:

The last Minister interviewed by the commission on the application of the principle of *laïcité* in the Republic on the morning of Friday, November 14, Dominique Perben, cited the importance of French society's "cohesion" in expressing his reticence regarding a law that would prohibit religious symbols in schools. . . . While preoccupied with "condemning communalism—without stigmatizing any community," Mr. Perben nevertheless recommended avoiding "all solutions that appear discriminatory towards Muslims" who, in his estimation, must "see the exercise of their faith protected."[57]

In their arguments regarding stigmatization, politicians again invoked the duty to protect republicanism from communalism, just as their colleagues had in arguing for a ban. They moved away from arguments that presented the headscarf as a *direct* communalist threat to republicanism and laïcité and instead stressed the need to protect faith, which can be understood as a *private,* and therefore allowable, expression of religion within French laïcité. Thus, by provoking debates about a ban that stigmatized Muslims, the headscarf became an indirect threat to the French national narrative. Some of these arguments were purely political instruments that political actors mobilized to gain support from Muslim voters or, alternatively, from right-wing voters who feared Islam but did not want to lose support for their Christian religious heritage.[58] At a meta-level, both the arguments for and those against a ban had the effect of reinforcing the centrality of republicanism, laïcité, and (opposition to) communalism as key concepts in the French national narrative, even as they were mobilized to different ends.

Some took the argument regarding stigmatization one step further, stating that headscarf-wearing girls should be allowed in schools so they could be trained in good republican citizenship. In these arguments, communalism was directly linked to radical Islam. In a rare article focusing on the experiences of Muslim women, a veiled high school student told a *Le Monde* reporter, "'I'm accused of being an apologist for fundamentalists, but to the contrary,' she argues, 'it's by permitting veiled girls to study with us that they develop a critical spirit and emancipate themselves. I know of some people that would be only too happy to pick them up, people who practice a radical strain of Islam.'"[59] Jean Glavany, one of the twenty Stasi Committee members, initially voiced a similar sentiment, although later all Stasi Committee members unanimously voted for the proposal to ban headscarves in schools: "'We are all opposed to the scarf in school. But the Republic's values are better suited to tolerance than to exclusion. Where will the girls who are expelled go? To Islamic centers?' asks Mr. Glavany."[60] From this perspective, a headscarf ban would prevent schools from performing their function in educating students in republican, laïc citizenship, fostering instead a sense of belonging based on students' particularistic, Islamic identities.

Representatives of Muslim organizations also reinforced the argument that stigmatization would foster communalism while they defended republicanism and laïcité. One of Sarkozy's accomplishments as Interior Minister was to bring together an umbrella organization for French Muslims that could serve as a "privileged interlocutor" in government dealings with (religious) Muslims.[61] The left subsequently criticized Sarkozy (and the UMP) because, they argued, organizations like the *Conseil francais de culte musulman* (French Council of the Muslim Faith, henceforth CFCM) would continue to mark Muslims as different from "regular" French citizens, which would inspire discrimination against them and foster communalism in turn.[62] Regardless of how the CFCM was perceived politically, the organization's warnings about the potential for stigmatization reinforced the principles of republicanism and laïcité. Dalil Boubakeur, head of the Great Mosque of Paris and first president of the CFCM, stated his surprise at seeing Muslim women in France wearing headscarves, "given that women in the Maghreb are a lot less strict in their observance."[63] He explained the turn to the headscarf as Muslim women's "aggressive" response to perceived rejection by French society. Boubakeur thus made an argument against stigmatization. He then reinforced the centrality of republicanism, laïcité, and communalism in the French national narrative when he warned that

> by exceeding its aims, the scarf is no longer a protection of femininity, but has rather become an affirmation of religiosity, which is unacceptable in a balanced country such as France. The political acclamation of the headscarf is a form of fundamentalism that is unthinkable in a country that has, since the 19th century, understood that a free and compulsory education is of fundamental importance for all citizens, second alone to basic rights of subsistence and equality.[64]

In doing so, Boubakeur demonstrated that he was perfectly fluent in the French national narrative, even from his position at the margins of belonging. Speaking to the French public outside the banlieue, Boubakeur defended republicanism by pointing out that their rejection of French Muslims fostered "communalism." At the same time, he turned to those who were excluded from French belonging through "social rejection," telling Muslims that although the headscarf is an understandable response to racialization, wearing the headscarf as an emblem of religious identity was rightfully sanctioned, given the centrality of laïcité in the French national narrative.[65]

Other representatives of Muslim organizations took a different approach, trying to redefine these key concepts of the French national narrative. One of the largest organizations associated with the CFCM, the UOIF, recognized republicanism and laïcité as quintessentially French but argued for the possibility of supporting these values through religion, in effect extending arguments that laïcité can accommodate Catholicism to include Islam. Fouad Alaoui, the UOIF's secretary-general, linked the centrality of law in French republicanism to Islam by reiterating an assertion often heard among Muslims in Muslim-minority countries: that they are obligated to obey the laws of the land in which they live. As he phrased it, "Respecting the law is a religious duty."[66] Abdallah ben Mansour, former secretary-general of the UOIF, built on republican ideas about political participation, arguing that "a law once forced Jews to wear yellow stars, and was eliminated. . . . As long as the law prohibits the veil, we will respect it, but we will try to get it changed."[67] In this way, the UOIF voiced its critique of the headscarf ban by likening it to the worst atrocities committed on European soil. At the same time, these French Muslim interlocutors argued that, as republican citizens, Muslims should participate in the political sphere in order to prevent the passing of the law. In doing so, they emphasized French Muslims' capacity to be French and to participate in French politics. However, their approach to religion in the public sphere also challenged the interpretations of republicanism and laïcité advocated by French politicians and others in France's Muslim communities.

Although the UOIF was a minority voice, it was not the only one to make this kind of argument. Dounia Bouzar, a founding member of the CFCM and a public figure and commentator on issues related to Muslim integration in France, participated actively in public debate as an anthropologist with Algerian Muslim roots. Of all the participants in this debate, she most clearly asserted that it is possible to wear a headscarf in ways that are entirely compatible with French values. Although she herself did not wear the headscarf, she coauthored a book with Saïda Kada, a headscarf-wearing activist from Lyon and the only headscarf-wearing woman invited by the Stasi Commission for an interview. In their book, Bouzar and Kada aimed to demonstrate that there is no inherent contradiction between wearing the headscarf and being French. According to Le Monde, "For [Bouzar], the headscarf can be a part of redefining a modern, Muslim identity: 'These French Muslims want to join other French people on common ground, while drawing on Islam.'"[68] This reinterpretation of the limits of republicanism and laïcité was clearly a minority position in a debate that largely viewed the headscarf as a sign of either an inability or an unwillingness to participate in a manner consistent with these principles. Bouzar was quoted in a number of newspaper articles and was interviewed by the Stasi Commission, but her arguments lost some of their power when she resigned from the CFCM, of which she was one of the two female founding members. Her resignation was widely interpreted as an indication that her version of a republican laïc Islam did not find widespread support among French Muslims.

Ultimately, most interlocutors in these debates agreed that schools were the sites of republican laïc education. What they disagreed on was whether the school could transform headscarf-wearing students into French laïcité-supporting republicans, or whether taking the headscarf off was a prerequisite for creating a space in which to transmit key elements of France's national narrative to the next generation. Some argued that the headscarf obstructed the transmission of republican laïc values; others took the girls' right to an education in republicanism and laïcité as superseding the state's right to close itself to the presence of these girls. However, no one argued that wearing the headscarf should itself be a protected practice, nor did these discourses reframe republicanism and laïcité as foundational to the French national narrative. These arguments did not shift the boundaries of belonging. One could not be French *and* wear a headscarf; rather, headscarf-wearing girls could at best *potentially* belong to the French nation.

The Veil as Expression of Women's Oppression in Islam

Arguments about whether to allow the headscarf in schools also built on post-World War II discourses about gender equality, reinforcing the importance of gender equality in the French national narrative. Generally, discussions of republicanism and laïcité contained little about the personal reasons some women and girls wore the headscarf. Instead, newspaper discussions largely focused on external perceptions of the headscarf as a threat to French republicanism and laïcité and to concomitant notions of French national belonging. Some argued that the headscarf was a violation of gender equality, presenting the garment as an *objective* symbol of women's repression and subservience within the Islamic faith. Headscarf-wearing women were rarely quoted in newspapers, except in a few cases, such as that of Alma and Lila Lévy, mentioned at the beginning of this chapter, which received significant media attention. Otherwise, headscarf-wearing women's subjective experiences and intentions rarely entered the discussion.

Newspapers encouraged this exclusion through stories in which headscarf-wearing Muslim women had no independence or agency. Some newspaper stories promoted the idea that women wore the headscarf only in response to pressure from family, particularly male members. An article in *Le Monde* based on an interview with Nadia, a veiled woman, recounts the journalist's experience when interviewing her:

During the whole conversation, the men of the family are present. Mohammed, the fiancé, is sitting next to her. Kamel, the elder brother, who wears a short beard, is standing in the doorframe. Nadia is the only girl of five children. At a certain point, the youngest brother arrives and whispers in his sister's ear: "Father is coming!" As Nadia doesn't move, he becomes more insistent: "Father is coming! Go make the coffee." After a final hesitation, the young girl gets up and goes to the kitchen, leaving her interlocutor.[69]

Such accounts portray Muslim fiancés and brothers, whom they mark as observant Muslims through references to short beards, as watchful and controlling figures who obstruct girls' ability to speak for themselves regarding their headscarves. Nadia's hesitation in getting up indicates her failed attempt to control the situation, further reinforcing the perception that she has little capacity to exert her will.

Prominent feminists drew on the image of the nonagentic Muslim girl or woman to reinforce the idea that Islam is inherently hostile to women.[70] Gisele Halimi, a woman of Jewish Algerian descent and a prominent writer, lawyer, and activist, as well as president of *Choisir la cause des femmes,*[71] a pro-choice organization she cofounded with Simone de Beauvoir and others in 1971, argued strenuously for a headscarf ban: "The veil is a terrible symbol of women's inferiorization. I don't need to elaborate—this is precisely the way it's intended by the Koran. Defined in relation to man, to his desires, to his compulsions, the woman must hide all that could seduce, that could indicate sexual transgression."[72] Such arguments privileged the interpretations of those seeing the headscarf rather than those wearing it. Whether or not Muslim women chose to wear these coverings did not matter; headscarves by definition represented an objective denial of women's equal status.

To the strongest opponents of the headscarf, the assertion that women might choose to wear this garment did nothing to detract from its nature as an objective form of domination. These interlocutors rejected arguments made by girls like Alma and Lila Lévy, who said they had freely chosen to wear the scarf, and by the young women who protested when the ban was passed with slogans like "the veil, my choice." Feminist activist scholars Anne Vigerie of the *Cercle d'étude de reformes féministes* and Anne Zelensky, president of the *Ligue du droit des femmes,* argued in the same newspaper article that religious women by definition did not have the capacity for agency: "Young girls or women wear it, invoking their freedom of religion. Wearing the veil isn't a sign of religious belonging. It symbolizes women's place in Islam as it is understood by Islam itself: shrouded in shadow, relegated to submission to men. The fact that women choose to wear it does nothing to change its meaning. . . . There is no surer oppression than self-oppression."[73]

Feminist activists such as Halimi, Vigerie, and Zelensky positioned themselves as knowledgeable about Islam and capable of interpreting the Koran, despite the body of research that provides far more nuanced and diverse interpretations of the headscarf.[74] They did so as defenders of the rights of all women, which they felt would be threatened if any group of women were systematically subjected to gender-unequal practices, as they believed Muslim women to be.

In December 2003, *Le Monde* reported that a group of prominent women—including well-known feminist activists, intellectuals, actresses, and academics—had published a statement in *Elle* magazine calling on Jacques Chirac to pass the law banning the headscarf. They argued that "the Islamic veil . . . subjects all women, Muslim and non-Muslim, to an intolerable discrimination. Any accommodation in this regard would be perceived by every woman in this country as a personal affront on her dignity and liberty. . . . To accept the Islamic veil in schools and in public administration is to legitimate a visible symbol of women's submission in spaces where the state must guarantee the strict equality of the sexes."[75] Portrayals of the headscarf as contradicting the equality of the sexes reinforced gender equality as a foundational principle of the French Republic. Furthermore, from this perspective, the headscarf becomes an agent in its own right (that is, it is not women who wear the headscarf who should be banned from schools, but the headscarf itself, thus removing subjectivity from Muslim women while imparting it to the veil!). According to this definition of gender equality, only those who already conform to a certain understanding of agency and embodiment in the public sphere are entitled to participate in public debate, and to take their place as republican citizens.[76] In the resulting narrative of belonging, being French cannot coincide with expressing adherence to Islamic beliefs in public.

The immigrant women's organization *Ni Putes Ni Soumises* (Neither Whores Nor Submissives, henceforth NPNS) was a particularly important generator of discourses that reinforced this interpretation of the relationship between gender equality and the headscarf.[77] NPNS was founded by Fadela Amara and Samira Bellil to address violence against women and girls in the *banlieues*. (Samira Bellil published a book recounting her experience of repeated gang rapes by young men in the *banlieue*, and Fadela Amara published a book entitled *Ni Putes, Ni Soumises*, in which she recounts the founding of NPNS.[78]) NPNS saw Islam as condoning such violence and argued that girls wore the headscarf to protect themselves from sexual violence.[79] This perspective led Fadela Amara to argue against any kind of communalist tolerance for the headscarf: "I do not accept that we should tolerate the veil under the pretext of respecting the cultures from which it originates."[80] As did the CFCM's warnings, this statement exemplifies immigrant activists' fluency in the vocabulary of the national narrative—in this case, the vocabulary of French republican feminism. This kind of exclusionary feminism, which takes the experiences of the dominant class of women as the benchmark for assessing equality, has been critiqued by many activists and scholars who are interested in analyzing the differences among women.[81] However, within the context of the French national narrative, the accommodation of difference is highly problematic, because it signifies a rejection of republicanism.[82] Furthermore, though no newspaper articles referred to it, the fact that gender equality is still a fragile and incomplete achievement in France (as elsewhere in the West) may have given an even stronger impetus to these feminist arguments.

Very few individuals disputed the interpretation of the headscarf as undermining the gender equality that has become a core element in the French national narrative. However, some suggested that it might be worthwhile to understand why girls wear the headscarf. Again, *Le Monde* cited Dounia Bouzar: "Mrs. Bouzar insists that the debate should consider the values defended by these young women, rather than becoming fixated on the headscarf as a symbol. 'These women aren't determined by the headscarf or by their choice of clothes, but by the beliefs they hold.'"[83] Bouzar suggested that until these girls are asked about their actual beliefs, which are protected in the 1905 law regulating the relationship between religion and the state, it is wrong to decide for them whether the headscarf signifies a lack of agency. Thus, Bouzar opened the door to the possibility that some girls might be agentic, countering the headscarf-equals-no-agency argument so powerfully presented by Vigerie and Zelensky.

The arguments linking the headscarf to gender inequality had a profound impact on the creation of the law banning the headscarf in schools. Even before the Stasi Commission had published its findings, Bernard Stasi suggested to the French media that young women frequently wore the veil "because their parents, older brothers and religious groups obligate them to do so."[84] Patrick Weil, a historian of citizenship and member of the Stasi Commission, testified that the argument that girls wore the veil to protect themselves from the sexual aggression of boys and men in the *banlieues* had a particularly strong influence on the Commission's recommendations.[85] Politicians were particularly taken with Muslim women's arguments against the headscarf, and the NPNS and its leader Fadela Amara were among the most-cited referents in the parliamentary debates that immediately preceded the adoption of the headscarf ban.[86]

The concept of gender equality had a lot of traction in the debate, with politicians citing it as a justification for the proposed headscarf law. In doing so, however, they gave a different meaning to this key concept in the French national narrative: they were more likely to focus on headscarf-wearing women's lack of dignity than on their lack of agency. In addition, they linked gender equality with integration of immigrants. For example, during the headscarf debate, Dominique Perben argued that "to accept the veil is to accept a conception of woman that is fundamentally contrary to her dignity. . . . Any solution must take the equality of the sexes to heart. . . . social integration occurs through women."[87] The difference between arguments that link gender equality with agency and those that link gender equality with dignity is that *agency* refers to women's capacity to act whereas, at least in the headscarf debate, *dignity* refers to having respect for women but not necessarily seeing them as equal to men. Perben was one of many politicians to reference women's dignity: for him and many others, shrouding women meant not appreciating them as persons. It prevented them from operating on equal footing with men (who are seen as persons). Thus, dignity became dependent on a kind of republican sameness, knitting gender equality ever more tightly into the French national narrative.

At the same time, the reference to integration reinforces the distinction between women and men; it echoes arguments made in other national contexts, such as in the Netherlands and Germany, in which integrationist discourses often position immigrant women as the conduits of their children's integration, reinforcing gendered understandings of parenting and mothering in the production of nationhood.[88]

It is almost a cliché to suggest that these kinds of arguments regarding women's agency and dignity foster old colonial discourses about "saving" women from men (whether brown or Muslim).[89] Yet such arguments clearly reinforce the notion that immigrant communities are backward and that the state is responsible for enabling women to enact their civilizing influence on children and men.[90] As demonstrated by Perben's quote, these fantasies of rescue reinforce gendered differences even as they purport to undermine them. The ubiquity of such gendered frames enforces homogeneity in the articulation of national belonging.

The French debates surrounding the ban of religious symbols in elementary and secondary schools illustrate how debates that are ostensibly about the management of difference can come to reinforce commonality.

The French case shows how a number of key concepts form the explicit discursive anchors in debates over national belonging. By mobilizing these core concepts, discussions about what appear to be social fractures become exercises in the production of social cohesion.[91] Yet this is only the case because of the flexibility of concepts such as republicanism, communalism, *laïcité,* and gender equality. We further demonstrate both the flexibility and the strength of these concepts in our analysis of the burka and niqab debates, to which we now turn.

Banning the Burka and Niqab from the Public Sphere

As noted earlier, the public headscarf debate died down once the law against ostentatious religious symbols in schools was adopted. Between mid-April 2003, when Nicolas Sarkozy inadvertently ignited the headscarf debate, and March 15, 2004, when the "Stasi law" was approved by France's parliament, *Le Monde* printed 185 articles about girls and women and the Muslim headscarf; 100 articles appeared from October through December 2003 alone, when the debate peaked. In contrast, only 113 articles appeared on the same topic over the next five years, from October 2004 until May 2009, and almost all of these were related to social integration in other European countries, or they were human-interest stories about Muslim-dominated states. With a few minor exceptions, the French headscarf debate fell out of the public view during those years. This trend held until June 2009, when Nicolas Sarkozy, in his new role as president, responded to requests by fifty-nine parliamentarians to create a commission to address the burka; he did so as part of a historic speech to both houses of parliament (the first time a president had addressed both houses since 1873) in which he said that "the burka is not welcome on the territory of the French Republic."[92] Evidently the debate about the place of religious coverings within the French national narrative of belonging was not over after all.

The impulse to ban the burka and niqab likely came from a July 2008 ruling by the Conseil d'État to let stand a decision not to grant citizenship to a niqab-wearing Moroccan woman, Faiza M., married to a French citizen.[93] Despite the fact that she had lived in France for years and had three children who were French citizens, the Conseil d'État took Faiza M.'s choice to wear the burka as evidence of her failure to assimilate to French norms. It declared that she had "adopted, in conformity to a radical strain of her religious faith, a practice that is incompatible with essential values of the French community, namely, the principle of the equality of sexes."[94] The issue did not generate significant media attention; instead, the uncontroversial response to the decision showed how firmly established was the idea that being French meant supporting gender equality in the French national narrative.

The issue of Islamic face coverings stayed out of public debate until June 2009, when communist MP André Gerin, former mayor of Vénissieux, a suburb of Lyon that had seen extensive controversy over headscarves in schools, proposed a commission of inquiry into the issue.[95] Sarkozy approved the proposal on June 25, 2009, and the Commission, to be headed by Gerin, was launched on July 1, 2009.[96] The Commission's goal was to investigate the most appropriate response to the burka and niqab. Unlike in the headscarf debate, the investigation was centered not on *whether* to ban, but *where* to ban. The resulting discussions enabled a revisiting and extension of many of the defining elements in the French national narrative put forth in the headscarf debate. However, in the case of the burka and niqab, there was no need even to entertain the possibility that these garments could be compatible with the French narrative of belonging.

On October 25, 2009, Éric Besson, Minister of Immigration, Integration, and National Identity for the UMP, summarized the general sentiment when it came to the burka: "When asked about the wearing of the burka, the minister judged it to be 'contrary to the values of the national identity.' 'We can debate the possibility of a law . . . but on the principles involved, there's no debate: the burka is unacceptable and contrary to the values of the national identity.'"[97] The stakes were clear. The burka was unacceptable in France, and the question was simply in which parts of the public sphere the burka, and niqab, should be banned: in hospitals, in government buildings, on the street? The answer depended on how people interpreted "sameness" within the French public sphere. Could this "sameness" accommodate the burka and niqab in certain places, or should the burka be entirely removed from French soil? Hence, the burka and niqab debate, even more than the debate over the headscarf, portrayed these practices as symbolizing the rejection of all things French. Indeed, in the article just cited, Besson also announced the "launch, in early November, of a 'great debate' with 'the country's working population,' aiming to 'reaffirm the values of national identity, and pride in being French.'"[98] Thus the debate on the presence of the burka and niqab in the public sphere became another opportunity to define the national narrative of belonging to France.

The burka and niqab debate differed from the earlier headscarf debate in that it was even more marked by political opportunism (*Libération* was particularly critical of this). Besson was not the only politician who, by starting his own inquiry, tried to exploit the issue for instrumental political gain. On December 23, 2009, amid intensive debate about "the burka and national identity," Jean-François Copé, president of the then-governing UMP, announced that his party would push for a law entirely banning the burka and niqab in France (not just in government spaces such as hospitals and other government buildings, but everywhere, including on the street). This enraged almost all parliamentarians, who, unlike Copé, had been waiting for the results of the Gerin Commission. Copé's declaration clearly undermined Sarkozy's authority as French president. This political maneuvering was resoundingly criticized. Such criticisms reinforced the perception of the burka and niqab debate as a moment in which to reaffirm French notions of national belonging. This political gains-making was made possible exactly because wearing the burka and niqab touched on so many aspects of the French national narrative.

The politicking continued after the release of the Gerin Commission's report (on January 26, 2010), which recommended a partial ban of the burka (and niqab) in civic institutions (a decision that reflected disagreements between Commission members regarding the extent of the ban). Sarkozy's government then took a few months to develop a draft law for parliamentary approval. In the interim, on March 14 and 21, France held its regional elections. The UMP lost votes to Jean-Marie Le Pen's ultraright Front National and was soundly beaten by left-leaning parties, who benefitted from this split among the right; the Socialist Party won in all but two of France's twenty-six regions. In what was largely understood as an attempt to gain votes from the right, Sarkozy declared on March 24 that his government would introduce a "burka-banning" law, without specifying how broad the ban would be.

As in Germany and the Netherlands, the idea of a complete ban on the burka and niqab was appealing to some but raised concerns regarding constitutional rights—mainly freedom of conscience, expression, and movement. To determine how far a ban could go, François Fillon, France's prime minister, tasked the Conseil d'État with investigating the most extensive burka-banning law options possible, although he echoed the concern about stigmatization previously raised in the headscarf debate by stressing it should be done "without harming our Muslim compatriots."[99] The Conseil d'État came down against a full ban, which they maintained would have insufficient legal-constitutional grounds. Drawing on the idea that French belonging can be taught (which had informed the headscarf debates), the Conseil d'État argued for a "pedagogical" rather than legalistic approach to the problem of the burka and niqab, warning that a total ban would have the effect of victimizing the women it intended to, in the Conseil d'État's phrasing, "rescue." The Conseil also asserted that public security and fraud prevention provided the only legal grounds for a (partial) ban. Principles of laïcité could not serve the purpose, because laïcité governs officials' actions in the *public* sphere, not the behavior or choices of private individuals (which contrasts with how the concept was applied in the headscarf debate).

In addition, the Conseil warned that the legal justification of protecting human dignity, as proposed by some parliamentarians, stood in direct contradiction with the principle of private autonomy also enshrined in France's constitution. For example, some politicians argued that a legal ruling prohibiting the carnival activity of dwarf tossing, even if the dwarfs in question consented to being tossed, could serve as precedent for a complete ban on the burka and niqab, which they portrayed as similar affronts to general human dignity. Nonetheless, the Conseil warned that a burka and niqab ban needed to be limited to specific places if it was to be constitutional. However, the Conseil d'État's arguments, only advisory, did not prevent Prime Minister Fillon from stating on March 29, 2010, that the government would pursue a law "going as far as possible toward total interdiction within the boundaries of respect for general principles of right."[100]

On April 21, 2010, President Sarkozy declared that the government would propose a law instituting a total ban on the burka in all public spaces in France. The law would be presented to the National Assembly in the first week of July and, in Prime Minister Fillon's words, would be "simple, short, based on the respect for the dignity of the person, on the equality of men and women, and lastly, on the issue of security, which can solidify the juridical grounding for the law without being at the heart of the debate."[101] The law took the Conseil d'État's arguments (though not its conclusions) to heart: although the law was intended to address the dignity of persons and gender equality, its legal justification rested on appeals to security and fraud prevention.

By designating the wearing of the burka as a political expression rather than as a symbol of individual religious commitment, the French state had no obligation to protect it under article 1 of the 1905 law guaranteeing freedom of conscience. In fact, the law could be used to prohibit practices associated with this political symbol on the grounds that they threaten public order, which is a recognized prerequisite for the functioning of a republican public sphere (or any liberal democratic state). At the same time, the law banned all "face coverings," not the burka specifically, thus ensuring that it would not violate international human rights law, which might treat the burka as a religious expression.

As mentioned in the introductory section of this chapter, the law that was passed instituted a 150 euro fine for wearing the burka or niqab in public, in addition to the possible requirement of attending a "citizenship class," and a maximum fine of 15,000 euros and up to a year in jail for those forcing women to wear the burka or niqab. The law was to be preceded by a six-month "education period" during which no charges would be laid for wearing an Islamic face covering, and during which the organization Ni Putes Ni Soumises would be responsible for "educating" women not to wear the burka or niqab. The law passed in the National Assembly with overwhelming support, on July 13, 2010, and on Tuesday, September 14, 2010, the Senate approved it with a number of abstentions from left-leaning senators. The law came into full effect on April 11, 2011, at which point the "education" period ceased and legal enforcement came into full effect.

Under the ban, only police officers can confront a woman wearing a burka or niqab, and they have to refer her to a judge, who will decide on the punishment.[102] Though a number of women have been taken to the police station, a year after the law took effect only two had appeared before a judge and both vowed to take their case to the European Court of Human Rights (ECtHR).[103] The Council of Europe Commissioner for Human Rights, Thomas Hammarberg, has taken a strong stance against the general type of "burka bans" passed by France.[104] Indeed, reports suggest that women who wear the burka or niqab face increased harassment and assault when they venture onto the streets of France because French citizens take the law as license to harass niqab-wearing women.[105] Reports on fines applied to niqab-wearing women suggest that the ban is not leading them to leave the public sphere. Rather, police officers are asking these women to reveal their faces for identity checks and then fining them.[106]

Analysis of the National Narrative: Burkas in the French Newspapers

What came to be known internationally as the "French burka ban" really referred to a ban on the niqab, which, unlike the burka, leaves the eyes uncovered. Although only a very small number of French women wore the burka (or more accurately, the niqab), it represented a multi-faceted threat, which made it a symbol that propelled a restrictive reiteration of the French national narrative. As in the headscarf debates, French newspapers discussed the ban in terms of the French national narrative of republicanism, secularism—laïcité—and communalism combined with gender equality. However, the burka and niqab debate emphasized different aspects of these concepts. First, wearing the burka or niqab was framed as a political rather than a religious choice. This issue had arisen in the headscarf debate but was now far more starkly articulated, with the burka and niqab being framed as a communalist threat to the entire French public sphere (rather than limited to education in French schools). Second, gender equality again played a key role. This time, however, the notion of women's dignity, rather than women's agency, was at the forefront of the discussion. Finally, the stigmatization argument resurfaced, this time not to prevent but to try and circumscribe the extent of the ban. During the burka debate, the same key concepts of the national narrative resurfaced but were now given even more exclusionary meanings than in the headscarf debates.

Republicanism, Laïcité, and Communalism: The Burka as a Political Choice

Whereas the headscarf operated as both a religious and a political symbol, the burka, or niqab, was widely perceived as solely a political, rather than a religious, sign.[107] Often associated with Salafism—itself perceived as a global political movement to widely institute Islamic law (though this is contested by Salafists themselves, who argue that they are a piety movement)[108]—wearing the burka, or niqab, was seen as an expression of political Islam that explicitly rejected French national values and practices by situating itself outside the French national narrative. The 2008 Conseil d'État decision in the Faiza M. citizenship case set the tone: "The Conseil [d'État] . . . regards the burka as anything but a banal religious symbol of personal choice or freedom of conscience. To the contrary, it sees it as an important symbol for a militant minority of Muslims who advocate a radical practice of their faith."[109] The Conseil's decision to deny Faiza M. French citizenship set the stage for arguments that the burka was an intentional social disruption, enacted as a political challenge to the French body politic.

In the headscarf debate, a few participants argued that laïcité could accommodate headscarves in schools. No such argument was made regarding the possibility of accommodating the burka or niqab. Rather, perceived as a singular sign of communalism, these garments inspired a spirited defense of republicanism and laïcité. Indeed, an editorial published in *Le Monde* shortly after the appointment of the Gerin Commission argued that "for years, our secular Republic has endured the assaults of the most radical Muslims, whose provocations have no other goal but to test our resistance and our capacity to defend our republican values. . . . It's time to face up to the rise of communalism and to affirm our attachment to republican egalitarianism and laïcité, the non-negotiable foundation of our society."[110] News reporting highlighted that the 2009 Gerin Commission's mandate in investigating the burka's place in France was to "limit this communalist deviation contrary to the principle of laïcité, to our values of freedom, equality and human dignity."[111] Like the headscarf debate, the debate on the burka reaffirmed the centrality of laïcité to French republicanism. However, the debate over how to regulate Islamic face coverings shifted the focus of the discussion to physical space and embodiment.

Most politicians and others participating in the public debate took the position that safeguarding the Republic required that the burka, or niqab, be worn only in private spaces. The initial discussion of the burka ban consistently used the word *territory* when describing the issue at hand. Even representatives of Muslim organizations used this language when interviewed by the Gerin Commission: "'This is an extreme practice that does not permit living a normal social life and we do not want it to become established on the *national territory*,' said Mr. Moussaoui [of the CFCM]. . . . 'The full veil is incompatible with the French context and living together,' said Anwar Kbibech also, representing the Gathering of the Muslims of France, part of the CFCM."[112] Thus politicians as well as representatives of Muslim organizations rejected the "full veil" as a communalist political statement counter to republican values. Simultaneously, they described the burka, or niqab, as a sectarian cult practice, which undermined any arguments for its protection on the grounds of religious freedom or freedom of conscience. The dominant tenor of the debate was that the French public should not have to encounter this embodied practice and the threat to French values it represented.

Unlike the headscarf debate, the debates on full face coverings turned to the communicative requirements of a republican public sphere. Arguing that republican practice demanded open face-to-face communication in order to counter the threat of communalism, Michèle Alliot-Marie, then Minister of Justice and Freedoms, claimed that the draft law being debated in parliament was not excessive, despite its application to merely two thousand women:

> At stake are the foundations of the Republic and of living together. This [draft law], I support it in the name of national unity. It is not a question of the veil in the draft law, but of the willful concealment of the face by any means. It is very important: it is not a question of religion. We affirm a principle, which is that the Republic is lived with an uncovered face. It is part of the Republican pact. The Republic rejects communalism, and concealing one's face [and] refusing to belong to society is the foundation of communalism.[113]

From this perspective, the covered face did not simply belong to the woman wearing a burka or niqab; it was really the face of the Republic: "For [Jean-François Copé,] the leader of UMP deputies, 'the full veil is not a garment, but a permanent mask, which constitutes a threat to our society.' And, he insists, 'we cannot let the full veil cover the face of our Republic.' 'This practice is the antithesis of our Republican values,' Colette Le Moal (Yvelines, Nouveau Centre) further affirmed."[114] These defenses of republicanism object to the burka, even more so than to the headscarf, as a *visible* sign of difference. Conversely, the ban on Islamic face coverings in all aspects of the public sphere fosters the *appearance* of sameness. In the process, republicanism and laïcité become embodied practices, and belonging to France gains an explicit physical manifestation. In this way, the burka debate reinforced the key elements in the French national narrative, but this time by tying republicanism to open communication (and the concomitant public order) in the public sphere.

The Burka as Expression of Women's Oppression in Islam

Only a year after the Conseil d'État's decision in the Faiza M. case, Benoît Hamon, spokesperson for the Socialist Party, argued in *Le Monde* that wearing the burka "is the practice of a very small, and rather sectarian, branch of politicized Islam, with all that this implies in terms of women's submission."[115] Echoing the French headscarf debates, the debate on the burka and niqab again made women the objects of French values, and allusions to gender equality again played a primary role in the way the debate delineated the French national narrative.

However, unlike the reasons presented in the headscarf debates, in which arguments about republicanism and laïcité were clearly separated from arguments about gender equality, the reasons given for banning the burka almost always focused on all of these issues simultaneously, demonstrating that by the time the "burka-ban" debate unfolded, gender equality had become imbricated with republicanism and laïcité. It seemed that the work performed by feminist interlocutors during the headscarf debates was now taken up by all interlocutors in the burka debate. Whereas various feminist public intellectuals and organizations took very clear positions in the headscarf debate, newspapers did not focus on concerted, explicitly feminist efforts to make the point that the presence of the burka or niqab should be understood as oppressing all women. The idea of gender equality had become firmly part of the French national narrative of belonging.

As in the headscarf debate, in this debate the burka or niqab were perceived rarely as a woman's choice but rather as the deliberate imposition by men belonging to a political-religious sect on a woman's everyday practices. However, instead of focusing on agency, as feminist interlocutors in the headscarf debate did, initial statements about the burka tended to place the protection of women and their dignity front and center. As noted in the introduction to this chapter, in his proposal to institute a parliamentary commission to study the issue, Gerin asserted that the burka forced women to live in "an unbearable situation of reclusion, exclusion and humiliation. [Their] very existence is denied."[116] Others reinforced this imagery. Abdelwahab Meddeb, a French Muslim writer and public intellectual, claimed that burkas are an affront to human dignity and have nothing to do with Islam: "The niqab or burka, the extension of the hijab, is a crime that kills the face, perpetually barring access to the other. It is a fabric that transforms women into a prison or a mobile coffin, bringing to the hearts of our cities ghosts that bar entry to invisible visible truths."[117] This kind of imagery presented the burka as a form of violence against women that, if not killing them directly, killed women's ability to communicate. The Muslim men who purportedly force women into these garments are the implied perpetrators of this crime, and the French public is called on to rescue the women thus violated in the name of rescuing the French public sphere from violation.

When Socialist deputies in the National Assembly hesitated to institute a full ban on the burka, Sihem Habchi, head of NPNS, and Naïma
Charaï, regional councilor of Aquitaine, forcefully argued for the ban, citing
women's freedom of expression: "Today, in our country, many women and
young girls are not free: free to choose their life, free to enjoy the same rights
as their brothers, free to dress as they want. The pressures they face lead
them too often to feel ashamed of their femininity, to camouflage it, sometimes even to deny it."[118] Highly gender-differentiated understandings of
women's personhood undergirded such arguments, with many politicians,
including Gerin and Sarkozy, echoing the claim that the burka obstructs
women's personhood and expression of femininity—in other words, the
essence of their existence.[119] From this perspective, unveiling women would
not make them the same as men. Indeed, as Scott argues, women's personhood rests in their feminine difference, and republican gender equality is
based on the right to express femininity.[120]

These interpretations of women's veiling gave rise to questions about
who is denying the burka-wearing woman her existence: the men who
ostensibly veil her, or the French politicians, activists, and public intellectuals who do not want to see her in public if she wears a burka or niqab?
The argument that the burka, or niqab, denies personhood was used to
justify denying these women a right to be recognized as public persons
by the state. Shortly after Gerin proposed a commission to investigate
the burka, Sarkozy, in his speech to the joint houses of Parliament, stated,
"We cannot, in our country, accept women imprisoned behind a screen,
cut off from all social life, deprived of all identity. This does not conform
to our idea of a woman's dignity."[121] Again, this line of reasoning gives
rise to the question, where is the freedom in conforming to someone else's
idea of dignity?

Overall, both the headscarf and "burka-ban" debates were concerned
with gender equality, but the burka debate placed less emphasis on women's
agency and more on women's appearance and dignity. In the resulting articulation of the French national narrative, politicians and others drew from
existing ideas about gender equality to predicate women's equality, women's
rights, and the continued existence of the Republic on women's free expression of their femininity. The headscarf brought into question whether
Muslim women could act independently from their religion and their men.
Apparently headscarf-wearing school-age girls could not, but adult women
could. The burka debates answered the question with a resounding no

across the public sphere. Here the issue was more about what was hidden underneath the burka. The answer: women's capacity to express themselves as feminine beings. Another issue was how women could be liberated. The answer was fully in line with the position of the state in the national narrative: through law. However, the law could have unintended consequences, which led to renewed discussions of stigmatization and the role of law with regard to including subjects in the French national narrative.

The Burka Ban, the Stigmatization of French Muslims, and the Idea of Law

Not all politicians supported the full ban on the burka. About one hundred deputies, mostly from the left, abstained from the final vote. A few weeks before the submission of the Gerin report, some noted, "'If a law is submitted, the communist deputies will oppose it,' says Roland Muzeau. 'We should not create a stigmatizing law,' repeats the head of the communists, Marie-George Buffet, who repeatedly brings up the subject. 'To avoid having this phenomenon develop, let's stop pointing fingers at these women. This especially runs the risk of pushing them into even greater conditions of reclusion.'"[122] During the headscarf debate, the discussion of stigmatization revolved around the place of schools in teaching republicanism and laïcité; in the burka debates, the relationship between law and the regulation of public space took central stage.

The French national narrative treats the law as an arbiter of the boundaries of belonging. The question was how to negotiate these boundaries without excluding those who ought to be included in the French national narrative because they have embraced both the spirit of the law and the idea that being French means respecting the law. An editorial in *Libération* responded to the proposal of a full ban by simultaneously rejecting the burka and opposing the law, which it claimed set Muslims apart from French society:

No one, outside fundamentalist circles, defends the full veil, which hampers the principles of secularism and women's emancipation. A ban in public services would have won broad consensus. Total prohibition, i.e. in the street, where the police (who apparently have nothing better to do) will have to bring charges, bears the mark of a damaging identity intolerance, coupled with clear electoral calculation. The vast majority of Muslims condemns this symbol of dress and will accept the law. But what will these peaceful believers think of this use of the highest authorities of the State to pass a special law that refers to them, once again, as citizens set apart, suspect and subject to special treatment that is perhaps a bit paranoid?[123]

This editorial seems to suggest that these "highest authorities" practice a form of communalism as they target specific groups in society, in the process calling such groups into being. This critique echoes arguments about stigmatization made in the headscarf debate. Like many of the interlocutors in that debate, the *Libération* editorial clearly suggests the general argument that the "full veil" hampers "principles of secularism and woman's emancipation." Yet it challenges the proposed solution, echoing arguments that stigmatization will worsen, not lessen, the threat of communalism.

Representatives from Muslim organizations were similarly adamant that stigmatizing laws would retard integration and foster, rather than prevent, communalism. They returned to the educational dimension of French republicanism, arguing that although the burka is "bad," it ought not be addressed by law but rather by public education: "The CFCM will not ask French society to accept the burka, but will rather support a pedagogical dialogue aiming to convince burka-wearing women to adopt a more centrist, moderate practice of Islam—that adopted by the vast majority of Muslims in France—and to abandon this garb, the symbol of a practice that can only contribute to stigmatizing Islam in France."[124] The UOIF similarly proposed that the burka be addressed and gradually eliminated through education and prevention efforts by France's Muslim community. In doing so, they reinforced the notion that French Muslims have the capacity not only to be good republican citizens but also to (re)produce such citizens. Spokespersons for these diverse Muslim organizations claimed that the "pedagogical period" in the proposed law was an important avenue for addressing stigmatization and fostering integration; they argued that the law alone would push women further into reclusion. However, the organization in charge of providing education, Ni Putes Ni Soumises, whose members had been very vocal supporters of the headscarf ban in schools, had little influence in the communities that were the targets of education.[125] Whereas lawmakers saw NPNS representatives as model French Muslims, their reception among segments of the Muslim and immigrant population was far less favorable, raising the issue of whether lawmakers had instrumentally appointed this group to be responsible for the education.

The recurring key concepts in the debates on the headscarf and burka—republicanism, laïcité, and gender equality—represent ideal types. A brief analysis of French politics and society reveals a multiplicity of political and other groupings that operate within the French public sphere and seem to make distinct demands on behalf of women, workers, teachers, retired persons, and even Muslims. However, discrimination based on group membership is difficult to address within the context of republican abstract universalism.[126] Under the republican ideal, these demands can be couched only in terms of the need to recognize obstacles placed in front of these groups that prevent their equal participation in the public sphere. Republicanism and the attendant notion of laïcité, then, are ideals that hold considerable power. They are important discursive resources in arguments against recognizing practices portrayed as individual particularities (such as wearing the headscarf, burka, and niqab) in the public sphere because they position these practices as sources of nonparticipation. Rather than portray the responses of non-Muslims and nonreligious Muslims to these practices as evidence of discrimination, the debate defines the headscarf, burka, and niqab as prime causes of Muslims' purported failure to participate.

In the end, both the headscarf and burka debates were marked by a great degree of consensus about how these garments threatened republican values, undermined laïcité, and retarded, if not altogether reversed, the achievement of gender equality in France. Within this context, we found very few attempts to expand the boundaries of belonging as delineated by the French national narrative. Where these attempts did take place, they focused largely on direct denials of the claims made by politicians and others. Rarely did anyone interpret the underlying problems associated with the headscarf, burka, or niqab in a way that shifted the national narrative. The political participation of one headscarf-wearing French woman illustrates how limited is the capacity to articulate alternative visions of belonging in France.

The Nouveau Parti Anticapitaliste Candidacy of Ilham Moussaïd

As the burka debate unfolded, a story about a young headscarf-wearing French woman briefly grabbed the French headlines. Her name was Ilham Moussaïd and she was the daughter of Algerian immigrants to France. She became a candidate for France's Nouveau Parti Anticapitaliste (New Anticapitalist Party, NPA) in the 2010 regional elections, the same elections that partially determined the outcome of the burka debates. Moussaïd contradicted many of the dominant tropes discussed in this chapter: she wore a headscarf but behaved with agency, her engagement in party politics was certainly the hallmark of French republicanism, and she was a candidate for a party that focused on class rather than on the potentially communalist religious or political dimensions of being Muslim in the French *banlieues*. Moussaïd (aged twenty-one at the time) became involved in politics when the Ligue communiste révolutionnaire (Revolutionary Communist League, LCR) reached out to an antiracist youth community organization in which she was involved. As another activist described the context of Moussaïd's candidacy, "Politicians had abandoned the neighborhood, there was nothing but policing left. With community organizing, we could apply Band-Aids here and there, that was all."[127] By joining the LCR, Moussaïd and others felt empowered to change things. They also shared the LCR's views on Palestine and other political matters. Moussaïd was treasurer of the newly formed NPA for a year before submitting her candidacy and winning the nomination.

In the brief publicity of Moussaïd's candidacy, she became a media example of someone who identifies as perfectly French and has every right to "be French" yet wears a headscarf. Her candidacy led to a number of articles focusing on how a young, headscarf-wearing woman could become the representative of a left-wing, laïc political party. Dounia Bouzar used her as an example to argue for the compatibility of laïcité and Islam, again claiming that veiled women can also be laïc and feminist. Discussing Ilham Moussaïd's candidacy, Bouzar wrote:

Can one be at the same time veiled and a feminist? . . . Could a small "French-style" headscarf harbor an emancipatory spirit? Is it the scarf that determines the woman or is it the woman who determines the meaning of her scarf? . . . There are as many different personalities as there are colors of headscarf. Some are victims of social pressure, others are entrapped by tradition, but still others have reappropriated their own reading of Islam, wrenching it away from men's monopolizing, masculinist interpretations. The headscarf provides this latter group with a symbolic resource enabling them to redefine themselves: one can be both Muslim and modern. We ought to let this candidate [Moussaïd] define herself freely, without thinking in her place. It would hardly be democratic, and entirely un-feminist, to define her by precisely the kind of subjection against which she struggles.[128]

Bouzar supported the idea that, as this quote suggests, Islam needed to be "wrenched" away from men but at the same time allowed that women might have their own, independent interpretations of the religion by wearing a "French-style" headscarf (with the adjective *small* suggesting the desire to protect femininity, a theme that echoed throughout these debates). Unlike the gender equality discourses in which the headscarf represented an inability to think for oneself, Bouzar suggested that women such as Ilham Moussaïd presented France with a different image of democracy, an image that politicians should take far more seriously if they are truly dedicated to liberation and defining republicanism as a particular way of participating rather than as a particular way of dressing. In short, Bouzar argued that Ilham Moussaïd's political candidacy signaled the embodiment of an alternative interpretation of the key concepts in the French national narrative.

Most commentators, however, did not interpret Moussaïd's role in terms of the possibilities her actions revealed. They focused instead on whether she should be used as an example of an empowered woman, particularly by those who cannot see a headscarf and agency at the same time. According to an article in *Le Monde:* "'The reaction from feminists has been the hardest to take,' reveals the young woman [Moussaïd], who has clearly stated her support for contraception and abortion rights. 'Despite my explaining that I'm not oppressed, and I think that that's pretty clear, there remains a lot of incomprehension.'"[129]

Through this *Le Monde* article, Moussaïd demonstrated her fluency in the French national narrative. At the same time, she tried to change the meanings of key concepts by attacking French feminist discourses about gender equality for not leaving many openings for headscarf-wearing women to express their own interpretations of their actions. Moussaïd reinterpreted not only gender equality itself but also laïcité and the link between femininity and republicanism by stating, "Feminism can itself be a cudgel to force women to act in certain ways, according to certain norms, rather than enabling their emancipation—there isn't, and there shouldn't be, just *one* way to be feminist [and] laïcité isn't a principle that outlaws religion, but rather that separates church and state—one can be *laïc* and Muslim at the same time."[130] This interpretation of laïcité echoes some Turkish efforts to reinterpret secularism as being able to accommodate the participation of religious people in the public sphere and politics. When voicing her political opinions, not only about the headscarf but also about a wide variety of other issues, as Ilham Moussaïd did eloquently,[131] she was met with incomprehension. For many, Moussaïd's headscarf symbolized her incapacity to think and to engage in the kind of critical analysis that had prompted her to run as a candidate for the NPA.

Moussaïd's redefinition of secularism even led Ni Putes Ni Soumises to go so far as to file a complaint against the NPA for supporting "open laïcité": "'In choosing to endorse 'open' laïcité, the NPA is perverting the values of the Republic and suggesting we reread them in a manner which conforms with regressive visions of women,' said the *Ni Putes Ni Soumises* (Neither Whores Nor Submissives) association in a statement."[132] The judge threw out the case due to lack of grounds for prosecution. However, this case exemplifies the intensity of the rejection that headscarf-wearing women face, particularly when they seek to recharacterize the French national narrative, the boundaries of which were reinforced during the burka debates that unfolded at the same time as Moussaïd's ultimately unsuccessful candidacy for political office.

Some individuals interpreted Ilham Moussaïd's candidacy as progress toward an era of greater freedom of expression:

If a majority [of the NPA] finally decided to support a veiled candidate, it was also to allow a new generation to accede to its responsibilities, a generation for whom the veil has a different meaning than it did ten years ago. As Nadia El Bouroumi, a municipal councilor (PS [*Parti socialiste*]) from Avignon, notes, "Muslims of my generation tried at all costs to be like others. Ilhem's generation doesn't have such complexes."[133]

By wearing a religious symbol that French politicians wanted to relegate to the private sphere while actively participating in French politics, Ilham Moussaïd exemplified the kind of woman who was excluded from belonging in the notion of France produced during the headscarf and burka debates.

As Moussaïd's brief appearance in French public debate suggests, whether the French national narrative leaves room for Muslims to become French remains a key question. Indeed, the French headscarf debates are not over. During 2013, an increasingly intense debate focused on the right to wear a headscarf in private employment, particularly when the employee interacts with (small) children. In December 2008, Baby Loup, a daycare provider in a banlieu outside Paris, fired Fatima Atif for wearing her headscarf at work. Atif fought the dismissal as a form of religious discrimination and the case has been wending its way through various courts for the past five years. After losing her case a number of times, on March 19, 2013, the Court of Cassation granted that Atif had indeed been wrongfully dismissed. However, on November 27 of the same year, the Paris Court of Appeals took seriously the Attorney General's argument that young children (up to age three) are "particularly impressionable" and that those attending Baby Loup come from "socially fragile families, which makes them even more receptive to [role] models" (such as headscarf-wearing women) and the Court of Appeals ruled that the firing was not discriminatory.[134] Socialist President François Hollande appointed new members to the observatory for laïcité (observatoire de la laïcité) in April 2013 and tasked them with assessing whether a new law was necessary to safeguard laïcité in private employment. A number of opposition UMP politicians argued for such a law, as did some members of Hollande's own party. In the end, the observatory declared, on October 15, 2013, that existing laws were sufficient to curtail religious expression in private workplaces, but this pronouncement was met with strong opposition, including from dissenting members of the observatory itself.[135] As this case suggests, the French continue to turn to regulating the headscarf as a way to reinforce the centrality of republicanism, laïcité, and gender equality in the French national narrative of belonging.

As suggested earlier, the niqab ban has led to increased harassment of niqab-wearing women. Even in its formal application by police, the niqab ban caused unrest. In the summer of 2013, the application of the law led to riots in French banlieues.[136] On July 18, 2013, shortly before people were about to break their Ramadan fast, Cassandra Belin was out walking with her husband, Michaël Khiri, their baby, and Belin's mother in Trappes, a banlieu outside of Paris. Three police officers asked her to remove her face veil for an identity check. What followed is under debate. Newspapers report that, according to the police, Mr. Khiri assaulted them, attempting to strangle one of the officers and hitting them on their cheeks. Mr. Khiri was then arrested and detained. Mrs. Belin and Mr. Khiri, however, gave a different account of the events to the media. Claiming that Mrs. Belin's identity had been checked a number of times and that they had paid the fine for wearing a niqab in a public space more than once without any violence resulting, they argued that this time the police had shoved Mrs. Belin's mother and insulted Mrs. Belin and Mr. Khiri. In response, Mr. Khiri had tried to defend his wife and mother-in-law.[137]

On the evening following Mr. Khiri's arrest, a group of people protested peacefully in front of the police bureau to demand his release. Later that night, a group of between two- and four-hundred youths rioted in Trappes, burning trashcans and bus stops and throwing rocks at the police.

A smaller group repeated the riots the night after, burning fifteen cars and again throwing rocks. Images of burning cars and police in riot gear dominated the French press for days. In November 2013, Mr. Khiri was sentenced to three months in jail and a fine of one thousand euros, leading to another round of reporting, including the news that one of the three officers involved in the initial altercation was under investigation for posting potentially racist comments on his private Facebook account.[138] Both the riots (as well as a smaller riot for a similar reason in Argenteuil earlier in the summer) and the sentencing inspired renewed discussions about the place of Muslims in the French narrative of belonging. *Le Monde* gave voice to some criticisms of the implementation of the niqab ban, though the general thrust was that republicanism needed to be protected. One author, sociologist Hugues LaGrange, argued that these riots needed to be understood within the context of the social and economic exclusion of Muslims in France; another author, political scientist Jacques de Maillard, argued in an article entitled "The Veil Reveals the Failings of the Republican Pact" that a growing sense of alienation from the forces of law contributes to Muslim youths' distrust of the police.[139]

Though much of this ongoing debate focuses on the headscarf, burka, and niqab as threats to French public life, a number of Muslims have participated in these debates, which suggests that Muslim participation in the French public sphere is not an impossibility. These Muslims come from a wide range of backgrounds, though many of them occupy elite positions in French political and educational institutions. The Muslims who have participated in public debate have exhibited a great degree of fluency in French republican and laïc discourses. Their participation illustrates that the fear of social fissures associated with the headscarf, burka, and niqab has generated a process that has actually strengthened French discourses of belonging and participation. Given this fluency, it is not surprising that the national narrative produced in these debates has contained relatively few discordant notes, with general agreement about the importance for citizenship of a strong separation between church and state, and a dominant (though not completely shared) French national narrative that is rooted in the French Revolution's version of republicanism and subsequent formulations of laïc and gender-equality values. Indeed, polls suggest that many French Muslims agree with the headscarf ban in schools (with 42 percent of all French Muslims and 49 percent of all Muslim women agreeing with the 2004 ban [see Endnote 3]). The fact that 82 percent of the French population support the niqab ban suggests that it has support among French Muslims as well.[140] Organizations such as Ni Putes Ni Soumises, composed of immigrant women fighting for a particular interpretation of gender equality, produced discourses that reinforced French constructions of republicanism and laïcité and strongly supported banning the headscarf in its various manifestations.

Some Muslim feminists engage in forms of political activism that push the boundaries of belonging by seeking to carve out a niche for "modern," Islamic, French, veiled women. The debates about Ilham Moussaïd's candidacy in the 2010 regional elections illustrate how such women might provide a political challenge to the French national narrative of republicanism and laïcité by advocating for veiled women's capacity to operate as active republican citizens. At the same time, Moussaïd's work has not led to a fundamental questioning of French understandings of gender equality. Instead, it draws on a specifically French feminist discourse to combine "Frenchness" with being Muslim, arguing for a "French style headscarf with an emancipatory spirit."[141] The July 2013 riots in Trappes suggest that the niqab moves too far away from this French-style headscarf. They indicate that French Muslims in the banlieues, whose voices are largely absent from public debate, have heard the message embedded in these headscarf debates loud and clear: you cannot be French and exhibit outward signs of your religiosity. According to Minister of the Interior Manuel Valls, this strategy of protest indicates an inability to live in accordance with the rule of law.[142] We suggest instead that the Trappes protests signified that these protesters had very limited avenues for inserting themselves into French debates about national belonging, and they revealed their disenfranchisement from the French public sphere.

3

Reinventing the Headscarf in Turkey

FOUNDED IN 1923 by Kemal Atatürk on secular principles, the Republic of Turkey has historically produced a sense of national belonging by tightly controlling religious manifestations in the public sphere. Clothing has been regulated since the beginning of the Republic, with Atatürk introducing two reforms, in 1925 and 1934, jointly known as the Hat and Clothing Laws. This law forbade the wearing in public of religiously inspired clothing, such as the *çarşaf* (similar to the niqab) and the *fes* (the dark red brimless hat with a tassel that men wore during the Ottoman Empire). Though the law was unclear about scarves that covered women's hair and neck but not the face, a number of local authorities did not permit the wearing of headscarves. These regulations (and their local interpretations) aimed to create a secular public sphere as part of a process of Westernization initiated by the founders of the Republic. Indeed, men and women were encouraged to wear Western dress. During the first years of the Republic, those who did not obey these laws could be sanctioned—including execution of those wearing religious attire—by the Independence Courts that were in operation at the time.[1]

Although the general headscarf ban was lifted by the current government in the fall of 2013, the headscarf continues to be a contentious garment in the Turkish national narrative of belonging, where it has symbolized the Islam that secularists want to keep out of the public sphere. Over the past decades, headscarf debates have proliferated in the streets and in Turkey's parliament (*Türkiye Büyük Millet Meclisi*, or the Grand National Assembly), and these debates continue although the headscarf ban has been lifted. The stakes of these debates have come to the fore in recent discussions of the historic decisions of the Independence Courts.[2] Ayşe Böhürler, a prominent journalist, linked what happened to headscarf-wearing women during the founding of the Republic to the plight of Turkish headscarf-wearing women today:

According to the statistics of the Independence Courts, within the two and a half months after the Hat Act had been accepted, fifty-seven people were executed, and hundreds were imprisoned. The execution of an itinerant woman who sold clothes and scarves [bohçacı] who on her way to the scaffold asked with surprise, "Women are not wearing hats, why is my execution?" was interpreted by some as a means to prepare women to start wearing hats. . . . This woman, two meters tall, scarfaced, with her snakelike braids, black scarf [puşu], and her belief in patience, was Şalcı Bacı. . . . Perhaps on this occasion we find the opportunity to confront another trauma, which continues to be inflicted on women today. We perhaps arrive at the unopened graves of the clothing torture, which was done for the sake of the regime.[3]

Böhürler links the dead body of Şalcı Bacı to the continuing pain inflicted on religious women by political attempts to safeguard secularism in Turkish society through the ongoing regulation of women's clothing. The majority of Turkish women have always worn a headscarf and these restrictive regulations against religious clothing have had a profound impact on these women's socioeconomic standing,[4] as well as on their political participation and their felt sense of belonging. The legal bases for these exclusions have often been unclear and ad hoc: the interpretation of the secularism clause of the Turkish Constitution by people in positions of power, such as deans, heads of university departments, and heads of various other state institutions, as well as by members of the army, the parliament, and the governing executive.[5]

The debate over the place of the headscarf in Turkish politics and society has taken place in the many spaces in which the secular state is present, including the civil service, military compounds, and the parliament. However, the most forceful and persistent debates concerning the headscarf has taken place in Turkish universities.[6] Though this issue has been hotly debated since the 1960s, headscarves were banned outright only in 1982 by the *Yüksek Ögretim Kurumu* (Higher Education Council).

The stakes in these debates are high: it is through the universities that headscarf-wearing women gain the educational and employment-related resources that will allow them access to the middle and upper classes that have historically been occupied by pro-secular Turkish citizens. Merve Kavakçı-İslam, a politician who in 1998 was denied her place in the parliament when she was not allowed to take the oath of office while wearing the headscarf, argues that some pro-seculars[7] would not be bothered if a woman who is wearing a headscarf is a cleaning lady; however, they are bothered when a person overrides class boundaries and appears to be in an equal position with a secular woman.[8] Here, the use of the terms *başörtüsü* (kerchief) and *türban* (turban) mark an important distinction in the debate. Many pro-seculars see the former as an innocuous head covering, reminiscent of the cleaning lady, and the latter as a political statement whereas many pro-religious people use only *başörtüsü* but not *türban* in order to emphasize that their covering is religious and not political. Thus one can often interpret the positions people take from the term they use: the *türban* represents the woman who threatens the class boundaries that inform pro-secular national narratives whereas the *başörtüsü* is not considered a threat.

As in France, in political debates, media and personal accounts of the headscarf became a symbol of the struggle over the meaning of secularism in Turkey's national narrative. In photos from the 1920s we see Atatürk posing with Turkish women in Western-style clothing (skirts and dresses with no head covering) to model what it meant to belong to the new Turkish Republic.[9] These models were not uniformly embraced by the general public; women like Şalcı Bacı had been protesting the barriers to expressing religion publicly since the early years of the Republic. Oppositions between the pro-secular elite and the religious public produced a national narrative filled with tensions regarding the meaning of secularism, democracy, and Islam.

As we did for France, we analyze how these debates have defined Turkey's national narrative of belonging. The Republic was founded by a pro-secular elite who promoted a national narrative rooted in a strict interpretation of secularism as the absence of religion in the public sphere. This form of secularism was seen as a prerequisite for democracy. At the same time, a largely religious public continued to attempt to reinsert into the public sphere the religiosity sanctioned by the Ottoman Empire that preceded the Turkish Republic, generating the foundations for an alternative national narrative. As we show, over the past decade, this religious public started a pro-religious account of the Turkish national narrative.

In Turkey, being pro-secular has a strong basis in class politics. Whereas in France the debates have tended to frame headscarf-wearing Muslims as "immigrants" regardless of their citizenship status, the Turkish debates hinge on deeply entrenched class distinctions. Historical divisions have created a Turkish society segregated into a class of secular, urban ruling elites and a religious, rural underclass. Over time, Turkish pro-seculars have possessively invested in the institutions of the Turkish Republic: protecting its principles and values through legal and military force; safeguarding secular schools, neighborhoods, and government institutions from the possible threat of religious people; and constructing a "secular Turkishness" or a redefined form of being Muslim under the Turkish state that reflects the practices and attitudes of the Turkish governing elite. In this fashion, they have guaranteed secular supremacy—politically, economically, and socially—since the foundation of the Republic.

This pro-secular national narrative ultimately results in a society in which the benefits of being Turkish fall to its publicly secular citizens, who have been the ones to participate fully in Turkish institutions, whether the civil service, the schools, or the parliament.[10] When it comes to the headscarf as a symbol of religiosity, some pro-seculars have positioned women with headscarves as outsiders in Turkey, in recent years going so far as to explicitly state that such women belong to the Islamic Republic of Iran or to Saudi Arabia and should live there instead.[11] By excluding women with headscarves from the public sphere and denying them access to basic civil rights such as education and employment in civil services, some pro-seculars have attempted to unambiguously mark them as not belonging in Turkey.

In this conceptualization of being Turkish, belonging means that people can practice their religions privately while secular principles organize the public sphere. In these accounts, the pro-religious are the "other" of pro-secular politics. However, unlike in France, where "communalists" are the Republic's others, pro-religious actors have attained a much stronger political presence and have had a profound influence in shaping the contemporary Turkish national narrative. Shifting class boundaries have seen the rise of an Islamic elite who are impinging on spaces historically occupied by, even reserved for, seculars. These Islamic elites are adopting aspects of middle- and upper-class lifestyles, receiving university degrees as doctors, lawyers, and engineers, while maintaining their religious practices publicly. They go on vacations in five-star hotels, but they swim at gender-segregated beaches. Their daughters drive expensive cars but wear a headscarf while doing so. The rise of the Islamic elite has led many pro-seculars to see the pro-religious as a challenge to their elite status. In this context, the headscarf of religious women has become a symbol of political and socioeconomic threat for pro-secular actors and of ascent for pro-religious actors.

Critical to the new pro-religious national narrative emerging in Turkey is the Ak Party (*Adalet ve Kalkınma Partisi*, the Justice and Development Party), which entered the Turkish political scene in August 2001. Since it came to power after the 2002 elections, in part by promising to end the headscarf ban in universities, Ak Party politicians and supporters have aimed to end Turkey's pro-secular supremacy. They claim they want to erase class boundaries and establish a new sense of belonging based on an over-arching solidarity that would include both pro-secular and pro-religious people in Turkey.[12] Pro-religious party members continue to use concepts like democracy and secularism, around which the pro-secular elite built the national narrative, but they reinterpret them to fashion new understandings of national belonging. For the Ak Party and its supporters, this process of reinterpretation generates true democratization whereas the democracy of the pro-seculars generated its opposite: strict, exclusive, hierarchical forms of rule. According to pro-religious understandings of democracy and secularism, pro-religious citizens, specifically women with headscarves, should be able to enjoy rights similar to what pro-seculars enjoy, such as the right to be employed as a civil servant or to study at the universities. They argue for a sense of community and solidarity that is inclusive of all religious and nonreligious citizens[13] by pointing out (strategically) that women who wear the headscarf have been unfairly treated: publicly humiliated, excluded, and denied full access to their citizenship rights.

The secular national narrative had been buttressed by those in political power since the founding of the Republic, but the 2002 election of the religious Ak Party dramatically changed this. Accordingly, we focus on the period since 2002 to analyze how the Turkish national narrative has become so sharply divided between those who promoted the historically dominant understanding that the Turkish state requires secular democracy and those who developed a new understanding of the links between secularism, democracy, and Islam in the debates regarding the ban on headscarves in universities and other state institutions.

Drawing on public discourses, we show that the pro-seculars link secularism to Westernization, modernity, science, and reason, which produces a national narrative of belonging based on the argument that all of these elements are requirements for democracy. By contrast, the pro-religious promote an alternative interpretation and retell this national narrative by taking the Islamic religion as its basis. They do not reject the value of democracy but rather argue that democratic freedom requires full rights for religious people. The pro-religious politicians have borrowed concepts from liberal political discourse by linking support for diversity and an open civil society to democratic values of freedom of expression, including religious expression, thus combining an Islamic discourse with liberalism.[14]

By using the categories *pro-secular* and *pro-religious,* we do not aim to reproduce the dichotomies of those who are for or against secularism or for or against religion. In fact, as the large civil society protests that started in response to the proposed destruction of parts of Istanbul's Gezi Park in June 2013 show, many pro-seculars sympathize with pro-religious claims for freedom of religion, and many pro-religious people have joined pro-seculars in the protests against the Ak Party's politics of neoliberalism, gentrification, and cultural conservatism. In June 2013, a strong public resistance against the Ak Party government started in Gezi Park, an urban park in Taksim Square, Istanbul. Inhabitants of Taksim who started the initial resistance were against the proposed environmental destruction of Gezi Park in order to construct a shopping center in its place. In an attempt to stop the protesters who gathered in the park, the police used excessive amounts of tear gas, which they sprayed directly into people's faces. In response, the protests only grew larger, becoming a civil society movement with millions of people marching and protesting against the government's policies to destroy the environment and ignore women and minority rights, and against the government's efforts to erase lifestyle differences in Turkey. During this period, women with headscarves protested against the government's policies together with diverse groups of people ranging from environmentalists to gays and lesbians. The participation of diverse groups of people in the protests suggests that, in the face of an increasingly authoritarian government, the national narrative of Turkey is returning to questions about democracy that cut across a pro-secular versus pro-religious divide. Some pro-religious political actors have organized political groups such as Anticapitalist Muslims (*Antikapitalist Müslümanlar*) or Revolutionary Muslims (*Devrimci Müslümanlar*). These organizations are against the Ak Party's neoliberal economic policies and its monopoly over Islam in Turkey.

Just as pro-religious groups are diverse, so are the pro-seculars. Certainly some pro-seculars are strictly against all religious affiliations and symbols, as is Fazıl Say, a renowned classical and jazz pianist who publicly announced in 2013 that he is an atheist.[15] But pro-secular does not always mean being anti-Islamic, non-Muslim, or nonreligious. In fact, some pro-secular people pray, fast during Ramadan, and have a sacrifice during the Sacrifice Feast (*Kurban Bayramı*), thus fulfilling many of the requirements of the Islamic faith. What they object to is the politicization of Islam, and they fear political parties or state authorities that could enforce adherence to Islamic customs, laws, and values, such as Sharia courts, mandatory wearing of headscarves in public places, and Islamic education in schools. At the same time, many pro-secular people have a strong connection to an Anatolian-based Islam in which the cultural and traditional roots of Turkishness are constructed as intertwined with religion. For pro-seculars, however, democracy requires a secularism that precludes politics being informed by religion. Analogous to French republicanism's interdependence with *laïcité,* in Turkey, some pro-seculars argue that for those who want to keep the Islamic faith as something to be practiced in private and something that might have cultural resonance but never with the force of state law, democracy rests on secularism. Because some political claims of pro-religious and pro-secular groups overlap, in some public events, including the Gezi Park protests in 2013, many pro-secular and some pro-religious citizens of Turkey have cooperatively protested the government's politics, despite their differences in religious views.

Following the Gezi protests, on September 30, 2013, Prime Minister Erdoğan announced a new "Democratization Package,"[16] which included important changes for women who wear the headscarf. Headscarf-wearing women are now no longer prevented from entering public places where the state is present. In other words, headscarf-wearing women can now freely enter state offices, universities, and schools, and they can be employed in state offices while wearing a headscarf. The lifting of the headscarf ban signifies the triumph of one version of the pro-religious national narrative over the pro-secular one in that this religious attire can now become firmly ensconced as a symbol in the state's formerly secular spaces.

This chapter proceeds as follows: First, we give an overview of the major political and socioeconomic trends since the founding of the Turkish Republic in 1923 in order to analyze how these trends informed the Turkish national narrative, before outlining the role of the headscarf debate in this national narrative. Second, we turn to newspaper accounts of the headscarf from 2002 to 2011, as well as to interviews with a select number of headscarf-wearing political activists, to analyze the tensions in the contemporary Turkish national narrative, illuminating how the persistent conflicts between the pro-secular and pro-religious groups have fractured this narrative into two distinct accounts. We show how the pro-secular national narrative increasingly depends on secularism alone, losing sight of democracy as participation and relying on the law as a blunt instrument to enforce the secularist vision of Turkish national belonging. We then analyze pro-religious approaches to the headscarf to show how these constitute national belonging around religiosity and democracy. The pro-religious claim to represent the voice of civil society and to have taken over from the pro-seculars as protectors of democracy. However, the pro-religious claim to incorporate liberal principles regarding freedom of expression into Turkey's national narrative are marred by a gender politics, we argue, that reveals the exclusionary elements of the newly dominant pro-religious national narrative. Indeed, we can read the Ak Party's response to the Gezi protests and its new Democratization Package as a borrowing of the pro-seculars' blunt use of the force of law. Finally, we analyze how Turkish religious women who are active in civil society negotiate this terrain. On the one hand, headscarf-wearing women garner limited support from both pro-secular and pro-religious actors in their efforts to foreground the gender inequalities encountered by openly religious women. In their attempts to shape Turkish national narratives, these women critique both the secular Republic and the religious men in Turkey for using headscarf-wearing women strategically in their political fights while failing to grant these women full access to the public sphere (albeit for very different reasons). Ultimately, these women argue for more inclusiveness in Turkish society and politics. In the course of the Gezi Park protests against the Ak Party government in 2013, many groups, including some headscarf-wearing women, argued for a more inclusive society and respect for diversity. By lifting the headscarf ban on September 30, 2013, the Ak Party government showed its dedication to including headscarf-wearing women in the public sphere. Although the Democratization Package recognized some rights of Kurdish minority, showing similar sensitivity to other discriminated groups in Turkey (such as Alevis, the Greek Orthodox religious minority; Armenians; and other minorities in Turkey) is not on the Ak Party's political agenda. Therefore, the lifting of the headscarf ban is the continuation of the pro-religious Turkish national narrative, which defines national belonging through Islam and secularism.

The Narrative of National Belonging in Turkey: Secularism, Democracy, and Islam

The secular Turkish state was born out of the ashes of the Ottoman Empire. At the turn of the nineteenth century, a new generation of bureaucratic and military elites, known as the Young Turks (*Jeunes Turcs*) initiated a political and intellectual movement that challenged the religious foundations of Ottoman rule,[17] imagining a governing system based on secular principles and nationalist ideas. As their group name suggests, they were inspired by French nationalism as well as by French culture and literature. In 1923, after the collapse of the Ottoman Empire in 1917 and the four-year-long War of Independence, their ideas about nationalism, secularism, and modernization inspired Mustafa Kemal Atatürk as he founded the new Turkish Republic.

The ideas of the Jeunes Turcs were a political reflection of Turkey's position as both a bridge and a break between Europe and Asia. In the early years of the Republic, Turkish state authorities designed their political and governance strategies to be "European," turning away from Asia. Analogous to the secularization of nation-state formation in Europe, Atatürk and his followers created a new form of Turkishness based on an ethno-national rather than Islamic identity that they associated with the Ottoman Empire.[18]

Turkish secularism also echoes the French principle of laïcité, aiming at strict state neutrality in the public sphere in what Ahmet Kuru labels "assertive secularism."[19] However, unlike France, the Turkish state has control over religious affairs through its institutions, such as the Presidency of Religious Affairs (*Diyanet İşleri Başkanlığı*) established in 1924 after the caliphate was abolished. Turkey's elites felt that secularism was necessary to their nation-state project, yet they believed it to be fragile and under constant threat from a religious public. They therefore banned religiously oriented political parties, as well as all of the religious institutions that existed before the Republic, with a law that took effect in 1925. The Presidency of Religious Affairs was established instead by the state authorities, in order to have one state-controlled institution that managed all Islamic affairs in Turkey. Similarly, İmam Hatip schools[20] were established in 1924 by the government to train imams to be employed in mosques. State authorities monopolized their power over Islamic affairs through these institutions.

In 1937, the Turkish leadership identified six fundamental principles of the Kemalist state that tie secularism to statism, populism, republicanism, revolutionism, and nationalism[21]. These principles reflected the values of an intellectual urban elite and not necessarily those of the general Turkish public. Imposed on Turkish society from the top, the new social rules sharpened class distinctions and a rural/urban dichotomy, establishing the rule of this elite over those perceived as poor religious peasants from Anatolia (*taşralı*). From the start, therefore, the founders of the Turkish republican project resisted expressions of religiosity.[22] This resistance has produced contradictions in pro-seculars' avowed commitments to democracy as they have excluded and silenced people who do not belong to the urban intellectual ruling class.

Strict state control over religion somewhat loosened with the end of the single-party regime in 1946. The early years of Turkish democratic party politics saw a revival of religious values in the field of politics. The right-wing Democrat Party (*Demokrat Parti*) that came to power in 1950 criticized the secular ruling elite and appeared to gain popular support from pro-religious people, especially those in rural areas. Since then, the tension between secularism and religion that resulted from increased democratization of the political field has been a constitutive element of populist party politics in Turkey, used mostly by conservative-right parties (such as *Adalet Partisi*, the Justice Party). This tension intensified after the 1970s with the founding of the first political party established by the pro-religious groups, the National Order Party (*Milli Nizam Partisi*), in 1970. The National Order Party was closed down by the Constitutional Court within a year on the grounds that it violated the principle of secularism in the constitution, much as did its successor parties, the National Salvation Party (*Milli Selamet Partisi*), which existed from 1972 to 1980; the Welfare Party (*Refah Partisi*), which existed from 1983 to 1998; and finally the Virtue Party (*Fazilet Partisi*), which existed from 1998 to 2001. Although none of these parties gained a majority, they drew on the secular-religious tension in the Turkish national narrative and established a religious foothold in Turkish politics by positioning themselves as the champions of those disempowered by the anti-religious sentiments of the ruling elites.

Although these religious parties got their foothold in Turkish politics through democratic elections, their presence in politics also led to the intervention of the Turkish military, which acted as the protector of secular rule. Turkey's multiparty politics was interrupted four times by military coups d'état, each aiming to "correct" the path that Turkish democracy was taking. As the most important and powerful protector of the Turkish secular state, the military has been perceived as protecting not only the territorial unity of

Turkey but also its internal peace through its strong support of secularism. Thus the military became a protector of secularism, preventing pro-religious politicians from participating fully in Turkish politics. Through these coups, the military had a long-lasting effect on the meaning and practices of secularism and democracy. The 1980 military coup, which lasted three years, suspended practically all civil society initiatives and introduced a military constitution in 1982 that is still in use.[23] In an effort to enforce state-controlled Islam, as part of this constitution, religious courses that used to be electives in secondary schools were turned into compulsory courses.

Yet even the military has not been above using Islam to support its actions. During the 1980 military takeover, it attempted to resolve the political conflict generated by too strict interpretations of secularism by portraying Islam and Turkishness as unified identities, which had the potential to terminate the right-left conflict of the late 1970s and guarantee the survival of the state. This approach, later named the "Turkish-Islam synthesis," triggered the identity politics that came to dominate the Turkish national narrative in the following decades. Islamist ideology gained prominence, and Kurdish nationalism reemerged as a political movement that also undermined dominant definitions of democracy. Since then, Turkish society has increasingly divided into Turks versus Kurds and secularists versus Islamists.

The military, however, never fully supported religious political actors and the reinterpretation of secularism that enabled religiously informed political activity. On February 1997, what many called a "postmodern coup" took place. Different from other military coups in Turkey, this intervention was not abrupt and did not involve generally restricting the everyday lives of all Turkish citizens; instead, it was a slowly developing process of surveillance, interrogation, and imprisonment that targeted only the main actors of Islamist politics. At the time of the coup, President Necmettin Erbakan, leader of the Islamist Welfare Party (*Refah Partisi*), which had formed the biggest fraction in the parliament, with 21 percent of the popular vote, was presiding over a coalition government. This threat to secular supremacy proved to be too much for the military, which forced Erbakan to resign, and his party was closed down by the Constitutional Court in 1998. The military then instigated the widespread investigation, surveillance, and control of religious political actors and the "liberals" who supported them. Many who were regarded as pro-religious lost their jobs in military and civil service or were watched by government authorities supported by the military. The postmodern coup swung the political power pendulum back to pro-secular political actors. However, the pro-religious shifts in the national narrative that preceded the coup showed a great degree of resiliency.

Indeed, only five years after the postmodern coup, the pro-religious Ak Party was able to assume leadership on its own by gaining most of the votes, at 34 percent.[24] The Ak Party has its roots in the pro-religious political movement known as Milli Görüş, which literally means "National Vision." Milli Görüş had been the ideology of religious politics in Turkey since the formation of the National Order Party in 1970. After the Constitutional Court banned the religiously oriented Virtue Party from participating in politics in 2001, the Milli Görüş community was divided into two camps—conservatives and innovators (*yenilikçiler*). The conservatives supported Necmettin Erbakan, the spiritual leader of Milli Görüş. They founded the Felicity Party (*Saadet Partisi*) in 2001. The innovators supported Erdoğan, and his followers were the young generation within the Milli Görüş movement.[25] Ak Party leaders presented themselves as innovators in Turkish pro-religious politics as they started using concepts such as freedom and equality in their political campaigns and adapted neoliberal economic policies, which were new to the political tradition of the previous Milli Görüş parties. The Ak Party again received most of the votes (46.5 percent) in the 2007 and 2011 general elections (49.8 percent), becoming one of the longest reigning governing parties of the Turkish Republic.

Some pro-seculars experience the Ak Party's religiosity as a threat; they fear that political religiosity will become prescriptive of how people are to behave in general and that an Islamic way of life will be enforced through politics and law.[26] In fact, in 2008, the Ak Party's attempts to make changes to the Constitution in order to lift the headscarf ban in state institutions were harshly criticized by many pro-seculars. Perceiving this change as a threat to the secular principles of the Turkish state, the Ak Party had to face a Constitutional Court case for its efforts to lift the ban.

The pendulum between being religious and sending democratic messages has been the basis of the Ak Party's politics. Ak Party leaders argue that they are "conservative democrats," erasing the "Muslim" and "religious" dimensions from their party's political identity. Indeed, Ahmet Yükleyen, a professor of anthropology who has studied the religious influence on Turkish politics, labels the Ak Party "Muslim democrats," capturing the democratization process occurring among religious political elites, while recognizing the religious influence in the party.[27] This characterization corresponds to that of the Christian Democrats who have formed well-established political parties in a range of European countries, showing that even in secular states religiosity and democracy can coexist in the political sphere. From this perspective, the Ak Party is a religious, conservative, and democratic political party, as shown by the way they define secularism and democracy. Campaigning for the 2011 election, the Ak Party reinforced the dominance of its interpretation of secularism and democracy in the Turkish national narrative. By choosing the campaign slogan "It was a dream come true" (*Hayaldi gerçek oldu*), the Party referenced Martin Luther King Jr.'s revolutionary "I have a dream" speech, with its simultaneous appeals to religious inspiration and full democracy for all.

Ak Party politicians reinterpreted the meaning of secularism and democracy and argued that secularism, democracy, and Islam are compatible with each other.[28] This approach differed substantially from that of pro-secular political actors, who continued to promote the secular national narrative based on the principles of Kemalism that are foundational to the Republic. Furthermore, early on in the Ak Party's reign, the question was whether the pro-religious account could exist side-by-side with a pro-secular one or whether it was supplanting it. Many secular political actors seemed to have lost their credibility and their audience; the Turkish public had increasingly perceived the pro-secular interpretations of Turkishness as narrow, polemical, and out-of-date. When the Ak Party was elected to the government for a second time (in 2007), it was apparent that the secular political actors had lost the ability to determine the political agenda.

When it came to the everyday experience of living in Turkey, when the Ak Party came to power, many Turkish citizens had accepted that Turkey was a segregated society, divided along religious-secular and rural-urban lines and run by a pro-secular governing elite. But the Ak Party politicians constructed a new national narrative that portrayed the Ak Party as the savior of Turkey. Reframing the meaning of secularism and democracy (and building on Turkish economic successes), their national narrative portrayed Turkey as a new country with a sense of community and solidarity that is inclusive of all religious and nonreligious citizens.

Throughout the Ak Party's time in power, some pro-seculars have voiced their fear of the impact that the Ak Party's national narrative, which imagines Turkey as a community based on religious solidarity, could have on everyday life. They have argued that this narrative puts pressure on people to abandon secularist views in order to be included in the pro-religious trends in Turkish society. Such pro-secular journalists and authors have claimed that the dynamics of Turkish society were being turned upside down: religious people were now pressuring pro-seculars to conform to the religious rules if they wanted to keep their social status. In an intensive prosecution process known as the Ergenekon Affair, many pro-secular military officers were tried and imprisoned during the Ak Party's struggle to determine its political agenda.

However, the reality was even more complex than just pro-religious and pro-secular power struggles, as seen through the rise of new democratic movements against an increasingly authoritarian government. The Gezi Park protests, which brought Turkish people together to protest against the government's policies, are examples of public unrest toward neoliberal politics, gentrification, and attempts to erase differences in lifestyle, such as restricting alcohol consumption.

We now turn to an examination of the participation of headscarf-wearing women in such civil society movements, and of the meaning of this participation in the development of the Turkish national narrative. We first illustrate what their presence means in the development of the Turkish national narrative by outlining the history of the headscarf ban in Turkish universities between the early 1960s and 2001. We then turn to our analysis of the headscarf debates following the Ak Party's ascent to political power in order to analyze the ongoing transformations of Turkey's national narrative.

A Brief History of the Headscarf Ban in Turkish Universities

A look at the headscarf debate enables an analysis of how changes to the Turkish national narrative are unfolding. Clothing regulations have been part and parcel of the Turkish Republic since its foundation, with Atatürk passing the so-called Hat and Clothing Laws in 1925 and 1934. These reforms were a key element in the establishment of a secular Turkish public sphere where Western dress became a visual manifestation of the Turkish national narrative of belonging. During the 1960s, covered women were in principle to be expelled from the universities, because they did not comply with the general clothing regulation that had banned religious attire in Turkey since the early days of the Republic.[29] However, university administrators and professors exercised some discretion in placing limits on headscarf-wearing women in universities. For example, in 1964, a student of medicine at İstanbul University who wore the headscarf managed to attend lectures and exams and finished her degree as a top student. However, in the graduation ceremony, she was not allowed to give the valedictory speech, which a top student would normally give, so as not to give highly visible support to a nonsecular way of belonging to Turkey.

After the 1980 military coup, General Kenan Evren outright banned the wearing of headscarves by university students; this was followed in 1982 by a ban on headscarves for government officials. Moreover, the headscarf ban was implemented discretionally in high schools beginning in 1981[30] and in government offices beginning in 1982.[31] The years following the ban saw a great deal of ambivalence in terms of headscarf-wearing in public. In an ongoing struggle between religious university students, who claimed their right to freedom of expression, and the military, which saw itself as a protector of strict Turkish secularism, the ban was lifted and reinstated many times throughout the 1980s and 1990s. The Higher Education Council, established by the military government in 1980, introduced the headscarf ban into universities in 1982 but removed it in 1984. Students who wore the headscarf for religious reasons believed that the removal of the ban was due to their growing protests. In 1989, the country's Constitutional Court reinstated the ban after a complaint by President Evren, the general behind the 1980 military coup.[32] During the 1980s, the Higher Education Council added a number of clauses to its Code (1982, 1987, and 1988), first widening the scope for wearing a headscarf in universities, but ultimately narrowing it, after the Constitutional Court declared it a violation of secularism.[33] In 1990, a final legal arrangement was made and a new clause was added to the Higher Education Council's Code. The clause stated, "There is freedom of dress in institutions of higher learning unless it is a violation of the existing laws."[34]

It was during this period that people started to distinguish between *başörtüsü* as a neutral religious expression and the *türban* as an expression of pro-religious politics. Drawing on the secular national narrative, the president of the Higher Education Council, İhsan Doğramacı, was instrumental in differentiating between the two, asserting that the *başörtüsü* is more "modern" and therefore "acceptable" in the universities.[35] However, in 1992, pro-secular state authorities declared that "both *başörtüsü* and *türban* were antithetical to *laiklik* [secularism]."[36] In other words, according to the pro-secular national narrative, the headscarf, no matter what form it takes, is a threat to secularism and so should not be worn in state institutions and preferably not anywhere in public.

This declaration created a legal struggle between the parliament, led by then Prime Minister Turgut Özal,[37] leader of the mainstream conservative Motherland Party (*Anavatan Partisi*), and the head of state, President Evren. Prime Minister Özal argued for the inclusion of headscarf-wearing women in the universities as a matter of human rights[38] (an argument later picked up by the pro-religious), whereas President Evren argued against its presence at institutions of higher education. From 1991 through 1998, there was no ban on headscarves at universities, mostly because of the political strategies of mainstream conservative parties (such as the Motherland Party) to attract votes from the pro-religious electorate. However, after Prime Minister Erbakan's electoral victory and the establishment of an Islamist government under his rule, the Turkish military stepped in and deposed him during the so-called postmodern coup on February 28, 1997, in order to eliminate all Islamist movements.[39] It also reinstated the ban on headscarves in universities, and in 1998 the judges in the Turkish Constitutional Court supported this headscarf ban, determining that "in a secular state, religion cannot serve as a frame of reference."[40] The Higher Education Council then issued a ban to all the universities. All of a sudden, students found themselves not able to graduate because of the headscarf ban and they protested en masse in front of the universities.

Among these students was Leyla Şahin, who garnered national and international media attention when she took her case to the European Court of Human Rights (ECtHR)[41] in 1998.[42] Her case has played an important role in constructing the pro-religious Turkish national narrative by claiming that the headscarf ban was discriminatory against religious students and a violation of their freedom of religion. In 2004, the ECtHR decided against Leyla Şahin on the grounds that Turkey has secular universities, and that the headscarf as a religious symbol threatens public order. Furthermore, the judges stated,

In a country like Turkey, where the great majority of the population belong to a particular religion, measures taken in universities to prevent certain fundamentalist religious movements from exerting pressure on those who do not practice that religion . . . may be justified under Article 9 (2) of the Convention. In that context, secular universities may regulate manifestation of the rights and symbols of the said religion by imposing restrictions as to the place and manner of such manifestation with the aim of ensuring peaceful co-existence between students of various faiths and thus protecting public order and the beliefs of others.[43]

This decision is in line with the Court's tendency to determine narrowly its margins to intervene in a state's affairs, under the "margin of appreciation" doctrine.[44] After the Grand Chamber of the ECtHR gave its final decision, Prime Minister Recep Tayyip Erdoğan said, "The Court has nothing to say on this issue, we have to ask the *Ulama* [Muslim scholars]"[45]—in effect saying that religious authorities are more important for Turkey than the European judges, and implicitly condemning the pro-secular national narrative that glorified Western law and civilization over Islamic law. In this debate, prominent international politician Emine Bozkurt, a Dutch citizen who represents the Dutch Party of Labour in the European Union parliament, argued that Leyla Şahin's case showed that the headscarf controversy could not be solved externally by appealing to Europe; rather, it was an internal matter.[46]

The Ak Party established itself politically through its handling of the headscarf issue and made it an internal matter. During the Ak Party's rise to power, many aspects of secularism and religion were debated through discussions of whether headscarves should continue to be banned at universities. In their campaign speeches leading up to the November 2002 election, Ak Party candidates said that solving the headscarf issue was a priority.[47] When Şahin's appeal to the European Courts did not meet with success, the Ak Party government decided to solve the headscarf issue through an internal legal struggle. In 2008, this led the Ak Party to propose changes to the Constitution—changes that failed to pass, however. They would have lifted the ban on the headscarf in higher education by adding clauses to two articles in the Constitution, Article 42 and Article 10, which ensure equal opportunity in education and gender equality. Article 10 states, "Men and women possess equal rights. The state is responsible for ensuring that this equality is realized in practice." The article also asserts that "state organs and administrative offices shall proceed according to the principle of equality before the law," to which would have been added "in receiving any kind of public service." To Article 42, which said that no one shall be deprived of his right to education, the Ak Party proposed adding the following clause: "No one shall be deprived of his right to higher education for any kind of reason unless it is specified by law. The limits to use of this right are defined by law." This clause would have guaranteed that the lifting of the ban would have been limited to higher education.[48] Combined, these clauses aimed to introduce a distinction between receiving and giving service within the state, so that women with headscarves would be able to enter higher education as receivers of a public service. These proposed changes to the Constitution caused massive protests in the streets of Turkey's major cities, by both those for and those against them. In the end, the Ak Party failed to get these additions past a pro-secular judiciary, and arguably the proposed constitutional amendments showed the continuing deep fissures within Turkish society's understanding of the place of religion in national narratives of belonging.

The president of the Constitutional Commission of Parliament, Burhan Kuzu, one of Turkey's preeminent constitutional law professors, gave a convincing speech on why the proposed amendments were not against the first three articles of the Constitution, which by law cannot be amended.[49] In addition, the amendments would have brought Turkey's Constitution in line with the Committee on the Elimination of Discrimination against Women (CEDAW) Convention, as well as other international human rights conventions. These conventions recognized the right to education as a basic human right and the proposed amendments would have removed the violation of the Conventions.

The proposed amendments initially passed the parliament on February 6 and 9, 2008, just before the start of the second semester in the Turkish universities. Many universities lifted the headscarf ban without waiting for the official decision of the Constitutional Court; however, some universities and departments continued not to accept students who wore headscarves. In fact, Turkish newspapers reported on the universities and their specific departments that did not allow students with headscarves on their premises.[50] Then, on March 6, 2008, the opposition Republican People's Party (*Cumhuriyet Halk Partisi,* henceforth CHP) made an official complaint to the Constitutional Court that lifting the headscarf ban would be against secularism. On June 5, 2008, the Constitutional Court annulled the amendments, in line with the pro-secular national narrative that such amendments would undermine secularism and Article 2 of the Constitution. In addition, on March 14, 2008, the Constitutional Court threatened the Ak Party with closure and with banning its politicians from politics.

At this point, the Higher Education Council unofficially lifted the headscarf ban. In 2010, Yusuf Ziya Özcan, professor of sociology at the Middle East Technical University and former head of the Higher Education Council, issued a new regulation that the Council would not permit religious students to be removed from their classrooms. Similarly Zafer Üskül, professor of constitutional law and former head of the Human Rights Commission in the Turkish parliament, said that university professors should not be policing students with headscarves.[51] With these new Higher Education Council regulations in place, backed by prominent politicians, students with headscarves could attend universities, although sometimes they still encountered difficulties at the university gates or in the lecture halls.[52]

Then, on September 30, 2013, Prime Minister Erdoğan announced the Democratization Package and officially lifted the headscarf ban in Turkey. Headscarf-wearing women can now officially be employed in state offices (except those that require special uniforms, such as the military and the police) and study at universities without any restrictions. Although some pro-secular politicians criticized the lifting of the ban and called on the Constitutional Court to intervene, as of December 2013 there has been no attempt at intervention.

Transformations in the Turkish National Narrative: The Turkish Media

In order to trace what the headscarf debates can show us about transformations in the Turkish national narrative, we turned to three national newspapers (*Hürriyet, Cumhuriyet,* and *Zaman*) and analyze reporting regarding the headscarf between 2002 and 2011 (with updates on selected events until 2013). The ownership and readership of these papers represent the various ways in which the Turkish national narrative of belonging is articulated, in part because the media are closely tied to specific political actors and appeal to their specific audiences. In addition, we interviewed a small number of key civil society actors in the debate, including politically active headscarf-wearing women. In our analysis, we show that rather than producing two versions of the Turkish national narrative, the pro-secular and pro-religious articulations increasingly look like two competing Turkish national narratives that build on alternative interpretations of Turkish history and politics. Our interviews reveal some of the tensions between these diverging pro-secular and pro-religious accounts of the Turkish national narrative. However, our brief analysis of the 2013 protests against the Ak Party government, which brought together some pro-religious and pro-secular people, suggests that a new national narrative may be emerging out of the protests.[53]

Zaman, the country's largest newspaper, has a pro-religious perspective. *Zaman* is politically supported by Fethullah Gülen, a powerful religious actor with extensive global networks who condemns violence in the

name of religion and supports interreligious dialogue and religious education.[54] Gülen started out in the 1960s as a religious rather than a political
leader. Eventually, he became the leader of a socioreligious movement that
established educational institutions around the world that promoted Turkish Islamic education.[55] As a result of these and other efforts, Fethullah
Gülen became politically influential in Turkey. He is in favor of women's se-
clusion, especially of wearing of headscarves, and this is reflected in *Zaman*.

Although *Zaman* has been published in Turkey since 1986, it did
not have powerful political influence prior to the election of the Ak Party,
which *Zaman* supports in its humanist and conservative religiosity. *Zaman*
appeals to an educated, urban, religious readership, reporting in detail on
international events and including intellectual and academic articles written by or translated from established scholars. Published in fifteen countries and distributed in many others, *Zaman* now enjoys a considerable
readership both in and outside Turkey; about eight hundred thousand
papers are circulated per day. To ensure that we fully captured the pro-
religious perspective on the headscarf debates, we cross-checked key parts
of *Zaman*'s reporting and editorials with two smaller pro-religious newspapers, *Vakit* and *Yeni Şafak*.

In order to understand pro-secular narratives, we collected data from
the pro-secular *Hürriyet* newspaper, which has an estimated circulation of
half a million. *Hürriyet* has historically represented the voice of the traditional political elite. For many years, *Hürriyet* used Atatürk's profile on
a Turkish flag as its logo, along with the statement, "Turkey belongs to
Turks." *Hürriyet* also represents a newsmaking legacy: it was founded in
1948 by the Simavis, a pre-eminent Turkish media family. *Hürriyet* has
always had a tendency to be more populist than the other papers; it is
written in simple language and contains large colored pictures. Especially
since it joined the Doğan Media Group owned by businessman Aydın
Doğan in 1994, the paper has fiercely defended a liberal, secular, and antireligious position. The Doğan Media Group is highly influential, own-
ing many widely circulated newspapers and popular TV channels, such as
CNN Türk. Until 2011, it also owned *Milliyet*, a slightly more highbrow
paper that we turned to in order to flesh out some of *Hürriyet*'s reporting.
With the rise of the Ak Party, the nationalist and pro-secular *Hürriyet* as
well as *Milliyet* have had to compete with *Zaman* for dominance in the
media field. Although not an open supporter of a political party, *Hürriyet*
(and *Milliyet*) has been clearly critical of the government, representing the

different points of view of the pro-secular public. Recently, negotiations between the Doğan Media Group and the government have led to a tempering of *Hürriyet*'s critical stance toward the government.[56]

Of the three main newspapers we analyzed, perhaps the most controversial is *Cumhuriyet*. Founded in 1924 right after the establishment of the Republic, *Cumhuriyet* was the leading center-left newspaper during the Cold War era; it has since become a platform for the most outspoken pro-seculars, specifically Kemalists, incorporating extreme antireligious and anti–Ak Party accounts into its pages. *Cumhuriyet* has always had a small circulation (approximately fifty thousand in 2010), because of its appeal to a small group of educated, left-wing readers; but its participation in media debates is of interest because it represents the limits of public discourse on the pro-secular side. *Cumhuriyet* has always been a threat to powerful elements of Turkey's politics and society. In the 1980s and 1990s, some of its writers were assassinated. In 1993, Uğur Mumcu, a well-known writer in *Cumhuriyet*, who was researching Islamic movements in Turkey, was killed by a car bomb. In a move that shows the tension surrounding religion in Turkish politics, in the 1990s the government banned *Cumhuriyet* from daily circulation because of its provocative anti-Islamic content. For example, it once published a translation of part of *The Satanic Verses* by Salman Rushdie, a book considered anti-Islamic, illustrating that *Cumhuriyet*'s pro-secularism went beyond that deemed acceptable even to the secular powers of the time. *Cumhuriyet* continues to represent the limits of pro-secular arguments, at times coming close to defaming the pro-religious government currently in power.

We also interviewed five people. In Istanbul, we interviewed Ayşe Böhürler, a journalist and film producer. She represents a critical stance in the media, although she is involved in the Ak Party. We also interviewed Atilla Yayla, a professor of political science at Plato University, a newly founded private university in Balat, Istanbul. He provided us with insights into the liberal perspectives of Ak Party supporters. In Ankara we spoke with Hidayet Şefkatli Tuksal, a critical journalist and writer especially known for her critical stand against the instrumentalization of the headscarf. Tuksal introduced us to the Başkent Women's Platform. We also interviewed Berrin Sönmez, chair of the Başkent Women's Platform, in Ankara. Sönmez is leader of a group of women who supported the "No headscarf, no vote!" campaign that aimed to increase the number of headscarf-wearing women in the parliament during the national elections of 2011. Finally, Zeynep Göknil Şanal, from the General Directorate on the Status of Women (part of the Ministry of Family in Turkey) and affiliated with the Başkent Women's Platform, introduced us to the history of the headscarf debate in Turkish universities, which had unfolded when she was a student. In these interviews, we gained firsthand information from academics, social activists, and journalists engaged in the headscarf debate in Turkey.

Pro-Secular Arguments in the Headscarf Debate: Producing a Fragile National Narrative

As our label itself suggests, pro-secular arguments regarding the headscarf are primarily concerned with the centrality of secularism as the cornerstone of the Turkish national narrative. In its almost exclusionary focus on this dimension, the pro-secular account of Turkish belonging is becoming increasingly narrow and, as a result, fragile, capturing the sentiments of a declining albeit very vocal and historically powerful segment of the population.

Pro-seculars put forward two arguments against the headscarf. In the first argument, the headscarf symbolizes a rejection of the enlightenment, including rational thought and scientific inquiry. In the second, wearing the headscarf is a practice that breaks the law. Finally, we show how gender equality arguments enter the debate through the interventions of pro-secular women.

The Headscarf as Rejection of Enlightenment Thought

The argument regarding the enlightenment is directly aimed at the wearing of headscarves in the university. For example, the late İlhan Selçuk, an influential political cartoonist and a veteran writer for *Cumhuriyet*, referred to Galileo's comment that the Bible cannot replace science, making the following analogy with the Turkish case:

Today Turkey is going through the historical tragedy of Galileo Galilei in a different way. How? Turkey's Prime Minister Erdoğan was educated in an imam school; he became the head of the government, where he should have belonged to the clergy. . . . If a young girl covers her head because of her faith, no one has a word to say; but wearing a headscarf does not go with the concept of university. A person who covers her hair will certainly argue against the theory of evolution; it is natural that she holds religious beliefs above scientific freedom. . . . [Therefore] the headscarf in the university means the end of scientific freedom.[57]

For pro-secular writers like Selçuk, having a religious prime minister who advocates for allowing religious expression in the public sphere did not signal liberal freedoms of expression and religion. Rather, he saw this as an attempt to move backward to an era preceding the Turkish Republic in which religious doctrine guided governance and in which scientific inquiry was an impossibility in light of religious teachings regarding creation. Selçuk did not reject the idea that religious people belong in Turkey per se. Rather, he argued that one can act religiously only in a role that is outside the sphere of politics. That is, Erdoğan can be an imam and belong to Turkey but he cannot be a religious prime minister in the secular Turkish state. Selçuk thus rejected the possibility of multiplicity in identity—to be religious is to be so in all facets of life. The possibility that a young headscarf-wearing woman might also be a physician, or studying biology and life sciences to become one, would be an impossibility from this perspective. Because of this imputed impossibility, creating space for headscarves on university campuses would threaten the very foundations of the Turkish Republic, with its grounding in enlightenment ideas of scientific inquiry and rational governance.

This pro-secular emphasis on the enlightenment, on linking positivistic science to secularism, reverberates throughout the public statements of pro-secular politicians, writers, and newsmakers. Perhaps its most important expression occurred in the 2008 Constitutional Court statements banning the headscarf.[58] In its decision, the Constitutional Court stated that secularism has its roots in "Renaissance, Reformation, and Enlightenment,"[59] historical processes that unfolded beyond Turkey's European borders and became orienting points for the Turkish national narrative only with the founding of the Turkish Republic. Yet, as contemporary political developments in Turkey make clear, these reference points resonate primarily for a Turkish elite, such as the judges and lawyers who write legal decisions, and not necessarily for the general public.

In the Constitutional Court decision and in ongoing editorials in the pro-secular media, the headscarf is presented as a symbol of religious dogma that does not fit into the universities as institutions of scientific freedom. As the allusions to the Renaissance, Reformation and, Enlightenment in these arguments make clear, pro-seculars continued in the tradition of Atatürk to root the Turkish national narrative in a Western history and intellectual development that have occurred largely outside Turkey's borders.

Headscarf-Wearers as Law Breakers

Many editorials in the pro-secular media have emphasized that wearing the headscarf in the university is a form of lawbreaking. Furthermore, they have argued that it undermines the constitutional legal principle of secularism, which pro-seculars have interpreted as the strict separation of religion and the state, meaning that no religious symbols should be worn in institutions of the state. In part because its roots are outside the history that preceded the establishment of the Turkish Republic, secularism has become a fragile foundation for the Turkish national narrative. Pro-secular arguments have reflected this fragility in an almost hectoring insistence that secularism is the law, something to be enforced by legal authorities. Pro-seculars making such arguments clearly do not feel they can appeal to secularism as a deeply embedded discourse defining Turkish belonging. In the early 2000s, during the period immediately following the ascendancy of the Ak Party, a few key political actors as well as some newsmakers equated headscarf-wearing and lawbreaking in order to promote the argument that the headscarf was against the law and to make it a symbol of the possible collapse of the Turkish Republic. President of Istanbul University Kemal Alemdaroğlu, a strong proponent of pro-secular arguments, said that "the *türban* is outlawed by the Constitutional Court and the Council of the State. It is outlawed by the European Court of Human Rights. The *türban* is a symbol. It is the symbol of fundamentalism. This [entry of fundamentalist Islam into the institutions of higher education] is not possible."[60] In this equation of the headscarf with fundamentalist Islam, a political movement that would build a state on religious rather than secular principles, fundamentalism is held in check by the principle of the rule of law, not by the will of the people bound together by a widely shared national narrative.

Similarly, Ahmet Necdet Sezer, president of Turkey from 2000 to 2007 and a strong proponent of the secular Turkish national narrative, pointedly did not invite the headscarf-wearing wives of Ak Party ministers to the presidential residence for important celebrations, such as the anniversary of the foundation of the Republic on October 29, 2003. Of this event, he said, "The Turkish Republic is a secular, democratic and social state of law [*sic*].[61] Recently, there has been an intention to take a stance against the secular character of the state. I did not want to give them [members of the Ak Party government] this opportunity."[62] By linking secularism and democracy to the rule of law, Sezer inferred that wearing the headscarf rejects the state of law, presumably replacing it with a state of religion. Indeed, for men like Alemdaroğlu and Sezer, headscarves are by definition antisecular, and therefore state institutions, including state buildings, should be protected from women with headscarves.

Indeed, when the ECtHR decided against Leyla Şahin in 2004, prosecular Republic President Ahmet Necdet Sezer issued an official letter in which he aligned the decisions related to the headscarf ban in higher education made by the Constitutional Court and the Council of the State with the ECtHR. He underlined that the ECtHR decided in accordance with Turkish domestic law that secular universities must impose sanctions on students who do not comply with the regulations.[63] Sezer used the ECtHR decision to further confirm that women with headscarves are in breach of the secular regulations. During the parliamentary discussions of this decision, the main opposition party, CHP, warned the Ak Party government that it should not expect support from Europe for its antisecular attempts. This warning further reinforced the pro-seculars' alliance with European culture, history, and legal systems in their account of the Turkish national narrative.

Cumhuriyet has also given voice to the deeply held fears inspired by the headscarf throughout the period of Ak Party rule. During the 2008 debate regarding the Ak Party's proposed changes to the Constitution to allow women to wear the headscarf in state institutions, veteran journalist Orhan Bursalı argued that "to introduce [the] headscarf as a constitutional right is a general threat! To enforce the headscarf throughout the country is the biggest step toward bringing religion into the country's legal system and to bury secularism in the grave."[64] Interestingly, Bursalı equates the *right* to wear a headscarf to an *enforcement* of wearing the headscarf, again with implied references to fundamentalism as not allowing any other worldview to inform who belongs to Turkey. Indeed, in the arguments put forth by Alemdaroğlu, Sezer, Bursalı, and other pro-seculars, religion is seen not as something one chooses to express, but rather as a force that could transform an entire people and its society. In an interview published in *Hürriyet*, well-known Turkish scholar Şerif Mardin called the force of religion a "neighborhood pressure" (*mahalle baskısı*) under which everyone has to conform to societal norms.[65] If pro-religious power were to rise, people would be pressured to fast during Ramadan not because they were believers but because if one did not fast, neighbors, friends, and colleagues would exclude one from their social circles. Similarly, one of the main discussions in the pro-secular Turkish newspapers focused on peer pressure in the universities, arguing that nonreligious women who did not wear headscarves would be discriminated against in the universities if the headscarf ban were to be lifted. According to many secular Turks, this would in turn mean the end of secularism, the central principle in the pro-secular Turkish national narrative.

For pro-seculars, the social pressure of religion needs to be checked with legal instruments of power and control. However, the implication of taking such a position is that it moves secularism away from being a discourse of belonging with wide subjective appeal to being one of using force against those who want to express their religiosity publicly. As a result, such arguments are likely to appeal solely to those who already object to the headscarf and to other forms of religious expression. As an indication of how fractured the Turkish national narrative has become, *Cumhuriyet* writers have often cited parliamentarians from the CHP opposition party, who have warned that a problematic "counterrevolution" is occurring.[66] This counterrevolution, they have suggested, threatens to undermine the historic Atatürk revolution and its insistence on secularism as the founding principle of the Turkish Republic.

The resulting pro-secular national narrative portrays women with headscarves and their supporters as lawbreakers, threats to secularism, and promoters of fundamentalist Islam. By disseminating this image of religious women as threats against the secular state, pro-secular state authorities have separated themselves from the religious public, using the legal system—judges, courts, and legal processes—as a protector of secular rule, and using the law to justify their power over religious people.

Pro-Secular Women and Gender Equality Arguments

Although gender equality played an important role in the articulation of the French national narrative (and as we will see, in the Dutch and German narratives), it was far more latent in the pro-secular articulation of the Turkish national narrative. Pro-secular women were the ones to insert the idea of gender equality into the pro-secular version of the Turkish national narrative. These women supported Westernization and saw secularism in particular as the guarantor of gender equality in Turkey.[67] In fact, many pro-secular women believed they owed their very existence to Kemalism.[68]

Showing similarity with their European counterparts, female pro-secular political actors often argued that the headscarf represented back-wardness and women's oppression. Furthermore, Turkish women working actively against the headscarf joined their male counterparts in drawing on legal arguments to try to reinforce a secular Turkish national narrative. These women argued that the headscarf fell outside the law, not only in the Turkish context but in general—rejecting that it could ever be a woman's human right to wear one. In the 1990s, Nur Serter had actively enforced the headscarf ban in universities as vice president of İstanbul University. In 2008, in her capacity as a parliament member for the CHP, she argued, "The headscarf cannot be interpreted in basic rights and freedoms. It is a clothing style that reduces woman to a second-class person. Freedoms are advancements."[69] Necla Arat, professor of philosophy and founder of the first women's studies program in İstanbul University, as well as a CHP member of the parliament, made a similarly forceful argument: "The de-ception of 'freedom for the *türban'* is nothing but disrespect to the state and the constitution. . . . the *türban* [is] not a problem of 'freedom and human rights of women'; it is actually an escape from freedom, a volun-tary abandoning of acquired rights and a choice of voluntary servitude."[70] As in the French case, such arguments did not attribute agency to wear-ing the headscarf, seeing it instead as a sign of submission and debase-ment. Although these particular Turkish women's voices were not central in the mainstream debates, they lent support to accounts that gave pride of place to secularism in the Turkish narrative of belonging. Yet this narrative showed its internal fragility in its appeal to law as a way to force people to enact Turkishness, which in turn opened a path for a pro-religious rewrit-ing of the Turkish national narrative of belonging.

Reinterpreting Secularism: Democracy Requires Religious Freedom

Turkish pro-religious actors are creating a new narrative of belonging. Rather than retelling the old story and adjusting it to the contemporary so-cial context, as we saw in the French case, they have woven democracy and Islam together in a way that has effectively negated the interpretation of sec-ularism that was so central to the pro-secular national narrative of belonging to Turkey. Before developing a new narrative, the Ak Party and others who argued for the right to wear headscarves in universities started out referring to religious obligations, seemingly justifying pro-secular fears regarding the inclusion of religion in governance. As we mentioned earlier, in 2004 Erdoğan responded to the ECtHR decision in the Şahin case by stating, "The Court [ECtHR] has nothing to say on this issue, we have to ask the Ulama."[71] This statement suggested that he placed religious law over international human rights law, and in doing so he confirmed pro-secular fears. Similarly, in the 2002 election campaign, Ak Party member and chairman of the parliament Bülent Arınç referred to the headscarf as a reflection of honor (*namus*[72]), promising voters to protect and defend it: "The headscarf problem is an issue of honor. We will solve it!"[73] Although the use of patriarchal terminology was challenged by some pro-religious writers who supported the Ak Party, Arınç's promise was widely circulated in the media as election campaign material, reinforcing the notion that the headscarf symbolized a threat to the secular, rational foundations of the Turkish nation.

Since then, the Ak Party, along with its supporters and the pro-religious media, have adopted a different terminology, emphasizing "democratic freedom" or "freedom of expression" in its pro-headscarf arguments instead of saying that wearing the headscarf is a religious obligation. In doing so, they are constructing a new Turkish national narrative. For example, in January 2008, Prime Minister Erdoğan gave a speech in Madrid in which he argued that political Islam and its supporters *should* enter Turkish universities. Rewriting the meaning of secularism by drawing on liberal discourses about freedom of expression, Erdoğan argued that although the headscarf could be a political symbol of fundamentalist Islam, this does not mean it should be banned: "Even if [women] wear it as a political symbol, can you consider wearing a political symbol as an offence? Do we see this kind of a ban anywhere in the world?"[74]

Whereas pro-seculars drew on a European enlightenment discourse to make their claims, Erdoğan turned to a universal ("anywhere in the world") human rights discourse, arguing that wearing political symbols is not inherently an offense against the secular state. Of course, in the Turkish context, this meant a radical reinterpretation of secularism, away from French-style laïcité, in which religiosity is expressed in private, toward what has elsewhere been called an "open secularism" that allows for a diversity of religious and nonreligious expression in the public sphere.[75]

For example, during the discussions in the Turkish parliament on the ECtHR's decision on Leyla Şahin's case, the opposition CHP used the law-breaking argument to call for the Ak Party's removal from government.[76]

The CHP argued that the Ak Party had contravened Turkish law, and they supported their claim by referencing the ECtHR's positive evaluation of the previous Minister of Foreign Affairs' argument that "the *türban* is the symbol of fundamentalism. . . . Turkish adjudication does not render it possible for this symbol to be used in the public sphere." In response, the Ak Party's Abdullah Gül, who was Minister of Foreign Affairs at the time and became president of the Republic in 2007, countered by stressing that the government "is on the side of freedoms, [and] does not favor the solution of such issues through bans."[77]

In making such arguments, Erdoğan, Gül, and other pro-religious actors countered pro-secular claims that secularism is the guarantor of "scientific freedom" in the universities and the bedrock of belonging in Turkey. Instead, pro-religious actors drew on the principle of democracy that, as we argued previously, gradually disappeared in pro-secular accounts of the Turkish national narrative. According to pro-religious actors, secularism as implemented in Turkey works against democratic freedoms, such as the freedom of expression, which is crucial to open dialogue and exchange of ideas in a university setting. By redefining secularism through the lens of liberal democracy, pro-religious actors reinterpreted the Turkish national narrative to the point of rewriting it.

Religious Freedom and the Voice of the People

The centrality of democracy in this new national narrative was bolstered by pro-religious claims to speak for civil society. Whereas pro-secular actors appealed to those who historically were in elite positions in the Turkish Republic, pro-religious actors claimed to give voice to the desires of "the public." From the pro-religious perspective, the problematic emphasis on secularism-as-law in the pro-secular account of the Turkish national narrative, showed an attempt to control the Turkish public rather than letting them be active participants in the public life of the nation. Mustafa Acar, a professor at Kırıkkale University, a newly founded state university located in the conservative city of Central Anatolia, cited a 2007 public poll that showed the "Turkish public" (*Türk halkı*) wants the ban lifted.[78] Acar used this poll to claim that the pro-secular state of law victimizes its citizens:

One last point is about the bleeding wound of the headscarf [*türban*] ban. This ban, which has no constitutional and legal basis, which became a gangrene because it is turned into an instrument of power struggle, and which is a shame for Turkey, is opposed by more than two thirds of the participants (66.9 percent) of this research. Once again, it is understood that this ridiculous ban at the universities is not approved by the Turkish people. The Turkish public expects that the new president of the Republic, the new government, and the new president of the Higher Education Council should, properly and smoothly, find a solution to this problem without offending the other political actors.[79]

Although Acar denied the constitutionality of the headscarf ban in universities, the thrust of his argument focused not on the legality of the ban itself but on the fact that it did not represent the will of the people. Conversely, pro-religious political actors, by drawing on the notion that they represent the general public, have consistently argued that religious expression in the public sphere is a democratic principle. Whereas the pro-seculars spoke for the Kemalist elite that ruled the Turkish Republic until 2002, the pro-religious electoral success, as well as polls like the one cited by Acar, gave weight to a new pro-religious national narrative in which democracy and Islam become compatible central principles.

Gender Equality: Respect for Gender Difference?

Women played a key role in this new narrative. Pro-religious political actors consistently argued that the headscarf ban victimizes women, making them vulnerable rather than empowered subjects of the state by limiting their freedom of religious expression and their ability to participate in the political, economic, and social life of the country. For example, after the 2011 elections, new discussions about changing the parliamentary dress code began, in part because of religious Muslim women who had advocated for their inclusion on the election slates of prominent political parties, though with no success. Surprisingly, after the Ak Party won a near majority in the election, *Cumhuriyet* gave voice to the Ak Party's vice president, Hüseyin Çelik, who argued, "In my opinion, just like we don't differentiate between blonde and brunette women, we cannot differentiate between women with headscarves and women without headscarves. . . . The majority of parliament members' wives have headscarves. They have the same worldview but women cannot enter [the parliament] where men can. This is an injustice to women."[80] According to Çelik, Turkey would overcome this problem, just as it had solved the problem in universities, where headscarves had been allowed first tacitly and then more overtly since 2010. The Ak Party's Democratization Package of 2013 included the lifting of this ban and strengthened the national narrative spearheaded by pro-religious politics. This regulation extended beyond the inclusion of women with headscarves at universities and enabled headscarf-wearing women to participate in formal politics.

Yet, although such statements and actions might create the impression that gender equality has become a key element in the pro-religious Turkish national narrative, we show that arguments about women's inclusion are not about gender equality per se, but rather about the right to express "innate" gender differences. Prime Minister Erdoğan, in a meeting with women's NGOs that took place in July 2010, stated that he did not believe in gender equality because it goes against the physical capacities of both sexes. He repeated this statement at his party's sixteenth Consultation and Evaluation Meeting in October 2012, where he argued that "some ladies are saying and demanding gender equality on television. This equality is acceptable for rights, but any other form is against creation. You women should first figure out equality amongst yourselves. You have yet to solve this [headscarf] issue, where is the justice in that?"[81]

Erdoğan has consistently argued that non-headscarf-wearing women need to show solidarity with their headscarf-wearing sisters. He draws on the Islamic idea of the *ummah,* or global Muslim community, and appeals to quotes from Persian poet and Sufi mystic Rumi such as "We love the created because of the Creator."[82]

Some headscarf-wearing women reinforce such arguments. For example, during the 2008 debate on changes to the Constitution, Nihal Bengisu Karaca, a headscarf-wearing writer and journalist, called for a solidarity demonstration between women who wear and women who do not wear a headscarf: "In this test of patience and freedom, women, with or without headscarves, will march together."[83] Such statements were directed at pro-secular women who had contributed to the pro-secular national narrative a gender equality argument in which religious women represented the negation of women's rights and freedoms.

Yet despite such appeals to solidarity, Erdoğan's public speeches also reinforced the schism between Turkish women along the lines of religion. In his claims for solidarity, Erdoğan failed to acknowledge the concerns of secular Turkish women and focused only on their lack of solidarity with their headscarf-wearing sisters: "A woman with a headscarf says that she would support the rights of a woman without the headscarf. . . . But on the other hand, my sister who doesn't cover her head cannot say that she would also struggle for the woman with the headscarf. This is the secret."[84]

Similarly, Nurhayat Kızılkan, a lecturer at the Gülen-funded Fatih University, argued that women in Turkey are divided by claiming that the "women who are in power in the Turkish women's movement" do not consider religious women their equals.[85] Kızılkan pointed out that in the March 8 International Women's Day celebrations, religious women's problems were not addressed and argued that this reflected the elitism of the (secular) women's movement in Turkey.[86] In her op-ed piece, Kızılkan referred to the inequality in the social and class positions of religious and nonreligious women, accusing nonreligious women of ignoring religious women, even though religious women constitute the majority in Turkey.

Overall, political actors like Erdoğan and Kızılkan tell pro-secular women not to be afraid of losing their rights, claiming to be inclusive by rewriting these rights through the lens of freedom of expression. However, in effect, their pro-religious gender arguments, which draw on the notions of the will of the public and freedom of expression, combine to marginalize a pro-secular account of belonging to Turkey.

Furthermore, within the Ak Party itself and among its members and voters, the solidarity between women who wear headscarves and women who don't is actually a contested issue.[87] Ak Party members questioned whether women with headscarves are indeed morally equal to women without headscarves. Showing this tension, Şerif Erdikici, writing for *Zaman,* emphasized that women who do not wear headscarves can be equal to headscarf-wearing women, but only if they are Ak Party supporters.[88] In other words, headscarf- and non-headscarf-wearing women have to show their morality through religious party membership.

While the Ak Party has used the headscarf issue to craft a national narrative around a pro-religious interpretation of democracy and human rights, the gender politics of the Ak Party and its supporters has increasingly reflected a negation of women's rights. In the late spring of 2012, Erdoğan gave a speech at the opening of a private hospital. He stated that abortion is murder and announced that the Ak Party government is preparing a new bill to ban abortions in Turkey.[89] After receiving opposition from both pro-secular and pro-religious women, there have been no further Ak Party comments on banning abortion.

On the independent web-based media outlet Bianet.org, Ferhunde Özbay, a veteran feminist and professor of sociology at Boğaziçi University, labeled the Ak Party's possible abortion ban a form of "population engineering," asking, "Why does the governing party aim to create religious housewives with children?"[90] Headscarf-wearing journalist Ayşe Böhürler admitted that she is against abortion but argued, "I wish it would not be discussed in this way."[91] The abortion issue suggests that the notion of gender difference put forth in the headscarf debates also informs an articulation of women's duty as that of childbearers. It seems that, over time, the pro-religious national narrative has increasingly constructed women as objects of the politics of nation building, first by referring to the headscarf as "honor," then by creating schisms based on the sexual moralities of women with or without headscarves, despite allusions to freedom of expression, and most recently by attempting to ban abortion in order to force women to be the bearers of the nation's offspring. In short, as the pro-religious rewrite the Turkish national narrative by treating democracy and religious expression as human rights, pro-religious gender politics show the possible contradictions in this account. In what follows, we show how Turkish Muslim women negotiate this tension to promote yet another, albeit it far less powerful, national narrative.

The Feminine National Narrative: The New Women of the Turkish Republic Wear the Headscarf

As the preceding analyses of the pro-secular and pro-religious national narrative suggest, politically active Muslim religious women cannot comfortably base their claims for belonging to Turkey in either camp. Both have clear exclusionary dimensions, and religious women argue that they are victimized not only by pro-religious Muslim men but also by pro-secular men.[92] The pro-secular national narrative unambiguously has no place for them: according to the pro-secular account of belonging, visibly religious women should not participate in the public sphere. At the same time, politically active religious women also contested the national narrative of belonging created, ostensibly on their behalf, by pro-religious actors, who are overwhelmingly men. They countered that the pro-religious national narrative instrumentalizes them for political gain while ultimately restricting women to conservative feminine roles, or as Özbay, quoted earlier, stated, as "religious housewives with children."[93]

Many prominent Muslim women who share these perspectives and are highly visible in the public sphere have been positioned in the media as counterweights to pro-secular women political actors. We interviewed two of them and draw from memoirs of one other, as well as from an afternoon spent with a group of politically active religious women, to show how these women used their religious perspective to reframe pro-secular and pro-religious national narratives.

Religious women in Turkey have struggled to make themselves heard in politics and the media, and a small minority has had some influence over the debates. For example, Ayşe Böhürler is a founding and active member of the Women's Branch of the Ak Party (*Ak Parti Kadın Kolları*). She has a media company and works as a filmmaker and journalist. She is known for her thirteen-episodes-long documentary, a comparative study of Muslim women's lives in a number of Muslim countries, called *Behind the Walls: Women in Muslim Countries,* and a related book.[94] Böhürler, who is also divorced with children, uses her status to represent the experiences of women who singly carry the double burden of income earning and childrearing. In 2003, Böhürler said: "We, as religious women with headscarves, are the grassroots in this country and the least alienated ones, but we have no value in the official platforms. Against this perception we have to be strong in number and in character. We have to take strength from each other."[95] In this statement made in an interview with journalist Şemsinur B. Özdemir, Böhürler referenced the pro-religious arguments that were based on popular support but instead argued that *women* represent civil society. She also argued that being in solidarity meant defending women's rights and promoting diversity rather than imposing a singular ideology to define the scope of women's participation in the public sphere, whether religious or nonreligious. Though she echoed Ak Party solidarity arguments, she gave them a stronger foundation in freedom-of-expression arguments, untempered by contradictory claims that only religious women have morality on their side.

In this sense, Böhürler does not draw solely from the pro-religious national narrative but combines it with elements of the pro-secular narrative. Here she references pro-secular arguments regarding the protection of gender equality that informed the foundation of the Republic and that historically used the appellation "woman of the Republic" (*Cumhuriyet kadını*). Böhürler claims that she represents a new woman of the Republic:

"Am I a woman of the Republic?" When I ask myself this question, my answer is "Yes" even if this leaves a sour taste in my mouth. In some of the portrayals of the Republican woman I feel that I have realized myself, in some others I feel I have gone beyond. In its educated, free in idea, free in conscience, enabling social participation part, I can say, "Yes, I am a woman of the Republic." However, in its part where this ideology imposes a female identity that is "submissive, unquestionably devoted to the Republic, that is, to home and to the national identity, patronizing, necessarily Western as well as uncovered," I can say, "I never feel like a Republican woman." There my national belonging is based on an emphasis on freely adopting my own female identity. I belong to an independent woman's identity.[96]

Yurdakul and our research assistant Özlem Kaya interviewed Ayşe Böhürler at her office in Istanbul.[97] We asked about this op-ed piece in *Yeni Şafak* from which we just quoted. In particular, we asked how she could bring the Republic and religiosity together in her identity, because ultimately the "Republic" to which she refers in her article asked her at that time to remove her headscarf, an integral part of her identity. In addition, her self-description reflects a multiplicity of identities that was both denied in the pro-secular national narrative and rendered problematic in the pro-religious one. She responded that she benefits from the political opportunity structures that the Republic provides for women, including their active participation in the public sphere, even while wearing a headscarf. From this perspective, the pro-secular national narrative of women's belonging to the Republic undeniably contributes to women's lives.

In addition, Böhürler experienced exclusion when trying to collaborate with pro-religious men in the media, in ways that led her to question the pro-religious national narrative. Elsewhere she has written,

Our Muslim male writers could not get used to work[ing] with conservative women. They found us too serious, sometimes boring and sometimes troubling. . . . The discourse of power was always patriarchal even when it was Muslim. And we were always aware of it. . . . If we [as Muslim women] exist in the media today, we achieved this not thanks to them but in spite of them.[98]

In order to understand herself as belonging to Turkey, Böhürler charted a course between the increasingly diverging pro-secular and pro-religious versions of the national narrative. She sought to combine the right to express herself religiously in the public sphere associated with the pro-religious accounts, with the avenues to women's participation that derived from the pro-secular accounts. The latter avenues to political participation are increasingly circumscribed in the pro-religious national narrative, as women's belonging is once again being associated with home and reproduction rather than with participation in the public sphere.

Although Böhürler does not identify as a feminist, because she does not accept "some of the features of feminism," in our interview with her

she said that "there are other religious women who say that they are Islamic feminists." Here Böhürler was referring to Hidayet Şefkatli Tuksal,
an influential and provocative writer known for her critical reading of the
Koran from an Islamic feminist perspective. Like Böhürler, who is critical
of the Muslim men who dominate media discussions, Tuksal argues that
Muslim women are doubly victimized, first by Muslim men and then by
secular men. She puts forth her own version of gender equality, which can
be distinguished from the "honor" discussed by Bülent Arınç in the early
Ak Party election campaigns, the gender difference protected by Erdoğan,
and the uncovered or even antireligious existence promoted by the pro-
secular national narrative. Tuksal argues instead that Muslim men are not
doing enough to support Muslim women and the headscarf:

> It is much more painful when people [with] whom we think we have the same cause
> exclude us. Sometimes we imagine the following scenario. Folks, let's get together, fifty
> women, go to these men, make our headscarves into balls and throw them at them:
> "Here, you have the headscarf!" Let's give them the headscarf as a gift and say, "Take
> it and deal with it for a while!"[99]

Arguably, by throwing her headscarf to these male political actors, Tuksal
wants to protest the instrumentalization of her headscarf for political purposes, an instrumentalization that does not grant her a full voice in political debates.

Similar to Tuksal and Böhürler, Merve Kavakçı-İslam experienced
double victimization in politics. In her book *Headscarf Politics in Turkey: A
Postcolonial Reading*, she describes being attacked in 1999 by secular members of the parliament after she was not allowed to take her seat as an
elected member because of her headscarf: "My name and picture were
taken out of the parliament's documents [and] I was erased from the parliament's history. The party also tried to move on, pretending that I did not
'happen.' Meanwhile, I was stripped of my citizenship and faced a set of
charges, including inciting hatred, discriminating against people, insulting
the dignity of the state, and attempting to overthrow the regime."[100] Her
victimization came from both sides of the political aisle: the pro-secular actors in the Turkish parliament were booing her while she was trying to take
her oath as an elected parliament member, and members of her own party,
the Virtue Party, a precursor to the Ak Party, did not support her either.

During the 2011 national elections, the headscarf debate in Turkey
took a surprising turn when a group of women wearing headscarves gath-

ered to initiate a campaign for the representation of headscarf-wearing women in the parliament, picking up where Merve Kavakçı-İslam had left off. They made an open call to the presidents of prominent political parties to nominate headscarf-wearing candidates and to list them in places where they could actually be elected. Engaging in a demonstration in front of the parliament building, they used the slogan "No candidate with headscarves, no vote!" (*Başörtülü aday yoksa, oy da yok!*). In these protests, they referred to the 1997 military memorandum known as the "February 28 Process" (which we referred to earlier by its other name, the "postmodern coup," in which the Turkish military exerted strong pressure on the government in 1997, which led to the resignation of the pro-religious prime minister, Necmettin Erbakan), as well as to the case of Merve Kavakçı-İslam. However, even though their argument was picked up by Ak Party Vice President Hüseyin Çelik after the election, it did not influence the election itself, and headscarf-wearing women continue to be absent from the Turkish parliament. This outcome suggests that although headscarf-wearing women can be a political symbol in both the pro-secular and pro-religious national narratives, until recently neither narrative has opened space for actual women to join in as active participants in the formal political process. However, the Democratization Package announced by Erdoğan on September 30, 2013, might open up this possibility.

On July 4, 2012, Yurdakul spent the day in Ankara with two women who played a significant role in organizing the "No headscarf, no vote!" campaign: Zeynep Göknil Şanal and Berrin Sönmez from the Başkent Women's Platform. In the interviews, both women argued that the Ak Party had used the headscarf as an instrument for its politics during the election campaigns, especially in 2011. Their evidence was that the Ak Party had nominated only one headscarf-wearing candidate, who was listed on the candidacy list in Antalya, an essentially pro-secular city. It was thus strategically unlikely for her to be elected.

Members of the Başkent Women's Platform, with or without headscarves, have diverse political opinions. But many of them are critical of the Ak Party, even though (or perhaps because) the Ak Party arguably won its first election in 2002 by promising to lift the ban on the headscarf in universities. Fatma Ünsal, a founding member of the Ak Party, chose to run as an independent candidate in the 2011 elections, which she lost despite women donating money to her election campaign. During the campaign, Ünsal was called "the unwanted voice in the AK party," meaning that she was "unwanted" by the higher ranking male politicians within the Ak Party, of whom she was critical. At the same time, it is very difficult for many of these critical women to reject the Ak Party fully, because they still credit it with providing them with an avenue for political participation. For example, Berrin Sönmez, chair of the Başkent Women's Platform, said that the Başkent Women's Platform supported the "No headscarf, no vote!" campaign only indirectly, because they did not want to harm the Ak Party members in their organization. According to Sönmez, the women who engaged with the campaign promoted an idea of belonging based on protection for multiple identities—defending not only the right to wear a headscarf but also the rights of gays and lesbians—and asking for constitutional change to protect a diversity of lifestyles.

For many years, both the secular and the Muslim patriarchies ignored the situation of all these religious women. Their double victimization discourse shows how both the pro-secular emphasis on secularism and law and the pro-religious discourse on democracy and freedom of religious expression in the context of women's traditional roles obscure these women's daily struggles to exist as religious women in Turkey. For religious women like Ayşe Böhürler, Hidayet Şefkatli Tuksal, Merve Kavakçı-İslam, and the women engaged in the "No headscarf, no vote!" campaign, the right to exist in the Turkish public sphere was more important than debates on whether secularism will survive in Turkey. At the same time, they resisted the traditional roles envisioned by the religious men who wanted to relegate them to childbearing. They promoted instead a vision of belonging to Turkey that falls within a much more postsecular national narrative— one in which a multiplicity of identities informs participation in the public sphere, and in which belonging is defined in maximally inclusive terms. The 2013 civil society movement, which started with the resistance in Gezi Park in Taksim, Istanbul, also reflects this version of a Turkish national narrative that is about a strong commitment to democracy and diversity.

Prime Minister Erdoğan apparently heeded this call with his 2013 Democratization Package. However, Erdoğan's understanding of democracy and diversity is much different than that of the Gezi protestors and the pro-religious women we interviewed. Although the Democratization Package officially recognized some rights of Kurds and lifted the headscarf ban in Turkey, other discriminated groups (such as Alevis and religious, ethnic, and sexual minorities) were largely ignored. Privileging Sunni Islamic groups over others caused severe discomfort among pro-seculars,

Ak Party critics (such as Anticapitalist Muslims), and discriminated-against minority groups.

On October 31, 2013, four headscarf-wearing women legislators for the Ak Party entered the Turkish parliament: Nurcan Dalbudak, Sevde Beyazıt Kaçar, Gülay Samancı, and Gönül Şahkulubey. This was the first time since the Merve Kavakçı-İslam incident in 1999 that headscarf-wearing women could enter the Turkish parliament. Their happiness did not last long. During their presence in the parliament, Şafak Pavey, a member of the parliament from the CHP, criticized the Ak Party members by saying they were concerned only about their own right to wear the headscarf in public places and not concerned about granting freedoms to other groups discriminated against in Turkey.

Many citizens of Turkey, including other parliament members from the CHP and headscarf-wearing women from diverse religious groups, such as the Anticapitalist Muslims, who are against the Ak Party's politics, as well as the pro-religious women we interviewed, produce a rendition of the Turkish national narrative that is distinct from both the pro-secular and the pro-religious ones. Here we see how globally relevant ideas, such as women's rights and minority rights, as well as the environmental concerns of the Gezi protesters, have become increasingly dominant in Turkey's national narrative.

4

Tolerating the Headscarf in the Netherlands

ON DECEMBER 20, 2005, Geert Wilders, populist anti-immigrant politician, at the time an independent member of parliament, put forth a motion to ban burkas from the public sphere. The left-of-center daily, *The Volkskrant,* quoted his argument:

The whole idea behind the burka contravenes the way in which we in the Netherlands treat women. Women don't have to be ashamed of how they look. The burka grows out of the Islam for which, here in the Netherlands, there is simply no place. In that sense, this [law] is about supporting the moderate Muslims in the Netherlands, who try hard to integrate properly. . . . [in addition] in these uncertain times, it's important that people are always identifiable when out in public. You have to be able to see who someone is.[1]

Wilders touched on a whole range of familiar tropes that at that point structured the Dutch debates on the headscarf, niqab, and burka—gender equality, Islam as outside the boundaries of belonging in the Netherlands, and facial recognition in a time of terror—but he also issued a plea for support for "moderate Muslims." Now, as leader of the Partij voor de Vrijheid (Party for Freedom, henceforth PVV), Wilders consistently argues that he has nothing against Muslims but he does not like their religion. This strategic nuance in his arguments, which enables him to claim to support "moderate Muslims," allows him to draw on two concepts well-entrenched in the Dutch national narrative, tolerance and pragmatism, to outline the contours of Dutch national belonging. In addition, in his focus on women's Islamic dress, he also mobilizes a newer trope in the Dutch national narrative, that of gender equality, which is situated in contemporary discourses of liberal freedoms. Wilders' actions have netted him tremendous political success, and in 2010 his Party for Freedom became the third largest party, at 23 out of 150 seats in the Dutch Second Chamber of Parliament. This suggests significant support for his rendition of the Dutch national narrative.

Wilders and his voters were responding to a transformation of Dutch society from a relatively homogeneous white, Christian country (although one with important internal differences, particularly along religious lines), to a much more racially and ethnically diverse society. Immigrants from predominantly Muslim countries such as Turkey and Morocco first came to the Netherlands in large numbers in the 1960s and early 1970s as "guest workers." Eventually, many of these (mostly male) immigrants brought over their families. Annual surveys conducted by the Central Bureau for Statistics (Centraal Bureau voor de Statistiek, or CBS) suggest that the adult children of immigrants feel more at home in the Netherlands than native-born Dutch of the same generation; however, the children of immigrants are not necessarily perceived by the nonimmigrant Dutch population as belonging to the Netherlands.[2] Discussions of Muslims' place in Dutch society continue to reinforce their "foreignness," in part by attaching the label *immigrant* to the children and grandchildren of the original immigrants.[3] In addition, Dutch Muslims continue to bring spouses from their parents' home country, with 85 percent of Moroccan immigration and 67 percent of Turkish immigration happening because of family formation or reunification.[4] The fact that net migration from Turkey was negative in 2012 (with three hundred more people emigrating from the Netherlands to Turkey than immigrated from Turkey to the Netherlands), and that net migration from Morocco was at three hundred persons among an overall Dutch population of 16.8 million, suggests that the label *immigrant* will become less and less accurate when discussing people in the Netherlands with a Turkish or Moroccan background.[5] Nevertheless, the prior migration waves have resulted in a profound change in the Dutch streetscape, particularly in the major cities, where those labeled *immigrant* now make up 50 percent of the inhabitants.[6] All these facts combine to generate continuing tensions over diversity and difference in the Netherlands. In this context, the headscarf, niqab, and burka have become symbols of a rejection of Dutch culture, with 40 percent of nonimmigrant Dutch agreeing that "Muslim women who wear a headscarf are not adjusting to our society."[7] This means that a sizeable number of Dutch Muslim women are placed outside the boundaries of Dutch belonging. Estimates put the number of women who actually wear a headscarf at 25 percent for women of Turkish background and 40 percent for women of Moroccan background,[8] with the estimate of niqab wearers hovering around three hundred.[9]

As in France and Germany, in the Netherlands, debates over immigrants' religious practices mask ongoing socioeconomic inequalities. The children of immigrants who were born or raised in the Netherlands are doing far better on various socioeconomic indicators than their parents, many of whom were brought over because of their capacity to do manual labor, not because of their educational attainment. Nonetheless, a continuing gap between the average educational and socioeconomic achievements of the second generation and those of nonimmigrant Dutch fuels discussions about the place of immigrants and their children in Dutch society.[10] By the late 1990s, Dutch integration debates had shifted from looking at socioeconomic barriers to placing the blame for lagging participation on immigrant culture.[11] The 1998 Dutch integration law was a first in Europe, mandating language and culture training for new immigrants. The passage of this law signified a shift in the public's focus from concern over immigrants' perceived lagging socioeconomic participation to concern over immigrant segregation and lack of cultural competencies.

In 1998, the Dutch state also became involved, for the first time, in legal debates regarding the headscarf, when teachers told a student's parents that the girl in question had to take off her headscarf for gym class. The parents took the case to the Equal Treatment Commission (henceforth ETC), which ruled in her favor, as did a court subsequently.[12] In France, similar cases ultimately led to the passage of the 2004 law banning headscarves in elementary and high schools. In the Dutch debates, however, this case signaled the beginning of a period, ongoing today, in which the ETC gives nonbinding advisory rulings on the limits of religious expression in the Dutch public sphere, including the worlds of work and education.[13] Unlike in France, then, there have been no legislative developments in which new laws were proposed to delineate the spaces in which the headscarf can be worn (although such directives are at times discussed in parliament). Rather, there is constant negotiation over the place of the headscarf in Dutch public spaces such as schools, government institutions, and sites of employment, against the background of a growing concern over immigrant integration.

The niqab, in contrast to the headscarf, has been subject to attempted bans since December 2005. As in other countries, newsmakers and politicians in the Netherlands have used the term *burka* to mean the niqab. When the Dutch debate a "burka ban," they are actually talking about the niqab; the burka is not worn by Dutch Muslims. Geert Wilders was the first to get a motion passed to ban the "burka" from the Dutch public sphere, which the Council of State declared unconstitutional. The issue did not go away, however, and the minority cabinet that ruled the Netherlands between 2010 and 2012 (with support from Geert Wilders' PVV) made passing it a promise in its governing agreement. In the fall of 2011, this government put forth a law to ban the burka. Despite the fact that the Council of State ruled that such a law would be unconstitutional (a ruling that is advisory rather than binding), the government moved ahead toward implementation in January 2012. The proposed law would have fined people who wore a face covering in public up to 380 euros.[14] However, the government fell in April 2012, before the law passed the Dutch Senate, leaving the legislation in limbo.

These ongoing legal cases and parliamentary debates generate a continuous stream of arguments that appeal implicitly to the concepts that have historically structured the Dutch national narrative, namely tolerance, pragmatism in everyday interactions, and strong support for liberal values, including gender equality and gay rights. These concepts help people negotiate what anthropologist Annelies Moors calls a "politics of discomfort," or the visceral negative reaction people experience when faced with a niqab-clad woman (which we argue extends to women in headscarves as well, albeit to a lesser degree).[15] ETC rulings and parliamentary debates become sites in which national belonging is delineated through arguments that use law as a reference point but that are often fueled by a deep-seated sense of unease, even anger, on the part of those who perceive the headscarf as a rejection of what it means to be Dutch. In these negotiations, debates over the headscarf and burka become debates over who sets the terms of belonging—those who see the headscarf as a symbol of Dutch tolerance or those who see it as a sign of intolerable otherness?

The ongoing debates regarding the regulation of head and face coverings produce an account of national belonging in which the headscarf becomes a symbol of either social disintegration or the potential for a reimagining of the meaning of being Dutch. Compared to France, in the Netherlands there is less uniformity in the resulting articulations of the national narrative. Particularly in the headscarf debates, tolerance, pragmatism, and gender equality are deployed to make opposing arguments about whether the headscarf has a place in the Netherlands. Yet the resulting different interpretations of the Dutch national narrative do not result in a Turkish-style fracture, though they do reflect greater tension than in the debates in France. As in France, in the Netherlands the niqab is uniformly rejected as an intolerable sign of women's oppression, though when it comes to the niqab, actors use different interpretations of Dutch pragmatism to give divergent meanings to national belonging.

In what follows, we analyze how these debates have produced these counterposed versions of the Dutch national narrative. First we describe the historical roots of the Dutch narrative of belonging. We then discuss our data sources, including newspapers, parliamentary debates, and interviews with three Dutch Muslim women who were actively politicking for the inclusion of Dutch headscarf-wearing women in Dutch society. The remainder of the chapter looks first at the headscarf, then at the burka and niqab, outlining legal and social developments before analyzing how actors articulated national belonging in the resulting headscarf and burka debates. We end the chapter with a discussion of how three women who are deeply engaged in Dutch politics, two of whom wear a headscarf, negotiate these national narratives of belonging; they are Muslims who represent full participation in Dutch society but at the same time are continuously confronted with others who reject their sense of belonging.

The Dutch National Narrative of Belonging: Tolerance, Pragmatism, and Equality Rights

The notion of tolerance that has been a core element of the Dutch national narrative pertains to a capacity to engage with those whose values or practices are at the limit abhorrent to those in the position to tolerate them.[16] In the Dutch national narrative, tolerance has historically promoted an even-keeled approach to managing difference in the public sphere.[17] The Dutch Republic, founded in 1581, consisted of a population that was highly diverse religiously, with varying Protestant sects in tension with each other and their Catholic counterparts; tolerance enabled these groups to live together. During the eighteenth and nineteenth centuries, Protestant and Catholic affiliations informed the foundation of tightly bounded religious communities that nonetheless coexisted peacefully. The principle of state neutrality in religion, which in the Dutch case means that all religions are supported equally by the state, derived from this process of facilitating coexistence.[18] Fred Bruinsma and Matthijs de Blois call this state involvement a form of "active pluralism."[19]

Unlike in France, tolerance for difference enabled a form of belonging to the Dutch nation through subgroup affiliation. This form of belonging provided the foundation for the pillarization of society and politics in the early twentieth century, or "a societal compartmentalization based on ideology or religion."[20] Pillarization amounted to the formation of something the Germans now call *parallelgeselschaften* (parallel societies) and the French capture with *communalism* but without the negative moral judgment attached to either term. From the early twentieth century until the mid-1960s, people joined churches and community groups, attended schools and social events, were cared for in hospitals and community organizations, and voted for political parties that were all formed around a particular set of religious or philosophical values. This included various Protestant sects and Catholics, but also socialists and humanists, who had their own pillars. Nobody disputed that belonging to one of these groups constituted belonging to the Netherlands. Only the elites of each pillar interacted with each other; ordinary people lived fully segregated lives, in accordance with the live-and-let-live approach to difference facilitated by the principle of tolerance.[21]

Pillarization and the concomitant segregation of people into (mostly religious) group affiliations ended by and large in the 1960s with the advent of far-reaching secularization and individualization. In 1970, more than 60 percent of the population was a member of a church; by 1999 this was 27 percent, with fewer than half of church members attending more than once every other week.[22] The process of secularization shifted the focus of tolerance from relations between groups to relations between individuals, as the Dutch increasingly valued individuation and self-expression.[23] As Ybo Buruma argues, "Without its religious background, tolerance had to take on a new, general meaning of acceptance of social and cultural differences in a pluralist society."[24] Indeed, even with the decline of religiosity in structuring society and everyday life, tolerance remained an important way to deal with increasing diversity in expressions of sexuality and shifting gender relations. Thus, while the way people lived their lives changed dramatically, tolerance continued to structure the narrative of Dutch belonging.

In the Dutch case, tolerance is not necessarily a deeply rooted moral belief but rather a pragmatic approach to dealing with difference.[25] Instead of engaging with the principles that inform people's group membership or their individual choices, tolerance promotes a form of *in*difference to difference, a sense that what motivates people is of no concern unless they start to infringe on each other's actions. Indeed, in contemporary retellings, the centrality of tolerance as a key concept in the Dutch national narrative is not the result of its moral weight but rather the application of a smart, pragmatic approach to problems of diversity, an approach that enabled the Dutch to overcome strife between Catholics and Protestants (and strife between various Protestant sects) and to accept the influx of Jews in the early 1600s, which then informed the advent of the Dutch Golden Age, or the rapid economic growth and its attendant sociocultural changes that the Dutch experienced during the seventeenth century. Thus, tolerance is also a political economic good. Some root this link between tolerance and pragmatism in the Dutch soil itself: reclaiming the land that was below sea level required that "hardworking people from all religions . . . work together—even if they considered one another heretics or heathens. Even in the twenty-first century, the Dutch use the term 'the polder system' to describe a political culture premised on the need to set aside sectional differences to address common problems."[26] This means that tolerance translates into a deeply rooted practice of pragmatism that structures everyday life as well as political, legislative, and legal processes. In the Dutch national narrative, then, practices of tolerance and pragmatism become a means to ensure that certain values are upheld, rather than constituting values in their own right. The resulting practices inform how people are woven into Dutch national belonging. However, this emphasis on tolerance as practice rather than as value also makes it fragile. When tolerance no longer seems practical, there is no moral scaffolding to uphold it and the boundaries of belonging can shift to exclude those previously tolerated.

The end of pillarization and an increasing emphasis on individual well-being, self-actualization, and autonomy led to just such a boundary shift, namely a decline in support for belonging as group-based membership rooted in religious values. Concomitantly, support for individualization or the expression of individuality by ensuring equality for women and men, as well as for gays and straights, increased. Equality rights became the normative end goal of Dutch practices of tolerance and pragmatism, creating a new base for belonging to Dutch society.

Although it might seem that such support for self-expression and self-actualization would lead to an extremely heterogeneous society, this is not the case. Historically, Dutch society has been structured by a great deal of value conformity, with national belonging rooted in shared values that crossed lines of group affiliation. When religious affiliation was the primary source of diversity, Calvinist values informed much of Dutch daily life. In other words, diversity was checked by the conformity of shared Calvinist values. As Peter Van der Veer argues, "although Catholics were a majority in the country before the 1960s, the Calvinist ethos of frugality and moral strictness had spread over the entire population, including Catholics, socialists, and communists."[27]

After the crumbling of the Dutch pillars, Calvinist values were replaced by the liberal values associated with freedom of expression, gender equality, and gay rights. These values have led many outsiders to think of the Netherlands as highly liberal in the colloquial sense—that is, very open regarding sexuality and promoting gender equality. However, the reality is that Dutch conformism shifted from being oriented toward strict religious values to a similarly strict adherence to these "liberal" values. The Dutch, then, are extremely "liberal," but also highly conformist.[28] Rather than generating wide diversity in values and practices as a result of this liberation, the Dutch continue to adhere to the national motto *doe maar gewoon, dan doe je al gek genoeg* (act normal, that's crazy enough).[29, 30]

As Sarah Bracke suggests, such consensus masks the incompleteness of women's emancipation and of the achievement of women's and LGBT rights, while positioning Muslims as dangerous others.[31] Elsewhere we have argued that discussions of purported "Muslim" practices such as "honor killing" draw bright boundaries of belonging by treating gender equality as an accomplishment threatened by Muslims' actions.[32] This treatment can lead to forms of intolerance under the guise of a defense of tolerance. Paul Mepschen, Jan Willem Duyvendak, and Evelien Tonkens show how the Dutch defense of gay rights and sexual freedom informs a particular kind of Islamophobia.[33] Tolerance is tightly bound up in this process: "In this context, expressions of homophobia have increasingly been represented as 'alien' to secular, Dutch 'traditions of tolerance.'"[34]

In the Dutch national narrative, then, tolerance has been buttressed not only by a highly pragmatic approach to difference, but also by an equally strong degree of conformity around the underlying values that should structure people's lives and public engagements. In the contemporary accounts of this national narrative, Dutch society had historically been able to manage difference through tolerance and pragmatism, and by the end of the 1960s it began to arrive at a consensus based on quite liberal (left) values. When around the same time large numbers of immigrants came from predominantly Muslim societies, religion again became the object of tolerance, but now religion was associated strongly with outsiders. Some of the practices ascribed to immigrants were experienced as either deeply offensive or dangerous to members of the Dutch majority society, who saw Muslims' religiosity as a threat to the achievement of liberal rights. Van der Veer sums it up thus: "The silent revolution of the 1960s is celebrated in the Netherlands as a liberation, especially from obstacles to enjoyment. . . . For the Dutch, Muslims stand for theft of enjoyment."[35] This perceived "theft" raised the question of at which point abhorrence could justify intolerance or exclusion from the public sphere in the Netherlands. To address this question, we turn to the headscarf and burka debates to analyze how the Dutch national narrative of belonging is being defined vis-à-vis new Dutch citizens with Muslim backgrounds.

Reinforcing the Dutch National Narrative

To trace the contours of the headscarf and burka debates, we looked at four national Dutch newspapers that span the political spectrum. The highbrow *NRC* is a centrist paper that appeals to an educated readership with in-depth analyses of issues. *De Volkskrant,* historically a Catholic paper, has represented the social-democratic left for decades. *Trouw,* a historically Christian paper with roots in Protestant resistance to German occupation in World War II, continues to discuss religious issues more extensively than other papers, giving voice to both antireligious, particularly anti-Islamic, and pro-religious perspectives. Finally, *De Telegraaf* represents a right-liberal stance and is the most populist of the four papers we analyzed. It also has the highest circulation of the four. Taken together, these newspapers cover the range of political stances and class positions in Dutch public debate. We collected all of the news and opinion articles on the headscarf, burka, and niqab for the period between 2004 and 2011, starting with when the culturalization of the integration debate was a fait accompli.

We also looked at a number of parliamentary debates, parliamentary questions, and legislative proposals. The Netherlands has a large array of political parties; about eleven or twelve of them tend to have seats in parliament in any particular governing period and coalition governments are the norm. These parties represent socialists (*Socialistische Partij*, Socialist Party, or SP), Greens (*GroenLinks*, or GreenLeft), labor and social democrats (*Partij van de Arbeid*, Party of Labor, or PvdA), centrist liberals (*Democraten 66*, Democrats 66, or D66), Christian democrats (*Christen-Democratisch Appèl*, Christian Democratic Appeal or CDA), Christians (*ChristenUnie*, or ChristianUnion, which is more on the left; and SGP, *Staatkundig Gereformeerde Partij*, or Reformed Political Party, which is more on the right of social issues), right-liberals (*Volkspartij voor Vrijheid en Democratie*, People's Party for Freedom and Democracy, or VVD), and the ultraright (*Partij voor de Vrijheid*, Party for Freedom or PVV), as well as a small animal-rights party (*Partij voor de Dieren*, Party for Animals, or PvdD). Politicians of these parties try to profile themselves by taking clearly identifiable stances on issues such as the head-scarf and burka, which makes these debates particularly interesting from the perspective of tracing the ongoing development of the Dutch national narrative. Politicians draw from the always circumscribed set of concepts that constitute such a narrative, reinforce or reinterpret them, at times even trying to add new concepts or new applications of old ones into the mix. We focus in particular on the parliamentary debate of the 2009 national budget, during which Geert Wilders proposed to institute a "headrag tax." Such moments show how various politicians draw on elements of the Dutch national narrative to articulate the boundaries of belonging in the Netherlands.

Unlike Muslim women in France and Germany, Dutch Muslim women actively participate in political and media discussions. Left parties like the PvdA, GreenLeft, and SP had strong Dutch Muslim women representatives in parliament during the period under study—including, for example, Naïma Azough for the GreenLeft, Saadet Karabulut for the SP, and Nebahat Albayrak for the PvdA, among others—while Ayaan Hirsi Ali of the VVD shaped much of the debate on gender and Islam on the right, until her departure from government in 2006. At the local political level, Fatima Elatik (of the PvdA), borough president of a large subsection of the city of Amsterdam, is a high-ranking headscarf-wearing politician in an executive role. In the media, women like Naema Tahir, Nehad Selim, and Nazmiye Oral write regular columns and shape the debate. Overall, prominent Dutch Muslim women represent a range of interpretations of Islam in Dutch society. All of these women illustrate agency; their participation in these debates contradicts the argument that Islam oppresses women. Even when their arguments are closely aligned with those who argue that they are fine with Muslims but reject Islam (the PVV line), as is the case for famous interlocutor Ayaan Hirsi Ali, many illustrate by their very actions that one can be both Muslim and an independent actor.[36] Furthermore, other Dutch Muslim women who have carved out a niche through alternative political action do not necessarily enter either parliamentary or media debate (or not often). In the concluding section of the chapter, we discuss two of these women's interventions, together with Korteweg's interview of Fatima Elatik, the highly successful head-scarf-wearing PvdA politician.

This array of Dutch Muslim women represents different aspects of Dutch Muslim culture and politics. Although Ayaan Hirsi Ali to some extent performs the role of "exceptional Muslim," or one who has liber-ated herself through the embrace of Western culture and thus appears to confirm the need to exclude nonreformed Muslims from public space,[37] we argue that many of the other Muslim women who participate in these public debates do so from more complex positions. These women navi-gate a far more complex set of relationships in the various communities to which they belong, and their interventions in the headscarf debates give a much more multi-faceted account of belonging in the Netherlands.

In general, the headscarf debate reflects a strong connection between what happens in parliament and media reporting. By far the majority of reporting on the headscarf and niqab in Dutch newspapers concerns their legal regulation, focusing on the spaces and places in which the headscarf and niqab can be worn and where wearing them needs to be curtailed. Media discussions address regulations proposed and adopted by government at both the municipal and national levels, including those associated with education, as well as cases that have been taken to the ETC. A small number of newspaper articles discuss labor market dis-crimination as reported by Muslim headscarf-wearing women, an issue that sometimes gets picked up in parliament as well. When reporting does not focus explicitly on regulation, it looks at the meaning of the headscarf, focusing on why women wear the headscarf and how the head-scarf should be interpreted symbolically. Although the women Korteweg interviewed became at times part of media and parliamentary discussions, their full story was rarely aired. As in France, debates on the headscarf in the Netherlands are distinct from those dealing with face covering. In the following pages, we turn first to the headscarf and then to the burka ban debates regarding the niqab.

Regulating the Headscarf in the Netherlands

In the Netherlands, formal regulation of the headscarf happens through targeted directives that provide guidelines for workplaces and public institutions. In addition, public discourse, whether put forth by politicians or civil society actors, produces informal regulation as it shapes what are considered appropriate responses to headscarf-wearing women.

Unlike in France, in the Netherlands there have been no attempts at passing laws that ban headscarves outright in a particular space such as schools or workplaces. Rather than being regulated from the perspective of space, the wearing of the headscarf is regulated in the intersection of space *and* practice. In other words, whether or not a headscarf is allowed depends on the space and the role of the person wearing it. So, although a judge is not allowed to wear a headscarf, a plaintiff can. As a rule, the greater the state-derived authority of the person, the less likely it is that they are allowed to wear a headscarf (so no headscarves for judges and police officers, but other government employees might be able to wear one on the job, particularly if there is no contact with the general public). This regulation shows that the decision-making positions or positions of authority are saved for people who are to some degree stripped of Muslim identity markers. Although this might look like an emphasis on sameness similar to the case in France and in some parts of Germany, Dutch regulations reflect a history of reinforcing class-based status distinctions that was built into the Dutch welfare state.[38] As in Turkey, the headscarf seems to become more problematic when middle- and upper-middle-class women start to wear it in the public sphere of work and politics.

A number of legal principles apply to the regulation of the headscarf. Three articles of the Dutch Constitution are particularly important: Article 1, which pertains to equal treatment and nondiscrimination; Article 6, on freedom of religion and belief; and Article 23, which addresses freedom of religious education and includes state financial support for religious schools.[39] In addition, the 1994 Law on Equal Treatment (Algemene Wet Gelijke Behandeling) came into force to outline in greater detail what the equality and antidiscrimination principles in the Constitution amounted to.

These laws continue to be worked out in practice. Between 1995 and 2012, the ETC, and since then the College of Human Rights, has adjudicated cases based on the Law on Equal Treatment. From 1995 to the middle of 2012, the ETC heard 121 cases. In its decisions, the ETC

applied the principle of state neutrality in religion by weighing two opposing principles: the appearance of state support for particular religious expressions that results from allowing the headscarf in various institutional
spaces, and the burden that would be placed on the exercise of freedom
of religion, and by extension the freedom to participate fully in public
life, if wearing the headscarf would be forbidden in those spaces. Here
the Dutch interpretation of state neutrality—what Fred Bruinsma and
Matthijs de Blois call "active pluralism"—led to context-specific rulings
based on the principle that state neutrality can be maintained through the
reasonable accommodation of religious practices.[40] More recently, however, in a context of increased public scrutiny regarding visible expressions
of religious difference, political actors have called for a narrower interpretation of state neutrality through calls for bans on government officials
wearing the headscarf and through successful proposals to ensure that police uniforms reflect "lifestyle neutrality." Thus, what we are witnessing
in the Dutch case is the transformation of a form of neutrality based on
tolerance for expression of religion in the public sphere into one that treats
tolerance and neutrality as oppositional. In this newer interpretation, neutrality comes to stand for the kind of strict secularism advocated in France
and by Turkish pro-seculars.[41]

The ETC's application of "active pluralism" to issues of state neutrality in matters of religion has inspired anti-immigrant politicians like
Geert Wilders to promote a French-style *laïc* understanding of secularism
by painting the ETC as an arm of "the Left Church." In the next sections,
we show how debates over the ETC's approach to the headscarf mirrored
the divide between the competing versions of the Dutch national narrative
articulated in public discussions of the headscarf.

The Headscarf and Two Versions of the Dutch National Narrative

Those who engaged in public discussions of the headscarf drew on
tolerance, pragmatism, and gender equality. However, they used these concepts to define national belonging in very different ways. In the end, the
actors who dominated the public debate generated two competing versions
of the Dutch national narrative. The first one reinforced Dutch liberal
values, particularly gender equality, but at the cost of an expansive notion
of tolerance. In the second version, a politics of discomfort regarding the

headscarf informed a weak defense of tolerance, even though the headscarf was perceived as an expression of gender inequality.

The Politics of Intolerance and the Defense of Gender Equality and Freedom from Religion

Outspoken Dutch Muslim women, such as Ayaan Hirsi Ali and Naema Tahir, among others, tried to sway the general public toward an interpretation of the headscarf that illustrated this garment as not belonging in the Netherlands. They did so by linking the headscarf to women's oppression and anti-Western forms of Islamic politics. They argued, albeit it in different ways, that the headscarf represented a rejection of Dutch values, which put the headscarf beyond what could be tolerated. The question of Muslim women's agency took center stage in these accounts of the headscarf.

In an opinion piece published in the NRC on April 13, 2004, Ayaan Hirsi Ali, then parliamentarian for the right-liberal VVD and their spokesperson on immigrant integration, argued that the laws then in place left too much room for conflict. She cited a list of decisions by the ETC and debates in the Second Chamber regarding a government proposal to provide prison guards with safe headscarves (which inmates could not use to strangle the guards). Hirsi Ali started by answering in the affirmative the question of whether or not we should concern ourselves with a small piece of fabric. Arguing that the government should clearly indicate when and where the headscarf could be worn, Hirsi Ali outlined the meaning of the headscarf:

Simply stated, Muslims argue as follows: the body of a woman inspires lust in a man. Men and women who are not first-degree family members and who are not married in accordance with the tenets of Islam should avoid each other completely. That is impossible; therefore a woman should dress herself in such a way that she does not [inspire] or barely inspires lust.

Two suppositions are the grounds for this. The first is that the man cannot control his sexual desires. The second is that the woman is responsible for the inner weakness of the man. Thus, she stays home and covers her body. This is all stated in the Koran and elaborated in the traditions of the prophet.[42]

Hirsi Ali further argued that Muslim women who try to free themselves from this oppressive interpretation of their sexuality, body, and personhood risked extreme violence by family members "hell bent" on enforcing these norms. Therefore, Hirsi Ali argued, the government needs to step in to ensure that Muslim women are protected when they express their selfhood by uncovering their hair, echoing French arguments that the headscarf can never be freely chosen.

For Hirsi Ali, the headscarf stands for a profound form of gender inequality in which men force women to live extremely circumscribed lives. She appealed to the Dutch value of gender equality to argue that the headscarf should as much as possible be eradicated from Dutch society. Although tolerance is core to the Dutch national narrative, for Hirsi Ali the headscarf crossed the boundaries of the tolerable because it threatened the hard-won liberal values, particularly those relating to gender equality, that are now at the heart of the Dutch national narrative. Hirsi Ali strategically used her background of growing up religiously Muslim to "explain" to a nonreligious audience why they should fear the headscarf and all it stood for.

Naema Tahir, a columnist and lawyer active in Dutch integration debates, also drew on her experience as a Muslim woman to put forth the headscarf as a symbol of gender inequality, but she did so differently than Hirsi Ali. In one column, Tahir responded to Muslim women's demonstrations in France against the headscarf ban. She stated, "It must feel very powerful, my sister," to be able to participate in making the headscarf "one of the most complicated pieces of clothing of our time."[43] Tahir then drew on her own childhood to explain to a Dutch audience the meaning of the headscarf as she saw it. Recounting her own experience wearing it during teenage years spent in Pakistan, she argued that the headscarf became a way of toying with men's sexual attention while overtly adhering to strictures of modesty: "My headscarf became a culturally determined expression of how I could express my sensuality," a way to get revenge on "my uncles and nephews, who in their tight western jeans, dictated how 'their women' should act, even though they did not restrict themselves in anything."[44] Unlike Hirsi Ali, who saw the headscarf solely as the forced covering of women's sexuality, Tahir suggested that there is some agency in donning the scarf. She gave a list of reasons why women in the Netherlands might be wearing the headscarf: as "a statement against Western society . . . a counterweight to the peer pressure in your own circle and as the winning prize: keeping the imam, your brother, your father and the jerk-calling-you-whore around the corner at bay."[45] By suggesting that this is agency in response to oppression, Tahir joined Hirsi Ali to argue for a similar exclusion of headscarf-wearing women from the Dutch landscape. Thus, regardless of whether they saw in women's actions just male power or some kind of agency, both Hirsi-Ali and Tahir agreed that the headscarf reflected a form of gender inequality not in line with Dutch values.

Gender equality was not the only value appealed to by those arguing for what amounted to an exclusionary interpretation of national belonging. Other arguments brought in religious values. For example, in 2011 the ETC ruled that a Catholic high school, the Don Bosco College, had unfairly asked a fourteen-year-old girl to either take off her headscarf or leave the school. This decision was in line with the idea of "active pluralism," in which "schools are obliged to pay attention to the religions and belief systems in Dutch society."[46] This means that nondenominational, publicly funded schools are not allowed to prevent students or teachers from wearing a headscarf. Publicly funded religious schools, however, do have that right, as long as they can show that this ban is required to protect the school's unique religious identity. Indeed, when Don Bosco College took the case to court for binding adjudication, the school won. The girl in question, Imane Mahssan, and her father fought the decision by taking it to a higher court. However, they lost again.

The Don Bosco case sparked rounds of editorializing on the place of Islam and Muslims in the Netherlands. Before the lower court ruled on the case, Geert Wilders and his party leader in the Dutch Senate, Michiel de Graaf, wrote an op-ed in support of the orthodox Christian party leader, André Rouvoet, who had suggested that Sharia law should be banned from the Netherlands. De Graaf and Wilders appealed to the Don Bosco College case to support this proposal, arguing that the "Sharia symbol *par excellence* is the headscarf." They continued:

It is not only about women. It's also about Christians, Jews, apostates, atheists, and gays. It's about all of us. For the survival of our values, our identity, our culture, and our freedom, it's of utmost importance to ban the Sharia in all its expressions: no new mosques and imams, no Islamic schools and burkas. There is no place for Sharia in free societies. A Sharia ban has to come.[47]

In sum, Wilders and his fellow politicians used the Don Bosco case to tie together key elements of the Dutch national narrative, arguing that the reigning interpretation of tolerance led to an assault on the values of gender equality, gay rights, and freedom of expression. Similarly, a columnist for *Trouw,* Elma Drayer, turned to the Don Bosco case to argue that we all know that Muslims of course have the right to wear the headscarf if they so choose. This is what "tolerance requires of us." At the same time, we all know, or so Drayer claimed, that by "wrapping themselves up," Muslim women promote "a conceptualization of humanity in which public space continues to belong to men." To remain free, we therefore have to ensure that the headscarf is not worn by anyone in a government position.[48] In this way, discussions of the headscarf quickly became discussions about "who we are" and what we can or should tolerate. The "we" in both Wilders' and Drayer's accounts was a "we" who did not include religious Muslim women. Although these women were to be tolerated, according to Drayer, Wilders wanted to see them in the Dutch public sphere only if they took off their headscarves.

By contrast, Imane Mahssan, the young student at the center of the Don Bosco College case, claimed that she belonged to the Netherlands by appealing publicly to her village roots—she was born and raised in the town of Volendam—and to what she felt was a right to be with her lifelong girlfriends. In doing so, Mahssan tried to carve out a space of belonging as a young Dutch Muslim woman: she was Volendams, Muslim, headscarf-wearing, tolerant of the Catholic faith, and accessing the Dutch courts to protect what she perceived to be her rights. However, in their account of the Dutch narrative of belonging, Wilders and Drayer denied Mahssan even the possibility of enacting such a subjectivity.

As Wilders' and Drayers' arguments show, the headscarf inspires visceral discomfort, which reinforces the interpretation of the Dutch national narrative of belonging as one in which liberal Dutch values need to be protected from an Islamic assault. Recalling Van der Veer's argument that "for the Dutch, Muslims stand for theft of enjoyment,"[49] a reader's comments on a blog post are illustrative. The website in question is hosted by a group of young Dutch Muslims who claim their belonging to the Netherlands by titling their site "we stay here."[50] One reader comments on the account of a young headscarf-wearing woman's difficulty getting a job as a checkout clerk in a Dutch supermarket:

I think Aldi [the supermarket] is exercising its rights. You are allowed to express neutrality as a company. What do I [do], as a customer, who is paying for his wine and a girl in a headscarf gives me the bill? I know because of her headscarf that in her eyes this is a great sin. That's not what I'm waiting for. Religion also means making choices that restrict your opportunities, but as a good believer you accept that and this works only to purify you. You don't want to have to have people pay for beer and wine.[51]

This reader assumes that the headscarf signals that the woman at the cash register will make a moral judgment regarding his purchases. The reader's comment shows how the headscarf debates continue to be informed by the echoes of the Christianity that for so long shaped the Dutch national narrative of belonging; the idea that the headscarf signifies a negative judgment of nonbelievers recalls the judgment in Calvinist interpretations of the righteous life that still inform Dutch everyday life, even though so many of the Dutch have ostensibly turned their back on religion. This same phenomenon is reflected in the court's judgment that the Don Bosco College could deny Imane Mahssan's *"claim* to express her religious beliefs" because it *"inescapably affects the feelings of others,* who believe they have the right to be free of such expressions."[52] This approach seems to establish a right to freedom from unwanted religious expression that seems more akin to the French than to the Dutch approach to secularism in the public sphere.

The discomfort that the headscarf inspired put it to some degree beyond the tolerable. The appeals of politicians, columnists, and judges to the defense of gender equality and freedom from religion reinforced the centrality of liberal Dutch values in the Dutch national narrative even as they reduced the scope of Dutch tolerance in assessing whether those who wear a headscarf could fully belong to Dutch society.

The Politics of Discomfort and the Defense of Tolerance

Discussions of the headscarf that privileged a defense of liberal values over the application of tolerance in the Dutch national narrative were countered by interlocutors, often women with a long track record in feminist and antiracist politics. These interlocutors argued for an interpretation of choice and freedom rooted in a historically more dominant account of Dutch tolerance and pragmatism. However, whereas those who called to ban the headscarf argued forcefully, inclusionary arguments were often more subdued and ambivalent. People who argued for tolerance and pragmatism often evinced a personal discomfort with the headscarf even as they argued for women's right to wear it. This qualified support for the headscarf (fine if you want to wear it, but it's not for me) is characteristically Dutch. A headscarf, after all, gets you attention, contradicting the informal Dutch national motto, "If you act normal, you're crazy enough," which signifies the centrality of conformity in the Dutch national narrative. In a variant, a small but noticeable trend in newspaper reporting discusses the headscarf as a fashion choice. Ultimately this discourse seemed an effort to reduce the threat of the headscarf (as outlined in the exclusionary claims made in the vein of Hirsi Ali and Wilders), turning it instead into an expression of youth not yet fully cowed by the mantra of normalcy that captures Dutch everyday national belonging.

Strong statements linking the headscarf to oppression of women were hard to negate even by those arguing for women's right to express their religiosity as they see fit. Although there is great conformity within the Netherlands on liberal values, the left has in recent history been the strongest home for those focusing on remedying gender inequality. When it came to the headscarf, this meant that those most likely to support pluralism were also those most likely to be directly engaged in anti-oppressive politics. This tension between support for pluralism and a narrow interpretation of gender equality informed a politics infused by feelings of discomfort. For example, Femke Halsema, leader of the GreenLeft, led a party that was the most likely to protect a multiculturalist interpretation of pluralism and to support multiculturalist integration policies. This also meant giving support to women wearing the headscarf in a wide range of government functions.[53] However, in an interview with *De Pers* (a free daily with a circulation of 200,000 published between January 2007 and March 2012) that was widely reported on in other newspapers, Halsema was asked what she personally thought of the headscarf:

Interviewer: What do you think of the headscarf?

Halsema: I have no problem with it, as long as it is put on in freedom.

Interviewer: What do you think of it?

Halsema: I think it's really sad that women hide their beautiful hair.

Interviewer: That's it?

Halsema: No. I say that playfully. When I go to my children's school, I find it difficult sometimes—I really do come out of the feminist movement—to find myself sitting between all those veiled women. I would not attack their rights. But I can't wait for the moment in which they fling off their scarves in freedom. I would most prefer to see every woman in the Netherlands without a headscarf. I don't believe that whichever God would have clothing rules. They are made by the men who explained the religion.

You can't force women's emancipation from above. It has to come from the women themselves. I have said that police officers should be able to wear headscarves. I have fought with Cisca Dresselhuys [publishing editor of a mainstream Dutch feminist magazine] when she did not want to hire women with a headscarf at *Opzij*. But that does not mean I do not have difficulty with the headscarf.[54]

This quote illustrates the difficult dance that ensues when people try to bring a feminist interpretation of the headscarf like the one promoted by Hirsi Ali and Tahir in line with a politics of tolerance, which values freedom of expression and choice. On the one hand, Halsema can support headscarf-wearing police officers (which makes her a minority on this issue) on the basis of a gender-neutral interpretation of tolerance; on the other hand, at the same time she can hold onto a gendered interpretation of the headscarf as "made by the men," which hews closely to the interpretation put forth by Hirsi Ali and Tahir. The resulting account reflects a narrative of belonging that has a place for headscarf-wearing women as on a path to Dutch interpretations of freedom. They are tolerated, but only because of the potential salutary effects of exposure to Dutch values and practices, which in Halsema's narrative ends with women "flinging off" their headscarves in a moment of (true) freedom.

Halsema's interview with *De Pers* caused a minor firestorm in the Dutch media. In an opinion piece responding to Halsema's claims, Jutta Chorus, journalist and author, argued that the Dutch debate on the headscarf is ossified by the positions put forth by Wilders and Hirsi Ali:

The left parties support the new cultures that entered the Netherlands, but they are stuck in a defensive mantra without their own new vision. Femke Halsema argued last week in *De Pers* that she has a personal problem with headscarves. . . .

That opinion is probably inspired by the streetscape of her Amsterdam neighborhood but in essence based on a feminist conceptualization of thirty years ago, and not on reality. In this way, she arrives, via the road of women's emancipation, at the same irritation as Wilders. . . .

Halsema, by the way, was immediately accused of treason by her party members. Negative utterances about headscarves, no matter how grounded in feminism, are apparently not left enough.[55]

Chorus's analysis puts the finger on the tension between various liberal values that confront left parties in the Netherlands. Chorus argued that even those who apply tolerance to wearing the headscarf hold an underlying sense of Dutch values that is very similar to that put forth by those who would exclude headscarf-wearing women from Dutch national belonging. Importantly, this tension results from a belief in personal choice, in line with the value that the Dutch have placed on individualism and self-expression in the post-1960s era, and a visceral distaste for the headscarf as signifying women who choose oppression.

Some try to avoid this tension between tolerance and a rejection of the values projected onto the headscarf by minimizing the meaning of the headscarf as a symbol of oppression. Portraying the headscarf as a sign of teenage rebellion (as Naema Tahir did) or as a sign of teenage confusion offers ways to accomplish this. Discussions of the headscarf as fashion (which is one continuing albeit small trend in Dutch reporting) reflect what we argue is a pragmatic strategy that makes the headscarf less meaningful politically and therefore more tolerable socially. One striking example comes from a short story published on the back page of the NRC, written by an Amsterdam high school teacher:

As long as she has been going to school with us, Melike has worn a headscarf. On a disco night organized by the school, a young girl with long, loose, black flowing hair stands out among the largely allochthone [of foreign descent] students. She wears a transparent blouse and a suggestively tight pair of pants. It is Melike. The next class, Melike reappears in her modest clothing with headscarf. I ask her why she did not cover her hair during the disco. She shrugs her shoulders and mumbles "oh miss." "But why is your hair covered now?" She looks at me surprised and answers, "If I want to do my hair properly in the morning, then I'd have to get up so early to get here on time."[56]

This short story suggests that the Dutch may be making a mountain out of a molehill. In the context of the Dutch headscarf debates, the teacher who wrote this story seems to want to defuse any sense that the headscarf could possibly threaten hard-won Dutch values. This girl is not going to undermine Dutch society; she can barely get out of bed on time. At the same time, the teacher who narrates this story gets to enact Dutch liberalism by being clearly open-minded (or what passes for it; why should this teacher be concerned with what her students wear?).

On the one hand, this seems like a lightweight story, but on the other hand, it shows that people who want to push back at the hysteria surrounding the headscarf do so by drawing quietly on these core practices of tolerance and pragmatism. Indeed, when Queen Beatrix was on a state visit to Oman in January 2012, PVV party members submitted formal questions to parliament on why she was wearing a headscarf when visiting a mosque. The newspaper reported that they asked "whether 'this sad spectacle could not have been prevented'" and "did the cabinet 'not realize that the head of state in this way legitimized women's oppression.'"[57] When asked for her response during a press conference at the end of her visit, the queen sighed and stated that this was all "such nonsense." The "sigh of Beatrix" became the hottest topic in the Dutch press that week and inspired countless editorials on the idiocy of the headscarf debates, in line with the Dutch tenet "if you act normal, it's crazy enough." Commentators largely sided with the queen, arguing nostalgically for a return to the time when the Dutch were more cosmopolitan in their outlook and understood that different people might have different customs. They longed for a return to an older Dutch narrative of tolerance, when one could shrug when seeing a headscarf.

The Dutch headscarf debates, then, were structured by the oppositional framing of the headscarf as, on the one hand, an enforced religious obligation signifying gender oppression and, on the other hand, an expression of free choice requiring Dutch tolerance and pragmatism. When people discussed the headscarf, two variants of the Dutch national narrative emerged. Both reinforced the centrality of key elements in the Dutch national narrative, but without producing a single, coherent story. For those like Hirsi Ali, Tahir, Wilders, and Drayer, the headscarf could not belong in the Netherlands because it was anathema to liberal values, particularly those associated with gender equality, and crossed the line of what can reasonably be tolerated in Dutch society. The need to protect Dutch identity required a pragmatic rejection of the headscarf and all for which it purportedly stood. However, many others felt torn between the personal discomfort generated by seeing women wearing the headscarf and the conflict generated by being intolerant of the difference the headscarf signifies. The latter interlocutors drew on the same elements of the Dutch national narrative as those who rejected headscarf-wearing women from Dutch national belonging, but tried nevertheless to find a space of inclusion. In some cases, this quest for inclusion involved depoliticizing any perceived threats caused by the headscarf by emphasizing its use in fashion. To show how this dualism informs the ongoing production of the Dutch national narrative, we turn to Geert Wilders' proposal to institute a "headrag tax."

The "Headrag" Tax:
Impossible Laws and the Limits of Tolerance

Every year in mid-September, the Dutch cabinet outlines its budget and policy proposals. The following day, the leaders of each party take the floor of the Second Chamber to outline their positions. These presentations are generally lively, with speakers interrupted by their colleagues asking questions during their statements. On September 17, 2009, Geert Wilders walked up to the microphone to outline his party's critique of the proposals made by the sitting cabinet of Christian Democrats and Social Democrats. He started his proposal to place a tax on wearing the head-scarf with an evocative image of the sitting cabinet as stuck in a car on the road to nowhere, fearful of what they might find if they stepped out. Then Wilders continued:

> But honesty requires [us to acknowledge] that the cabinet has also achieved certain things. It's going well with integration. At least with the integration of the Netherlands in the *dar al-islam,* the Islamic world. All over Europe, the elite is opening the gates. It will only be a little while and one in five people in the EU is Muslim. This is good news for the multiculti cabinet, which sees bowing for the horrors of Allah as its most important task.[58]

Wilders continued that, for this political elite, the diversification of the Dutch landscape represents an enrichment even if it means that "every once in a while there will be a dead body [in reference to the murder of filmmaker Theo van Gogh in 2004[59]], someone will get raped, and the country will in the long term go bankrupt." In making these statements, Wilders drew on "Eurabia" discourses that claim Europe is being overrun by Muslim immigrants.[60] These discourses were also referenced by Anders Breivik (who in the summer of 2011 murdered seventy-seven Norwegians in an attempt to fight multiculturalism and what he perceived as the Islamic takeover of Europe). In short, Wilders evoked a discourse on Islamic threat and conquest that informs transnational European right-wing discourses. This threat in turn needs to be staunched not by creating a pan-European identity but rather by protecting national distinctions, which in the Dutch case means protecting gender equality and gay rights (something that else-where might not be associated with repressive right-wing politics). In his parliamentary intervention, Wilders strategically positioned himself as the savior of the Dutch nation:

> A better environment begins with yourself [a Dutch environmental slogan]. Many Dutch people are annoyed at Islam's pollution of public space. In other words, in some places our streetscape looks more and more like Mecca and Tehran: headscarves, infested beards, burkas, and men in strange long white dresses. Let's do something about this. Let's reconquer our streets. Let's ensure that the Netherlands will look like the Netherlands again. Those headscarves are really a sign of oppression of the woman,

a sign of submission, a sign of conquest. They form a symbol of the ideology that is out to colonize us. That is why it's time for a spring cleanup of our streets. If our new Dutch so much want to show their love for a seventh-century desert ideology, they should go to an Islamic country, not here. Not in the Netherlands.[61]

These are stock phrases for Wilders, used to outline the threat of Islam as the eradication of "Dutch" culture, practices, and beliefs. In these accounts of the Islamic threat, Wilders first gives his interpretation of its severity (in his eyes, underestimated by the left) and then positions his party platform as the way to rescue the threatened Dutch nation-state. During this particular parliamentary debate, Wilders put forth the following "proposal: why not introduce a headscarf tax? I would like to call it a headrag tax. Just once a year, get a license. . . . It seems to me that euro 1,000 would be a nice sum. Then we'll finally get some payback for that which has cost us so much already. I would say: the polluter pays."[62] To solidify the connection between Islam and gender inequality, Wilders further suggested that the income from the €1,000 tax to wear the headscarf would be donated to women's shelters. Not surprisingly, even in the highly polarized political landscape of the Netherlands, this outlandish proposal sent the other parliamentarians reeling, trying to find ways to respond.

Wilders' success in public opinion polls was largely the result of his capacity to manipulate the press and set the tone of the debate by making the most quotable interventions in such debates. Even though much of the reporting of his proposals and statements has been critical, Wilders has nonetheless managed to produce the statements to which others, be they media, politicians, or public intellectuals, then had to respond. Highly mediatized events like these annual parliamentary debates require parliamentarians less skilled than Wilders in manipulating the debate to come up with pithy, quotable responses, which they did by appealing to elements of the Dutch national narrative. Agnes Kant, then parliamentary leader of the opposition Socialist Party and the first to take the interruption microphone, took the route of ridicule: "This is too absurd to react to, but I also propose a tax: a tax on peroxide to [bleach] hair, because I find that polluting."[63] Alexander Pechtold of the left-of-center D66 (at that time an opposition party) similarly asked Wilders if he thought he was in Leiden (rather than in The Hague), where the annual Dutch cabaret festival takes place, and questioned whether Wilders was proposing a special tax on the "hat of Minister [of Education] Plasterk" (known for always wearing a hat). The normal that is so highly valued in the Dutch context informed these responses.

Others tried to show the contradictions in Wilders' proposal, appealing to the levelheadedness required by pragmatism. For example, Femke Halsema (GreenLeft) asked Wilders how he could argue that he was for the environment and increasing tax revenue when he also proposed to reduce the tax on gasoline. Wilders did not take the bait but rather outlined how we need to tax Dutch Muslims, who cost the Dutch state so much: "They don't come here because they think it's such a beautiful country, filled with *kafirs*, unbelievers. They come here, for example, for the social assistance."

After a few rounds of ridicule and appeals to rational reasoning, to which Wilders responded that "the message of the Party for Freedom, for social policy and against Islamization, appeals to an increasing segment of the Dutch population," Pechtold got down to the heart of the matter as he perceived it, addressing Wilders directly: "As long as you try to divide the country in your way, with your xenophobic, racist expressions in the direction of [specific] groups of the population, I will stand here time and again."[64] By marking Wilders' utterances as divisive and racist, Pechtold opened the door to other serious critiques. For example, Arie Slob of the ChristianUnion, appealed to the Dutch history of religious tolerance and asked Wilders about his understanding of freedom and of treating others with respect: "You very often reference the Christian-Jewish traditions of our country. I believe that one of those traditions is that we treat each other with respect, even if we have differences of opinion. Why don't you practice this? I really don't understand. It's also a break with the way in which we have interacted in this country for centuries."[65] Femke Halsema of the GreenLeft party elaborated on this appeal to the Dutch national narrative, arguing that upon hearing Wilders' headrag tax proposal, her

first thought was of the religious persecution during the Reformation. That is in effect what you argue for: forbid the Koran, forbid the headscarf, put a tax on it. That is not much different from the Iconoclasm. For that we needed the Enlightenment. Then I thought a little more and arrived at only one equivalent [of your proposal]: Iran. What you want is the morality police. That is what you introduce. Shame on you![66]

Wilders replied that he wanted the opposite, to prevent the Netherlands from looking like Iran, but the comments from Halsema and Slob showed how Wilders crossed the lines drawn by Dutch principles of tolerance and pragmatism.

Finally, Halsema countered Wilders' claim that he wanted to discourage the wearing of the headscarf because it signifies women's oppression:

"According to me, the core of a civilized society should be that women are free to believe and to make their choices. You want to introduce a backward culture."[67]

Thus, Dutch politicians tried to counter Wilders' statements regarding the Islamic threat as embodied by headscarf-wearing women by appealing to long-standing traditions of tolerance and pragmatism. Both tolerance and pragmatism were motivated by an adherence to liberal values, in this case, gender equality, interpreted not as a singular way to act but as women's freedom to choose their actions. Wilders was unable to get his tax proposal passed (he later admitted he knew this would be the case). Yet his ability to introduce concepts like the headrag tax into Dutch political discourse reshaped the terms of the debate, even if the term *headrag* was largely used critically.[68] Thus, we see how even a failed proposal to regulate through law can introduce informal regulation by shaping discursive interaction in the public sphere.

Regulating the Burka and Niqab

Attempts to regulate the burka and niqab have followed a different pathway than attempts to regulate the headscarf. Both reporting on the issue and parliamentary debates have focused primarily on formal regulation. As in France, politicians and opinion makers focused on *where* rather than on *whether* or not to ban it. However, calls for such regulation have run into the same laws that make regulating the headscarf such a case-by-case affair. Insofar as the burka and niqab signify religious expression, wearing them is in principle protected unless those trying to limit this right can show reasonable grounds for doing so.

Annelies Moors, one of the first in the Netherlands to conduct systematic research on who wears the niqab in the Netherlands, shows that there are about three hundred women who wear the garment, many of them either converts or second-generation Moroccan women, with about half of them wearing it part-time rather than always.[69] The women Moors interviewed unanimously stated that they made a personal choice to wear the garment, contrary to the presuppositions of those pushing for a ban on the burka or niqab.

According to Moors, the first extensive public discussion of the burka or niqab happened in 2003–2004 when a postsecondary vocational school (Regional Education Centre, or ROC) tried to prevent three girls from wearing face veils on school grounds.[70] They had already agreed to take off their face coverings for classes, exams, and professional training, but they wanted to be allowed to wear them at other times. The ROC governing board did not want to allow this and the girls took their case to the ETC, arguing that they were treated differently than other pupils because of their religion, something that would hold water in the case of the headscarf.

Although the ETC had previously decided in a student's favor in a face-covering case in 2000, it did not do so now. Rather it accepted the ROC's arguments that the requirements of communication and safety in the educational setting trumped the rights of religious freedom and expression. The case was discussed in parliament, but both the national legislature and the Dutch cabinet decided not to intervene at this point, beyond requesting that then Minister of Education Maria van der Hoeven generate guidelines regarding dress policies at educational institutions. Following this case, a number of universities devised such policies, even if no students wore a face covering at the university in question. Some of these initial guidelines were generally restrictive while others suggested that individual faculty should decide what made sense given the instructional setting.

In 2005, Geert Wilders, who had just resigned from the right-liberal VVD because he opposed the party's support for Turkey's accession to the European Union, used the issue of face coverings to cement his position as a fighter of the Islamic threat in Dutch politics. Wilders proposed a ban on "burkas" across the entire public sphere. Following parliamentary debate, his motion passed with support from the two ruling parties, the VVD and the Christian democratic CDA. The accepted motion, however, did not lead to a law because it violated the Dutch constitutional principle of equal treatment for religious expression and Dutch interpretations of state neutrality in the public sphere—values analogous to those applied to the headscarf. Minister of Foreigner's Affairs Rita Verdonk announced a few days before the November 2007 elections that she would propose a burka ban that was in line with the Dutch Constitution. However, her party, the VVD, lost the elections and became an opposition party in the next government.

The cabinet that formed after the 2007 elections, composed of Christian Democrats, Social Democrats, and the Christian Union, agreed that face coverings could be prohibited from various sectors of the public sphere but they did not plan to implement a complete ban, which would have contravened the Dutch Constitution and European human rights regulations. Instead, they planned to focus on a ban in education and public service,[71] which has since been implemented.

After the June 2010 general elections, a minority government of VVD and CDA took power with the support of Geert Wilders' PVV, which made the biggest electoral gain in the election, coming in third with 15.5 percent of the popular vote. Wilders promised to support the minority government in return for a promise to ban the burka. On September 16, 2011, the Minister of Justice announced a complete ban on the burka, analogous to the French ban. Newspapers reported that in the press conference where he announced the "burka ban," Minister Donner had stated:

"Wearing a burka contradicts the way in which we interact in public space: recognizable and approachable." . . . "Almost everyone feels it like this: that's not how we interact with each other. People feel 'unheimisch' [literally, not at home]. . . . [Regulating clothing is not strange]: "You're not allowed to walk around naked on the street." Donner argued that 98 percent of women who are Islamic walk around without a burka. So the question is whether this is truly important for Islam. "And not everything you want to do by claiming freedom of religion is allowed. This freedom has to be able to be curtailed in the public interest."[72]

Donner justified the proposed ban primarily by arguing, on the one hand, that people feel uncomfortable, using the German-sounding word *unheimisch,* while on the other hand stating that public order required such a ban (even though he himself acknowledged that few women wear the burka). Donner's remarks suggested that discomfort apparently had become a real danger to "the public interest" in Dutch society. Even though the Dutch Council of State advised that the ban would violate the Dutch Constitution, the government chose to ignore that advice and officially adopted a "burka ban" in January 2012. However, the cabinet fell in April 2012, before the Dutch Senate approved the law, putting the regulation in limbo again.

The niqab has also been regulated at the municipal level. In particular, there are recurrent reports of municipal welfare offices penalizing niqab-wearing women, charging that these women's inability to find employment results from the willful donning of a face covering.

In the end, however, attempts to ban the niqab at the national level are complicated not by lack of will or desire on the part of politicians and government, though that plays a role, but by the Dutch Constitution, which makes banning Islamic face covering nearly impossible. As a result, the Dutch regulatory landscape is one of piecemeal bans at both the national and municipal levels.

The Burka and a (Largely) Shared Version of the Dutch National Narrative

The discomfort associated with the headscarf became outright aversion in the case of the burka. Discussing the general use of the term *burka* to describe all Islamic face coverings, Moors points out that Dutch women wear a niqab or chador rather than a burka.[73] She links the persistent use of the term *burka* to describe the niqab or chador, despite multiple attempts by a number of actors to rectify this misusage, to the association of the burka with the Taliban.[74] Moors argues that the term *burka* became common during the post-9/11 invasion of Afghanistan and that Dutch politicians use it—some purposefully, others more unthinkingly—to reinforce that association.[75] At the same time, although initially the spelling of *burka* varied, over time the dominant spelling became *boerka,* which embeds in the noun the Dutch word *boer* (farmer) and its association with a lack of sophistication. The aversion implicit in this appellation was reflected in the ways in which various actors drew on tolerance, pragmatism, and gender equality in the Dutch debates about where to ban the burka.

Tolerance, Pragmatism, Gender Equality, and Aversion to the Burka

Discussions of the burka in the media have reflected a general agreement that the burka is viscerally intolerable. For example, in a 2008 debate on a proposal to ban the burka in the public sphere, the news media quoted Socialist Party member Ronald van Raak's account of the one time he saw a "burka-wearing" woman in the park: "That was quite frankly uncomfortable. Here was a woman who did not want to make eye contact with me. We did not belong to each other."[76] Although many women do not meet the eyes of men who are strangers, for van Raak the act of wearing this garment made this avoidance explicit in a way that led him (and others) to associate the burka with a rejection of belonging in a shared community. The idea that the burka prevents communication and signifies a rejection of participation in Dutch society is largely stated as truth throughout news reporting on the issue.

The Dutch debates oscillate between confessions of aversion and considerations of tolerance and pragmatism in discussions of how the burka should be regulated. Geert Wilders has long agitated for banning the burka completely, proposing such a ban years before one passed in France, and arguing that the defense of Dutch values requires the—in his eyes—pragmatic rejection of tolerance for this garment. However, others have been less willing to link their personal experiences of aversion to justifications for suppression or intolerance. For example, then-mayor of Amsterdam and future leader of the PvdA Job Cohen stated his aversion to the burka and niqab but argued that this personal response did not indicate a need for state intervention: "Personally, I find it horrible to see a woman walking in a burka. But whether I like it or not is not a criterion to forbid it."[77]

This statement made it into the "quotes of the week" section of the NRC, most likely because of Cohen's reputation for being what many of his opponents saw as overly friendly with immigrants. Whereas in headscarf discussions acknowledging such visceral responses could get you into political hot water, as Femke Halsema's experience suggests, personal feeling-based rejections of the burka seem almost a mandatory element in Dutch burka discussions. The quote by Cohen shows that when they pertain to the burka and niqab, such expressions of aversion are completely acceptable and can even coincide with a claim to being tolerant. This stands in contrast to the headscarf debates, in which those who hold onto the traditional interpretation of core Dutch values and practices did not have space to voice their discomfort.

The tension between aversion and tolerance informed discussions of "burka bans" throughout the period under study. In 2008, the reigning cabinet, a coalition of the CDA, PvdA, and ChristenUnie parties argued that implementing a complete ban was against the Dutch Constitution and the European Convention of Human Rights. Therefore, they opted for partial bans in certain spaces, such as public transit, schools, and those spaces that would mostly affect government employees and users of government services (such as students and women receiving social assistance). Justifying such partial bans, Prime Minister Balkenende (CDA) argued that the burka is an "obstacle for communication." And Integration Minister Ella Vogelaar (PvdA) pointed out that although only a few women wear a burka, this "does not mean this is a marginal problem. The burka evokes fear. It is associated with radicalism. We need to take that seriously into account."[78]

As they did in much of the discussion of the headscarf, these politicians argued from the standpoint of the eye of the beholder rather than the wearer of the niqab. From this point of view, it was unclear whether burka-wearing women could belong in the Netherlands. The Ministers who held onto Dutch tolerance and pragmatism developed a solution to the problem of the burka that was almost republican, namely to allow it as a completely private practice while removing any suggestion of explicit state support. By banning the burka in government spaces, they in effect granted these women symbolic visitor status, rather than the full membership of belonging. Niqab-wearing women could travel in the Dutch public sphere, but they could not participate in state institutions.

The fact that only a small number of women actually wear a religious face covering also inspired clear expressions of Dutch pragmatism. For example, in 2008, five ministers visited the Second Chamber of parliament to explain the cabinet's partial-ban approach to the face coverings, such as banning the burka and niqab. One of the headlines in the reporting of the parliamentary discussion reads, "Five Ministers Spend the Afternoon to Discuss 100 Women Who Wear the Burka."[79] The article opened with the observation that this discussion created a ratio of one minister per twenty women, and that "few Dutch citizens will ever get that much attention from the cabinet,"[80] suggesting that the ministers had wasted their precious time on a practice adopted by a miniscule portion of the Dutch population. Indeed, the PvdA parliament member for integration at the time, Jeroen Dijsselbloem, asked VVD parliament member Henk Kamp "which problem are you trying to solve" if you ban face coverings, suggesting that the ministers and members of parliament have weightier issues to discuss.[81] This notion of spending time proportionate to the severity of an issue marks Dutch pragmatism. Of course, for those like Wilders, this *was* the most pressing problem in the Netherlands, whereas those like Dijsselbloem tried to argue that Dutch problems should be perceived differently. But even for Dijsselbloem's party, the PvdA, burka-wearing women could never fully belong in the Netherlands, and Dijsselbloem himself is on record as finding the burka "abhorrent."[82]

Very few interlocutors argued explicitly for tolerance or the right to wear a burka. Interventions from outside the mainstream media came the closest. For example, in an attempt to tackle the aversion associated with the burka, a collective of art academy students offered "the winter burka" for sale through a website, which shows a flowing garment that covers the head, face, and shoulders, leaving a fur-lined rectangular opening for the eyes. (The website has 250 likes on Facebook—not a large number, but an indication that they are getting some exposure.) These art students made a tongue-in-cheek pragmatic claim for the right to wear a burka: the need to cover one's face when riding a bike in the Dutch winter. Their website brings to mind the framing of the headscarf as a fashion statement.

The FAQ section of the website advertising these "winter burkas" addresses the legality of the garment: "Even though the media have popularized the term *burka ban*," it is juridically impossible in the Netherlands to ban the wearing of a specific garment. . . . Therefore, we believe that the wearing of the winter burka falls under the inalienable right to wear warm clothing."[83] The idea of the "winter burka" builds on the Dutch experience of bicycling in the cold, in order to normalize a garment and to prove that rather than being treated as foreign, it can in fact be useful in the Dutch winter. Clearly this lightly ironic expression of Dutch pragmatism nonetheless addressed an issue important to the people who put the website together: pragmatism, the right to self-determination and self-expression. Thus these students moved beyond the fashion stories in the newspapers to express an understanding of belonging that can include garments like the burka, by making the burka about covering your face against the cold, something that both Muslims and non-Muslims experience, rather than an expression of religious and other differences. In doing so, they tried to undermine the aversion to the burka that informs so much of the debate and develop a more relaxed, pragmatic, and tolerant stance toward it.

Arguments regarding gender equality undermined such attempts to apply principles of tolerance and pragmatism (channeled through irony) to the burka. In arguments about gender equality, the perceived lack of women's agency informed a high degree of aversion. This led interlocutors to redirect the practices of tolerance and pragmatism toward a full rejection of any claims to belonging on behalf of burka (niqab) wearers. Cisca Dresselhuys, former chief editor of the feminist magazine *Opzij* (freely translated as "move over"), recounted the following in an op-ed piece:

When I, in Amsterdam, encounter a woman in a burka—and luckily this happens only very rarely—I am scared to death. Not because I, like Geert Wilders, think that beneath that obscuring garment hides an Al-Qaida warrior with a Kalashnikov [rifle], but because it fills me with disgust to see a woman who, because forced by culture, religion, or man, makes herself so completely invisible. As a feminist who has spent a large part of her life [trying] to counter exactly that, I find the burka a very undesirable garment.[84]

Dresselhuys could not fathom (despite evidence to the contrary[85]) that wearing the niqab can be a woman's choice. As a result, she builds on an understanding of women's agency as determined by the tenets of individual, liberal freedom.[86] Dresselhuys also brings to the fore the association between the burka and terrorism, or public safety (an argument that indeed resonates with Wilders and the PVV platform), but rejects it for the—in her eyes—much more profound threat to Dutch gender equality that she believes the niqab signifies. This of course leads to the question of whether or not this gender equality is indeed so fragile. Might it be that this much-touted Dutch achievement is far less secure and stable as the rhetoric regarding burka (and headscarf) might lead one to suspect?

Articulations of Dissent: Art, Humor, and Dutch Sensibilities

Combining arguments regarding tolerance and pragmatism with a dry Dutch sense of humor, some Muslim women have intervened in the debates to posit an articulation of the Dutch national narrative alternative to the variants put forward by the actors who dominate the Dutch debate. These women's interventions communicated three messages: (1) the headscarf and burka debates contradict Dutch practices of tolerance and pragmatism, (2) one can wear a headscarf and belong in the Netherlands, and (3) the real problem with the headscarf is that it leads to labor market discrimination (which pragmatism and equality rights require to be redressed).

A Dutch volunteer organization for Muslim women, Al Nisa (Arabic for "the women"), took the idea of being Dutch while wearing the headscarf as the basis for a poster campaign named *Echt Nederlands* (Real Dutch). They used phrases uttered by Geert Wilders to show that *Moslimas* (Muslim women) of various backgrounds have a right to stake a claim of belonging in the Netherlands. In Korteweg's interview with Leyla Çakir, chair of Al Nisa, Çakir explained how the campaign came about. She recounted how Wilders had won significant victories in the municipal elections of March 2010. When these elections were followed by the announcement of early national elections, Çakir said to the women in Al Nisa, "Guys, we cannot remain silent," even though up until then that had been the strategy for dealing with Geert Wilders in an attempt to deflate the media attention he received. They brainstormed together and decided they wanted to show images to evoke discussion: "We also thought that it should be something ludic, something humorous, but also that it should be a powerful statement. And we thought about what we as Moslimas encounter, that people say 'you can't be Dutch and Moslima at the same time.'"[87] For Çakir and the women in Al Nisa, the headscarf debates were squarely about Dutch national belonging. Through their ad campaign, they aimed to assert their place in the Dutch national narrative by appealing to Dutch practices and values.

Their brainstorming led them to take a list of utterances by Geert Wilders, including his claim that he could take on Muslims "raw" (a Dutch expression that implies you are not afraid to take on a fight). Al Nisa turned that comment into a poster of a Muslim woman with a headscarf in a traditional blue and white pattern eating a raw herring, a traditional Dutch dish. The women from Al Nisa created three other posters, including one referring to the headrag tax debate in which a woman wears a headscarf with the words "tax free" on it and the caption "we can make it cozier" (*gezelliger,* an untranslatable Dutch word). This poster refers to an ad campaign of the Dutch tax revenue agency that used a slogan indicating that while they could not make paying taxes more fun, they could make it easier. The use of these stereotypically Dutch images shows a deep understanding of Dutch humor.

All of the posters were self-produced using donations of money, time, material, and services, in a strategic choice to avoid the taint of abuse of government largesse (though they were still accused in blog posts of benefiting from government subsidies). The women in all four posters are Muslim, including a blond woman drinking a cup of tea who invites people to join her in the mosque for this traditional Dutch but also Turkish and Moroccan drink.

Çakir recounted the many positive reactions to the campaign, including media attention and lots of requests for posters from schools, cafés, and community centers, and even for a high school social studies textbook; but she also cited the stream of negative reactions. She received e-mails asking, "Who do you think you are? You will never become Dutch, and that headscarf is really not Dutch."[88] People would write to her about terrorism and everything negative they associated with Islam. In the interview, it was clear that this did not faze Çakir. Rather, she took it as an opportunity to engage in conversation, going so far as to invite those negative correspondents "to meet and discuss this over a cup of tea," something a number took her up on, showing that Çakir enacted the Dutch "polder" model of dialogic pragmatism.

Based on the success of the Real Dutch campaign, Al Nisa also generated a cartoon in response to the proposed burka ban in 2011. Çakir told us that she read an interview with Wilders in which he argued that the burka is not Dutch, that in the Netherlands "you have to be able to look each other in the eye." She felt that this "argument was so weak" and she professed disbelief that "this would be [Wilders'] very last argument to throw at the battle, after six years."[89] The cartoon Al Nisa developed in response depicts Lady Justice wearing a niqab, showing her eyes but not her face, rather than a blindfold, with the words *fear* and *self-determination* in her scales, in an attempt, as Çakir put it, to communicate "yes to self-determination, no to fear."

In our conversation, Çakir brought up the idea of tolerance in her account of the proposed burka ban. First she pointed out that Minister of Justice Donner's arguments about face-to-face communication were insincere: "Let's be honest with each other, if he really thinks that in the Netherlands we should look each other in the eye, then we should also get rid of sunglasses and helmets. That's childish [to point that out], eh?" She continued:

But I think, actually, that to be really Dutch is to be tolerant. I say *tolerance* consciously, because tolerance also has something negative; after all, it means that you endure something. That is also the case in this case. It [the niqab] calls forth a feeling of unease, even among Muslims. I knew this action would get criticism from Muslims, because they agree with Donner; they also think that it does not belong here.[90]

The overall message that Çakir promoted, one of tolerance as inclusion for that which is scary, clearly provoked feelings of discomfort and aversion in both Muslims and non-Muslims. The burka action led people to think that Al Nisa was an association of niqab wearers, which in turn led Çakir to put a photograph of her board on her website (showing women with and without a headscarf, but no one with a face covering) to illustrate "how diverse we are."

Çakir works on these issues as a devout Muslim woman without a headscarf. Two other women Korteweg interviewed engage in these debates as headscarf-wearing women. Both of their political activities and embodied experiences shine light on the construction of national belonging in the Netherlands. In 2009, a small group of people started the Polder Moslima Headscarf Brigade (PMHB) in response to what they perceived as persistent labor market discrimination, particularly for headscarf-wearing women aspiring to professional positions. An increasing number of Dutch Muslim women are receiving postsecondary degrees, yet they encounter problems in the labor market. Nora el-Jebli, one of the PMHB's early members, recounted to us how her own experience of such discrimination led her to be a spokesperson for the organization. She had applied for a position as an accountant at a major Dutch company, speaking on the phone with their human resources department and e-mailing back and forth until they reached agreement on the terms of her employment. She described the moment when she came in to sign her contract:

When I entered I actually saw that the HR manager was shocked by my appearance. I'll never know for 100 percent sure, of course, but I think that she had a very different image of who I was . . . and then she said that she was being called and needed to step out for ten minutes. I said "no problem." And after ten minutes she came back, saying that she had just heard from her boss that they had hired someone else internally. And the position had been open for five months.[91]

El-Jebli did not complain or take the company to court, in part because she found another position two weeks later. The experience did lead El-Jebli to accept an invitation to join the PMHB. Their first action was to identify the company that was most positive toward employees who wear a headscarf. In 2009, PMHB handed out the first, and so far only, silver headscarf to a supermarket chain, for the ease with which women working at the cash register could wear a company headscarf. They added a gold lining for the fact that the chain also allowed the shop's floor managers to wear a headscarf. However, Nora el-Jebli recounted that they have been unable to find another employer who is positive toward headscarf-wearing women in higher managerial or professional positions (like the one she holds). They have polled their networks and asked as many people as they can, but they have not been able to identify such an employer.

El-Jebli, born and raised in Amsterdam to parents who came from Morocco, understood herself to be Dutch; both in her volunteer work with PMHB and in her work for an organization that tries to help immigrant youth navigate education and internships on the way to employment, she felt that Muslims' claim to belonging was constantly undermined. The women who came to her with accounts of not being able to wear a headscarf and find work (which they felt was already hard enough to do with a Moroccan or Turkish last name), and accounts of the inability of youth to find the internships that would allow them to obtain their high school degrees, reinforced that even though she felt she belonged, that was not the image reflected back to her by nonimmigrant Dutch. She recounted that the youth she works with respond to the obstacles they encounter by claiming they will "go back to Morocco or Turkey" even though they do not have strong ties to Morocco or Turkey anymore. Although Çakir fought back against such trends (which she too experienced), the fight seemed to have left El-Jebli, who was thinking about moving elsewhere in Europe in order to leave the Dutch debates behind.

Korteweg also interviewed one of the few Dutch politicians to wear a headscarf, Amsterdam borough president (*stadsdeelraadvoorzitter*) Fatima Elatik. In her capacity, she oversees a section of Amsterdam with 112,000 inhabitants, managing a staff of one thousand. A daughter of Moroccan parents who was herself born and bred in Amsterdam, she very much feels herself to be Dutch through-and-through. As an elected official, she was able to bypass some of the issues that El-Jebli described. Yet she too indicated that though she felt herself to be an Amsterdammer and Dutch in every fiber of her being, others have not always seen her that way.

Elatik is a passionate advocate of dialogue and conversation as a way to sort out conflicts of opinion or belief. She embraces friction in such dialogue, using the image of how pieces of sand in an oyster produce pearls. For example, while talking about the ETC, the question arose of whether the platform that ETC provides for an ongoing debate about whether or not to allow the headscarf in different parts of the public and private spheres might be detrimental to generating a notion of Dutch belonging that would include the headscarf. Elatik vehemently disagreed with people who put forth this framing. To the contrary, she argued, the ETC provides a platform for much needed discussion. Like Çakir, Elatik believes that dialogue is essential: it is only by articulating the frictions between them that people can move forward. In one example, she mentioned mediating between a young woman who was doing an internship at a day care center who refused to give male parents a handshake. The center's director asked Elatik for advice and Elatik spoke with the young woman in question. She explained to the young woman that she was taking care of the most precious person in a man's life; to not give a father a handshake would be very unsettling for him. The young woman agreed and changed her behavior. For Elatik, this shows that too often people jump to conclusions about what people do or believe without discussing the real possibilities that may exist. This understanding shows her faith in the Dutch pragmatic emphasis on dialogue in the face of conflict.

At the same time, Elatik pointed out that she had gotten tired of constantly being asked to explain her headscarf: "I am so much more than that scarf!" She recounted how she goes to cafés where alcohol is served, shakes hands with everybody, and told her father that if she sees a beautiful man, she will take a good look. In short, Elatik wears her headscarf (and cannot imagine doing anything else) but it does not necessarily mean that she engages in the list of practices so often associated with the garment, both by those who argue that such symbols of women's oppression should not be tolerated and by those who want to tolerate it but do so in the face of profound discomfort.

Elatik professed to taking a "ludic approach" to the headscarf issue, using the same word that both Çakir and El-Jebli applied to their interventions in public debate. A few months before our interview, a member of the PVV had claimed that Elatik should not be allowed in the provincial parliament building, that she had violated the clothing regulations. When she had to attend a meeting there, she sent a tweet, "let's see if they let me in." When the parliament was mired in questions about the Queen's headscarf, Elatik sent a tweet that she preferred the red one over the blue one, suggesting that this was a debate about nothing. Indeed, she told us that she "found the sigh of Queen Beatrix really beautiful; what those 150 cowards in parliament do not dare to say, she communicated with one sigh."

Elatik also showed a difference among the women Korteweg interviewed in her response to the ongoing headscarf debate. When PVV members of the provincial government publicly threatened not to let her into the provincial parliament building, she shrugged this off. Nora el-Jebli, by contrast, felt so worn down by the constant friction around her headscarf that she thought about leaving the Netherlands. Leyla Çakir is staying but clearly feels increasingly unsettled in the Netherlands. In an interview she had with Korteweg in 2008, she proclaimed herself to be unproblematically Dutch, but in our January 2012 conversation she used "they" to identify nonimmigrants. When asked how she saw the future, Çakir said that on the one hand she thought the Dutch would continue to argue, but that things would eventually normalize. However, she could also imagine much more severe forms of exclusion. She argued that World War II, in which the Dutch to some degree collaborated with the Germans, is truly not that distant, and that the fact that *apartheid* is a Dutch word denoting a political system propagated by descendants of the Dutch should give people pause.

These three women show the space for alternatives and the insertions of protest voices that are possible given the Dutch national narrative. In France, the story of Ilham Moussaïd showed the limits of participating in politics as a headscarf-wearing woman. In the Netherlands, by contrast, we see the actions of PMHB and Al-Nisa's campaigns, and the full participation of an influential politician with a headscarf. The assertions of all three women are highly intelligible within the Dutch national narrative; they focus on tolerance and pragmatism while using very Dutch humor, irony, and directness. But these ironic statements can mask real despair at not being able to participate over the long term, or a real sense of a decline in tolerance. Indeed, in a 2008 interview that Korteweg conducted with Naïma Azough (GreenLeft member of parliament and child of Dutch immigrants from Morocco), she reinforced the idea that young women choose to wear the headscarf and, like Çakir, El-Jebli, and Elatik, argued against making a too-easy connection between headscarves and gender inequality. Yet she also worried that for young Muslim women the headscarf was increasingly not a religious symbol as much as a sign of protest, "like the Mohawk"—a symbol that young Dutch Muslim women turned to out of rebellion against a society they feel does not accept them.

Although the dominant interpretations of the Dutch national narrative appear to generate a "balance" in voices "for" and "against" the wearing of Islamic garments in the public sphere, the accounts of these three Dutch Muslim women suggest that the inclusionary arguments barely manage to provide a counterweight to the exclusionary ones. At the same time, the debates have also created room for some headscarf-wearing Muslim women to insert their voices into the debate on their own terms. They do so with a typical, dry, in-your-face Dutch sense of humor, using artistic expression and public actions to make their point that headscarves have become as much a part of the Dutch landscape as dikes and windmills.

5

Negotiating the Headscarf in Germany

IN LATE 2003, a controversial public debate ignited in Germany about whether Muslim women teachers who wear headscarves could teach classes. A German schoolteacher of Afghan origin, Fereshta Ludin, was denied a teaching position at a school in Stuttgart in the state of Baden-Württemberg. She complained that she was being discriminated against on the grounds of her religious beliefs. When her case was brought before the Constitutional Court (*Bundesverfassungsgericht,* henceforth BVerfGe, which is at least as powerful as the American Supreme Court), the Court ruled that the school administration could not deny Ludin a job for wearing a headscarf; however, the Court still expressed fear that the headscarf as a religious symbol would, in and of itself, threaten the national educational mission. Presented as creating a "potential situation of danger" in German classrooms, the headscarf was regarded by the Court as a symbol of a profound social threat: "In the most recent times, it is seen increasingly as a political symbol of Islamic fundamentalism that expresses the separation from values of Western society."[1] However, the Court also argued that the laws in place at the time of Ludin's appeal did not clearly provide grounds for prohibiting the headscarf in the classroom. The Constitutional Court then encouraged the individual German states (known as *Länder,* singular *Land*) to decide whether or not wearing headscarves is acceptable in schools.[2] Since the Constitutional Court's decision in the Ludin case, each German state has developed its own policies on the issue, based on its historical background, its ethnoreligious composition, and most important, the state's currently ruling political powers.

As a result of the Ludin case, the headscarf became a focal point of integration debates that unfolded in Germany after the ascendance of the coalition government of the German Christian Democratic Union (henceforth CDU) and Social Democratic Party (Sozialdemokratische Partei Deutschlands, henceforth SPD) in 2004.[3] The actors in these integration debates articulated the national narrative of belonging by discussing how to turn Muslims into German citizens.[4] Until 2000, German citizenship was based on the *jus sanguinis* principle of descent by blood (which itself was based on laws originally introduced in 1904), giving clear evidence of how belonging was defined in Germany: namely, belonging was defined by the preservation of a homogeneous "German" identity. The debates on immigrant integration that took place in the first decade of the twenty-first century carry on this ideal of homogeneity, leaving little to no place for difference, particularly in the case of Muslims. Conversely, Muslims in Germany argue that the Muslim identity brings social and cultural richness to "Germanness" rather than posing a threat to the ideal of homogeneity. They have instead developed a narrative of diversity that has been taken up by some non-Muslim Germans as well. The headscarf debate reveals the tensions between these two interpretations of the national narrative regarding who belongs and who does not belong to Germany.

Although there is a national narrative of homogeneity, Germany is in fact a historic amalgam of culturally, politically, and socially diverse groups, signaled by the presence of many different cultures and ethnic groups, and two Christian denominations. A "late case" in terms of modern nationhood, many German states were countries in their own right with distinct cultural traits for much longer than the now 142-year-old German nation-state.[5] Even today, regional pride prevails, with citizens frequently identifying as Bavarians or Berliners rather than as Germans. This long-standing regional tradition is reflected in the federal system of governance and in the fact that many states are governed by political parties that have views opposed to those of the federal government. Differences in economic development among states have existed throughout the six decades of the post-World War II federal republic, with the southern states of Baden-Württemberg, Bavaria, and Hesse taking the lead for most of this time and acting as the economic locomotives of Germany. On the other end of the spectrum, states in the north and in the east (since unification in 1990) have been struggling. However, these economic differences are moderated by a constitutionally mandated solidarity system, the most important element being the state equalization payments (*Länderfinanz-ausgleich*), in which richer states have to give a share of their tax income to poorer states. In short, although its national narrative is based on constructing an imagined homogeneous German society, Germany is in reality a politically, historically, socially, and economically diverse country.

The latest source of diversity resulted from a large-scale influx of immigrants from predominantly Muslim countries, which started in the 1950s, when immigrants from Turkey and elsewhere came to Germany to work. At present, Muslims constitute the largest non-Christian group in Germany; the 4.3 million Muslims in Germany make up almost 5.2 percent of the German population, with 63 percent of the Muslim population originating in Turkey.[6] Germany's Muslim population also includes Iranians, Iraqis, Bosnians, Bulgarians, Albanians, Moroccans, Pakistanis, Palestinians, and Lebanese, as well as Muslims from other Arab, African, and Asian countries. Despite this diversity in origin countries, in many cases, "Muslim" is represented as "Turk" in Germany, and the two terms are often used interchangeably.

Germany's Muslims, particularly those of Turkish background, have not achieved parity with non-Muslims in terms of socioeconomic achievement. Children from Turkish immigrant families are low achievers in education: approximately 27 percent drop out of school in comparison to about 4 percent of nonmigrant Germans.[7] Some argue that there is discrimination against immigrant children in German schools, but to date no study has pinned down exactly where and how this discrimination is taking place, although there are several competing arguments.[8] Some blame the school system, some blame teachers, and some blame the German state for not introducing any special programs for immigrant children in recent decades. At the same time, a significant number of Turkish Germans are successful in tertiary (postsecondary) education.[9] There are also well-known German Turks in the political sphere (Cem Özdemir, co-leader of the Green Party), in media (Nazan Eckes, a popular TV personality), in the literary and art scenes (Emine Sevgi Özdamar, a famous literary author, and Fatih Akın, an internationally acclaimed film director), and in business (Vural Öger, founder of a major travel agency), although these are relatively few in number compared to the total population of German Turks.

The history of social and political diversity in Germany affects the debates on Muslim "integration."[10] According to the national narrative of belonging, Germany has managed its historical diversity by producing certain social norms, cultural symbols, and legal regulations that bind its residents. Some politicians argue that when every resident in Germany, especially Muslim immigrants, conforms to these predetermined norms, displays only certain cultural symbols, and respects the legal regulations of German society, then there will be no problems, and all immigrants will be *integrated* into Germany.

As Riem Spielhaus argues, *integration* is a problematic term, because it creates "we" and "others," where "others" have to find ways to be similar to "us."[11] According to Spielhaus, in many instances, politicians do not define *integration* or what one can do in order to "integrate," but instead use Muslims as examples of disintegration. For example, while referring to Muslims, the previous Federal Minister of the Interior, Thomas de Maizière, (CDU) used the term *Integrationsverweigerer* (integration deniers).[12] In another instance, Chancellor Angela Merkel (CDU) concluded that the only effective policy for remedying social problems is to "integrate" Muslims into German society, when she made the infamous statement, "Multiculturalism has utterly failed."[13]

In fact, multiculturalism has never been an official policy in Germany; it has been endorsed only by Germany's Green Party. Indeed, the current governing party, CDU, released to the federal commission on immigration its *Arbeitsgrundlage* (position paper) on immigration on November 6, 2000 (while it was an opposition party), concluding that

Germany is not a classical country of immigration and must not become one in the future. . . . Multiculturalism and parallel societies are not a model for the future. Our goal must be the culture of tolerance and togetherness—which is based on our constitutional values and consciousness of individual identity. In this sense, it should be understood, the recognition of these values is named as the leading culture [*Leitkultur*] in Germany.[14]

This attempt to revive an imagined homogeneous German society by referring to a leading culture continues to shape the CDU's approach to immigrant integration policymaking. In this and other press releases and in the public speeches of many CDU politicians, the main targets of Leitkultur debates are Muslims, mainly Turks and Arabs, who are identified as not adopting the German Leitkultur.

At the same time, many German Muslim organizations have tried to facilitate the participation of Muslim immigrants in German society, at times adopting the language of integration in order to be able to communicate with the German state. The most prominent Muslim organizations are known as the Islam Council (*Islamrat*) and the Central Council of Muslims (*Zentralrat der Muslime*), which are semi-officially recognized by the German government, because they are invited to the annual German Islam Conference (*Deutsche Islam Konferenz,* henceforth DIK) that was carried out by the government between 2006 and 2013.[15] Islam studies scholar Schirin Amir-Moazami shows in her analysis of this conference how government authorities are seeking ways to constitute a dialogue with various Muslim communities.[16] These Muslim communities likewise are interested in establishing themselves institutionally in Germany, something the government currently supports in its efforts to facilitate "integration."

This chapter shows how the German headscarf debates can be a lens through which we can understand how national belonging is constituted in Germany's "integration" debates, and how these debates can be a point of entry into understanding the ways in which conflicts of belonging play out in Germany. First, we discuss the historical transformation of the German national narrative of belonging from racial to cultural homogeneity. Then we discuss how the main actors in constructing the contemporary national narrative of belonging are constituted as "the Germans" versus "the Muslims." Next, we show how "the Germans" mobilize key concepts of the national narrative of belonging—namely state neutrality, *Leitkultur,* and gender equality—in attempts to remove the headscarf from women employed in the German public sector, especially in schools. Finally, we discuss another construction of Germanness, that of diversity, from the voices and writings of the ones who are labeled as "the Muslims," some of whom wear the headscarf.

The German National Narrative of Belonging: Homogeneity, State Neutrality in Religion, and Gender Equality

National narratives are always conflictual, developing out of tensions between different interpretations of belonging. In the case of the German national narrative, the burden of history makes discussing belonging in and of itself difficult. After the Holocaust, the German nation was faced with the difficult task of reconstituting itself. However, this did not necessarily amount to a complete rewriting of the German national narrative. Rather, elements that existed prior to 1933 and even those that were highlighted in the Nazi period (1933–1945) were redefined to constitute a national narrative that was ostensibly free of the justifications for genocide. Indeed, homogeneity, one of the threads that structure the German national narrative, spans the entire period of German national history, although with different meanings at different times, especially pre- and post-Holocaust.

From the late nineteenth century (with the establishment of the German nation-state in 1871) until the end of World War II, homogeneity was linked to an ethno-racial understanding of belonging. After the Holocaust, the concept of a "German race" was replaced with a potentially more open definition of "German culture" as including democratic values. Homogeneity has always been an achievement, never a given. Germany as a nation was created out of many diverse traditions, in the middle of Europe at the intersection of many trade routes, and with a population constituted of the descendants of foreign armies from the ancient Romans to the Swedish, as well as by immigrants from France to the Netherlands and Russia. The discourse of homogeneity was very much the result of a conscious construction through political campaigns, state institutions, and outright propaganda. Taking philosopher and sociologist Helmuth Plessner's perspective on Germany as a "belated nation"[17]—referring to the creation of a German nation-state in 1871—the discourse on homogeneity can be seen as designed to overcome an inferiority complex in comparison to the long-established European nation-states of France and Great Britain. Rather than embracing the historical cultural diversity resulting from being the amalgamation of a multitude of German-speaking countries, the new German nation-state emphasized homogeneity.

In 1871, after a decade of war, including one against the German-language-dominated Austrian-Hungarian Empire, Prussian Chancellor Otto von Bismarck consolidated the first German nation-state and became chancellor of the new empire. Prior to 1871, the idea of German nationhood was expressed through the notion of *Kulturnation,* which bound German peoples through shared culture and language, but did not make them a nation-state. Germany was a conglomerate of principalities, duchies, and city-states such as Lippe, Saxe-Weimar-Eisenach, and Lübeck. Of note is that Bismarck's consolidation of the new nation-state was a "small solution," in that it excluded the German-speaking parts of the Austrian-Hungarian Empire.[18] Bismarck tried to establish national unity by portraying certain groups as outsiders and threats to the nation—for example, the Rome-directed Catholic Church in the *Kulturkampf*,[19] or the Slavic minority of the Sorbs, whose language he banned from being spoken in schools.

Historically, then, the alleged homogeneity of the German nation-state was constructed quite explicitly vis-à-vis the idea of "the other." By the end of the nineteenth century and leading up to WWII, the nation's new "others" were the Polish workers in the coal mines and steel works in the Rhineland, and the poor Jewish immigrants (*Ostjuden*) who moved to Germany from the Russian Empire before World War I, all of whom were increasingly seen as racially different.[20] This "race thinking," in Hannah Arendt's terms, was cultivated by means of eugenics and theories on "racial hygiene" that were promoted both in politics and in academia.[21] Racial polarization resulted in hierarchies of "us" and "them" that were reinforced through notions of racial pollution. The idea that those labeled non-German were "threats to the nation," which was first developed during the Bismarck period, became justification for the National Socialist regime.[22]

After World War II, Germans turned their backs on the belief that the "German nation" was the expression of a "German race." Postwar public discourse avoided all notions of race and precluded the articulation of any narrative that would be associated with "race."[23] Instead, "Germanness" was defined as based on "collective guilt" and as a "community of fate,"[24] which indicates how carrying the responsibility for the Holocaust has become one of the main criteria for being German.[25] In fact, former Chancellor Helmut Kohl's public speech to the Israeli Knesset in 1984 on the "grace of late-birth,"[26] in which he insisted that the postwar generation of Germans should be exempted from carrying the burden of the Holocaust, was widely criticized in Germany with a reminder of "the responsibility" resulting from the murder of six million Jews.

Yet this move away from "race" did not actually negate concepts of "otherness." For example, during the Cold War period, the national imagination now emphasized "cultural" differences between West and East Germany in place of racial and ethnic differences. West Germany proclaimed national unity and solidarity with their "oppressed brothers and sisters" in the East—a perspective that enabled West Germans to look down on the poorer inhabitants of the "Zone" (short for eastern zone, a reference to the Soviet-occupied zone in Germany and a way to avoid calling the East German state by its official name).[27] This perspective strengthened West Germany's perception of itself as the only true German democracy.

Conversely, East Germany portrayed itself as a paradise for workers and farmers, and depicted West Germany as a haven for former Nazis and the epitome of cutthroat capitalism.

After reunification, the narrative again changed. West Germany was celebrated over East Germany, creating two types of Germanness along territorial and political lines: *Ossis* (former East Germans) and *Wessis* (West Germans). Ossis were represented in the West German media almost like an inferior ethnic group: "passive, pacifist, pessimistic, and paranoid" (*passiv, pazifistisch, pessimistisch und paranoid*).[28] Although they were clearly members of the same German nation, albeit separated by the partition of Germany and the creation of the Berlin Wall, they were stigmatized in the media and politics. For example, Thilo Sarrazin said in Panorama, a political program on German TV, on September 14, 2010, that Ossis were "dumber than West Germans" (*dümmer als Wessis*). Twenty-three years after the destruction of the Berlin Wall, stereotypes about *Ossis* still exist in German media and politics.

Whereas *Ossis* and *Wessis* were each other's "others," so to speak, new immigrants became the "other" for all Germans. Starting in 1956, a large number of foreign workers were hired and brought to West Germany under the "guest worker" program to support West Germany's "economic miracle" (*Wirtschaftswunder*[29]). The status of guest worker (*Gastarbeiter*) was created to mark these people as temporary "guests" in the new country with no intention of staying long-term,[30] a notion initially shared by both the foreign workers themselves and the Germans. Designed at first to include only southern European countries, similar invitations[31] were extended to additional countries such as Algeria, Morocco, and Turkey. Starting in 1961, workers from Turkey quickly became the largest group of immigrant workers in Germany. The label *guest worker* was extended to Turks who came to West Germany as political refugees after the Turkish military coup led by General Kenan Evren on September 12, 1980, that resulted in the massive destruction of the Turkish left.

When Germany unified, the East German economy collapsed. Although the West German social safety net protected the newly unemployed East Germans from severe economic hardship, the psychological impact of this transition, together with an already existing undercurrent of xenophobic tendencies, made many East Germans susceptible to neo-Nazi propaganda directed against immigrants. This in turn led to a series of violent attacks on foreigners, starting with the much-publicized incidents in the former Eastern German towns of Hoyerswerda (1991) and Rostock-Lichtenhagen (1992). On the West German side, the celebratory mood of the unification was replaced by a more downbeat perspective on the enormous costs of converting the former German Democratic Republic (GDR) into a competitive part of a Western-style economy. Growing unemployment, the economic recession of 1993, and increasing taxes started to shake voters' confidence in the Kohl government, which had ruled the country since 1982.[32] In order to find scapegoats for the failing economy, right-leaning politicians started to target migrants and refugees. They claimed that migrants were robbing Germans of their jobs while refugees were abusing the welfare system. The clear racist undertones of this political discourse can be seen as a trigger for the series of racist attacks against refugees and immigrants that culminated in the fire bombings of the houses of Turkish families in Mölln (November 23, 1992) and in Solingen (May 29, 1993), both in what had been West Germany. In fact, these events are still commemorated in order to attract public attention to the racism that continues to exist in German society.[33]

The attacks led to many public pronouncements in support of Turkish immigrants by ordinary German citizens as well as by politicians and public officials. One such statement was a street march organized by Turkish migrants in Berlin.[34] At the institutional level, new government programs to fight racism were also introduced during this time.

Meanwhile, Turkish residents of Germany faced declining access to economic opportunities, as well as the long-term impacts of hard physical labor and limited German language skills. As a result, it was difficult for many of the first-generation Turkish immigrants to stay connected with the changing German economy and society. Ultimately, the xenophobia and economic insecurity following the unification had a tremendous effect on this migrant population. There is a saying in Kreuzberg, the heavily Turkish neighborhood in Berlin that bordered the Wall before unification, that "when the Wall came down, it collapsed on Turks" (*duvar Türkler'in üzerine düştü*). Although second-generation Turks perform better than first-generation Turks in terms of language acquisition and everyday cultural knowledge, as Germans of immigrant background they are still underrepresented in the media, parliament, and civil administration. Cultural differences, especially between German Muslims and German Christians, continue to be regarded as "unbridgeable" by some political actors, especially the currently ruling CDU.[35] When Chancellor

Angela Merkel stated in 2010 that "multiculturalism has failed in Germany," she showed how the continuing desire for homogeneity forms the bedrock of German national belonging. This desire is expressed through the public devaluation of German multicultural diversity, particularly in right-leaning populist politics.

The continuing importance of homogeneity is also reflected in German citizenship law. According to "the ethnocultural understanding of nation-state membership" in German nationhood, belonging to a state (*Staatsangehörigkeit*) assumes belonging to an ethnocultural community (*Volkszugehörigkeit*).[36] Until 1999, this definition of ethnocultural nationhood shaped the citizenship law and excluded immigrants from collective incorporation. Unlike the state-centered French nationhood, which provided citizenship to immigrants in order to facilitate their assimilation into French society, the *Volk*-centered German nationhood made the naturalization of immigrants difficult.[37]

In 1999, the SPD/Green Party coalition government developed a new citizenship law (*Staatsangehörigkeitsgesetz*), for the first time bringing in birthright citizenship (*jus soli*), rather than solely basing citizenship on descent (jus sanguinis). However, the idea that immigrants in general and Turkish immigrants in particular could now obtain citizenship merely by being born in Germany faced strong opposition from the conservative CDU, which claimed to represent a significant portion of the German population. Because the citizenship law had to pass both parliamentary houses, and CDU had the majority in the second German chamber (the *Bundesrat,* roughly equivalent to the US Senate), the government had to agree to a compromise in order to get any kind of change passed. According to the new law, children born in Germany after the year 2000 can be granted dual citizenship: German citizenship and their parents' native citizenship. However, this major change from jus sanguinis to jus soli includes the following paradox as a result of the political compromise: in order to be granted German citizenship as a legal adult, a child born in Germany has to give up the citizenship of his or her parents' native country between the ages of eighteen and twenty-three.[38] Thus, even though this was a revolutionary change in German citizenship law, it reveals that the desire for homogeneity is still prevalent on the conservative side of the German political spectrum.

In this case, the opposite of the desire for homogeneity is the reality of diversity. Conservative-leaning Germans have especially struggled with the immigrant-related diversity that is the empirical reality of their society. When it comes to Turkish immigrants, two forms of difference receive particular attention: religion and gender. Accommodation of religious difference is discussed through the concept of *state neutrality* in religion, or the principle that state institutions should be neutral to make sure that all citizens are equal regardless of religious background. This idea is put into practice by following the French model of erasing all religious symbols from the public sphere.

Yet this neutrality is interrupted in practice by a strong defense of what is considered by some to be German culture. For example, whereas members of the Green Party and the SPD support banning all religious symbols in public schools, members of the Christian Democrats and right-leaning liberals from the Free Democratic Party (*Freie Democratische Partei,* henceforth FDP) treat Christian and, since the Holocaust, Jewish symbols as expressions of German culture that provide the basis for German national belonging.

Similarly, the idea that immigrants have problematic gender relations in which adherence to patriarchal norms leads to phenomena like honor killing[39] informs public support for a German version of gender equality. As Myra Marx Ferree notes, German feminism is based not on gender equality in a liberal sense, nor on the idea that women should be free to choose what they do with their own lives, but on the political assumptions of "social justice, family values and state responsibility for the common good."[40] Thus, Judeo-Christian forms of religious expression and a particular interpretation of gender equality are marked as culturally German.

After the partial softening of the jus sanguinis principle with the citizenship reform of 2000, the CDU and the Christian Socialist Union (henceforth CSU) parties started a debate on Leitkultur in Germany as they resigned themselves to the fact that Germany's immigrants were here to stay. However, rather than admit to being a country of immigration, they declared Germany a country of integration, in which immigrants should learn to organize their lives in accordance with German cultural precepts. According to the position statement of the CDU-CSU, immigrants should accept the German Leitkultur as their own and express their acceptance by learning German, being loyal to the German nation, and adapting to its political and legal institutions. Deconstructing this concept, Douglas Klusmeyer shows that the CDU-CSU's conceptualization of Leitkultur is based on the "foundations of European civilization" and inherently tied to Christian and Jewish traditions (*Christlich-Jüdische Leitkultur*).[41] The underlying political argument is that Europe in general, and Germany in particular, is a community of values (*Wertegemeinschaft*) that is under threat by Muslims and Eastern Europeans.[42]

Yet the concept of Leitkultur received criticism from critical and left-liberal Germans. For example, in 2010, Andrea Nahles, General Secretary of the SPD (then the center-left and largest opposition party in Germany) attacked the CDU's commitment to the idea that "the Judeo-Christian tradition, the Enlightenment and historical experiences are the basis for social cohesion and form the dominant culture [*Leitkultur*] in Germany."[43] Nahles critiqued the ways in which the CDU's message is exclusionary and increases the stigmatization of Muslims in German society: "Nothing connects so much as a common enemy, and this is particularly Islam. If one is to believe the accompanying battle cries, Muslims in general are people from 'foreign cultures,' they have different values, they do not accept our liberal democracy, are not enlightened, and undermine our legal system and settle in our social systems."[44] Nahles pointed out that the CDU's message of exclusion is actually contrary to the Judeo-Christian values of dignity and freedom for all. She also denounced this attempt to generate a sense of "we" against "the others" who are in conflict with Germany's secular order. Furthermore, she argued that the notion of Leitkultur—and the sense of us versus them that it inspires—is the wrong answer to the problem of organizing daily life together in Germany. Finally, Nahles remarked that the CDU's concept of Leitkultur is nebulous at best: "What exactly is meant [by Leitkultur]? The CDU has failed to deliver an answer to this question for years now."[45] Nahles here pinpointed a major problem with the CDU's concept of Leitkultur. After all, it is not so clear what Germanness is today.[46] This might also explain why, instead of a positive definition of Germanness (in defining what it *is* to be German), the CDU's Leitkultur offers a negative definition (what it is *not* to be German). On this basis, Muslims can become the "them" versus the "us" supported by images of stroller-pushing women with headscarves that evoke fears of an explosion in the numbers of the Muslim population as the German population is declining, and by the fear of Islamic terrorism evoked by the imagery of aggressive dark-skinned men. It is in this context, between conservative Leitkultur and multiculturalism (*Multikulti*), that the German debates on the headscarf unfold.

Regulating the Headscarf in Germany: Can Muslims Be German?

After the Constitutional Court's decision to let the specific German states decide whether or not they will allow teachers to wear headscarves in public schools, there was a long discussion in German media and politics about when and where headscarves can be banned or permitted. Fereshta Ludin's home state of Baden-Württemberg passed a law banning the headscarf. This prevented Ludin from wearing her headscarf while teaching. The regulation is part of the Education Act and applies specifically to teachers. Unlike in France and Turkey, in states like Baden-Württemberg, the focus is not on directly regulating students as future or present citizens, but rather on the teachers who train these students to become citizens. Only Hesse and Berlin have moved beyond regulating the headscarf in schools, expanding their headscarf bans to employees of the public service. Although consumers of public services, including students, are free to wear the headscarf, these German states are concerned with avoiding any perception of public support for Islam.

As we argued earlier, German homogeneity masks vast heterogeneities. This is particularly salient when it comes to understanding the regulations of federal states. Julia von Blumenthal, a political scientist specializing in issues of federalism in Germany, analyzes how the political processes in various German states have produced different approaches to regulating the headscarf.[47] She shows how each federal state deals differently with the headscarf, and by extension with diversity in the population. Von Blumenthal argues that both state and religious organizations in each state and the nature of German federalism, which gives to the German states exclusive powers on issues of education, are responsible for the various decisions in the headscarf debate. She suggests that the interaction of political party tensions and the cultural and historical background of the specific state affect the headscarf policies and laws in each state.[48] The various federal-state governments thus incorporate and enact different understandings of the German national narrative.

According to von Blumenthal, the states follow one of four models in regulating the headscarf. The first is the *liberal model*. In these states' parliaments there have been no decisions on religious symbols, and the headscarf issue is dealt with contextually if there is a dispute. This policy exists in the eastern states except for Berlin, and in Hamburg, Schleswig-Holstein, and

Rhineland-Palatinate. The second category is the *flexible regulation model*. In these states (Bremen and Lower Saxony) there is a ban on religious symbols; however, it is unclear whether the ban applies to Judeo-Christian symbols as well. The third category is the *Christian model*, which ostensibly bans religious symbols, arguing that they threaten state neutrality in religion. However, in these states, Judeo-Christian religious symbols, such as crosses and *kippot* (yarmulkes) are allowed in schools, because they are constructed as part of the cultural rather than religious traditions of Germany.[49] These policies are in effect in Bavaria, Baden-Württemberg, Saarland, North Rhine-Westphalia, and Hesse. The final category, the *secular model*, has been passed in the state of Berlin, mandating a total ban of all religious symbols for all civil servants.[50]

Clearly there is no unified political approach to dealing with the headscarf in Germany, so it is not possible to say that headscarves are completely banned at any particular site. Furthermore, neither the political affiliation of the party in governing power nor the political leanings of the state's voting population have automatically translated into more or less restrictive approaches. For example, the SPD in a number of states supported the prohibition laws (for example, in Baden-Württemberg and Lower Saxony). The change of government to a more left-leaning red-green coalition (the red represents the SPD and the green represents the Greens) in these states did not mean that their respective bans on teachers wearing headscarves were abolished. In turn, the Hamburg parliament did not adopt a headscarf ban during the CDU government, despite the fact that at the national level the CDU clearly advocated against practices like teachers wearing a headscarf.

Although Muslim women's wearing of the headscarf in German public schools has been the main controversial media and political debate in Germany, a less well-known discussion focuses on the labor market. Reporting on this issue shows that each state's political decisions on the headscarf had important social effects on headscarf-wearing women, which went beyond the immediate regulation of government employees. Indeed, a number of private employers began to argue that they would not employ women wearing headscarves. There are a few media reports and academic studies on labor market discrimination against headscarf-wearing women.[51] Some of these women have brought their cases to the courts, which have largely ruled in their favor, in line with a general trend of German regional courts ruling in favor of employees in discrimination cases. A well-known headscarf-related employment case involved a saleswoman who was denied further employment at a perfumery when she started wearing her headscarf.[52] The employer argued that her headscarf would affect sales negatively. Upon complaint, the Federal Labor Court (*das Bundesarbeitsgericht*) ruled that the woman had faced unfair dismissal.[53] When she returned to work, the employer placed the headscarf-wearing woman in another department so that she would not have direct relations with the public.[54] As Susan Rottmann and Myra Marx Ferree point out, the legal basis for these decisions is the right to freedom of religion versus the interest of the employers.[55] In addition, the 2006 antidiscrimination law has been used effectively to reach an overarching consensus that discrimination against religion is not acceptable in the German labor market.

What we see, then, are two opposing trends: one in which states regulate largely against the right of their own employees to wear a headscarf, while antidiscrimination laws are put into use in order to help women who are wearing headscarves in private employment. (A similar tension recently came to the fore in the French headscarf debates.) These opposing trends originate from the interpretation of state neutrality in religious matters. By extension, the interpretation of this neutrality impacts the degree to which individual German states enforce homogeneity in the public sphere (as opposed to the private sphere of paid work). Finally, as we show, such interpretations are informed by the particular understanding of gender equality in Germany.[56]

For headscarf-wearing women in Germany, the antidiscrimination protections appear to be tempered by the anti-headscarf regulations of many German states. In her article on headscarf-wearing women's counterstrategies for dealing with labor market discrimination, Islamic studies scholar Riem Spielhaus shows that women have not been able to develop adequate strategies to deal with such discrimination.[57] According to Spielhaus, women try to avoid discrimination by not applying to jobs because they assume they will not be hired, and when they do experience discrimination, they do not seek help or services.[58] Spielhaus focuses on how headscarf-wearing women assess their chances in the German labor market, and her work suggests that, like in the debates in the other countries discussed in this book, the German headscarf debates have a clear impact on headscarf-wearing women's practices.

Compared to the headscarf, the niqab has received relatively little attention in Germany. Following the "burka" bans in France and Belgium, some German political actors started to discuss a similar ban in the federal state of Hesse in 2011. The major controversy in this region was a German-Moroccan woman who was wearing a niqab while working in a municipal office in the city of Frankfurt. Following a ban imposed by local authorities, in February 2011 Hesse's Minister of the Interior, Boris Rhein (CDU), banned the burka for employees in public offices in his state. Currently there is no burka ban in other parts of Germany, nor is it being discussed. Calling the burka a "mobile prison," liberal (FDP) politician Silvana Koch-Mehrin, at the time a member of the European Parliament, along with several of her party members said that the burka has no place in Europe and advocated for a Europe-wide ban (clearly echoing the French niqab debate and extending the French arguments to the European political realm). However, this call has not been taken up either, and we leave the issue of the niqab aside in our analysis of the German case because it does not show a significant impact on the national narrative at this time.

In Germany, regulation of the headscarf occurs in the context of a larger debate on public and legal recognition for Islam. The Protestant Church (*Evangelische Kirche*) and the Catholic Church, as well as the Jewish religious community, have privileged legal status in German law. According to the 1949 constitution (*Grundgesetz für die Bundesrepublik Deutschland,* or the Basic Law for the Federal Republic of Germany, Article 140), religious associations can acquire the status of public law corporation provided that they guarantee continuity with their bylaws and the number of their members, as well as provide clear indications of the members' status. If these requirements are not met, religious denominations must organize themselves as mere associations under private law.

Islamic groups have been trying to obtain a preferred legal status for their religious communities in Germany since the early 1970s, but the courts have rejected their petitions. There have been several failed attempts to gain the status of corporation of public law (*Körperschaft des öffentlichen Rechts*) with the intent to have Islam publicly recognized and acknowledged as an organization equal before the law with the Christian churches.[59] The problem here was the discrepancy between the definition of this matter in German law, on the one hand, and the perception of what constitutes "official status," on the other hand. German legal experts argued that the German constitution does not require any kind of legal procedure for a religious community to be recognized. From this perspective, Islam was always officially recognized in Germany. The question of obtaining the status of a corporation under public law, which would entail certain legal and tax benefits, was an altogether different matter. The German constitution had specific requirements that interpreters argued had not been met by the applicants representing these Muslim organizations, and therefore these applications had to be rejected (until the success of the Ahmadiyya Muslim Jamaat, an international Muslim community associated with South Asia, in 2013).[60] The rejection was based on the argument that the applicant organizations were not able to demonstrate legally binding membership status for their members. German law requires that there be a way to verify this in the respective organization, and such memberships do not exist in many Muslim religious organizations.[61]

Those who were critical of such an application of German constitutional law argued that it was yet another way to enforce Germany homogeneity, this time at the organizational rather than individual level.[62] On the side of the German authorities, the lack of a body of representation for Muslims in Germany is also frequently lamented, because it makes it difficult to find organizational interlocutors to handle complex social issues. The federal-level DIK, discussed later in this chapter, brought together representatives of a diverse range of Muslim organizations to discuss ongoing issues with representatives of the federal government during the 2006–2012 period. Some German states have shown slow movement to incorporate Islamic religious expressions into education. Since 2008–2009, Alevis[63] in North Rhein-Westfalia and Bavaria have had the right to education under Basic Law (*Grundgesetz* Article 7 III), and since 2009 in Hesse. In Fall 2013, Hesse recognized Islamic classes for two Muslim organizations: DITIB (*Diyanet İşleri Türk İslam Birliği,* or the Religious Affairs Turkish Islamic Union, rooted in Turkey) and the Ahmadiyya Muslim Jamaat. North Rhein-Westfalia amended its school regulations in 2012 and introduced Islamic religious education on the basis of an advisory board consultation. In 2012, the Hamburg regional government signed an agreement with three Muslim religious organizations (two Sunnite and one Alevite), which introduced new rights and responsibilities on both sides. On the one hand, the Sunnite and Alevite organizations agreed to carry on effective integration strategies, as stated in the agreement. On the other hand, the Hamburg state government agreed to regulations in various social areas, such as Islamic education, burial according to Islamic rites, and others. This official agreement between a state government and Muslim organizations was the first of its kind in Germany.[64]

The battle for religious recognition reflects an ongoing struggle over what it means to be Muslim in Germany and over whether or not Germans can be Muslim. There have been positive changes with respect to religious recognition in several German states. However, as the following analysis of the headscarf debate shows, the "integration" of Muslim immigrants in Germany continues to be highly contested.

Analyzing the German Headscarf Debate

In the German case, we combine an analysis of newspaper data with material from the website of the DIK and interviews with a select number of women who are currently active in the headscarf debates. In terms of the newspapers, we focus on *die tageszeitung* (henceforth *taz*), *Süddeutsche Zeitung* (henceforth *SZ*) and *Frankfurter Allgemeine Zeitung* (henceforth *FAZ*), which are high-brow newspapers, for the period 2004 to 2011, as well as *BILD*,[65] a widely circulated tabloid, for the period 2006[66] to 2011 (updated for selected cases until 2013). At times we supplement these with material from other media sources, such as the weekly *Die Zeit* and a daily news site on the Internet, *Die Tagesschau*. The first paper, *taz*, is a Green-Left-oriented daily newspaper, generally immigrant friendly and published in and focused on Berlin, the city with the largest number of Muslim immigrants in Germany. *SZ* and *FAZ* are nationwide papers. *SZ* reaches highbrow left-liberal readers, and FAZ targets highly educated but more politically conservative liberal readers. The political views in *BILD* are generally regarded to be conservative and right-leaning, but at times *BILD* has demonstrated an astonishing flexibility in changing its position, for example, when it abandoned support for Helmut Kohl before the 1998 elections and embraced SPD candidate Gerhard Schröder for chancellor. It is the best-selling tabloid in Europe. By using newspapers that span the political spectrum (left, left-liberal, conservative-liberal, and populist), we ensure that our comparative conclusions in Germany are not the result of the political outlook of a given newspaper, but rather provide an overall analysis of the debate. Many social actors, including politicians, feminists, and members of the Muslim, especially Turkish, communities, and representatives of civil society organizations (both Muslim and non-Muslim) have their own ways of retelling the German national narrative of homogeneity, reflected in both op-ed pieces and factual reporting. We focus on the debates from 2004 onward, after the Ludin headscarf case led the various German states to legislate the issue.

The three broadsheet newspapers, *taz*, *FAZ*, and *SZ*, mostly discussed the headscarf ban in schools. Both *taz* and *FAZ* included interviews with prominent politicians, academics, and feminists who represented various positions in the debate. *Taz* was more open to diversity than the other newspapers, and its writers were more critical of restrictions on wearing the headscarf. This is not to say, however, that all *FAZ* writers supported such restrictions; there were some very critical opinion pieces in *FAZ*. *SZ* dedicated much less space to the topic than either *taz* or *FAZ*. Instead, many SZ articles were concerned with the headscarf debates in France, Turkey, and other European countries.

The most lively and surprising debates took place in *BILD*. Unlike the coverage of the headscarf debate in highbrow German newspapers, BILD's articles did not focus solely on banning the headscarf or the burka at schools or in the public service. Rather, *BILD* presented competing narratives of the headscarf, ranging from those that depicted the headscarf in a negative light (that is, as a political symbol of women's oppression, as representing violent and patriarchal non-Western practices, or as a sign of failed integration) and those that discussed discrimination against Muslim women with headscarves. For instance, the headscarf was mentioned in numerous reports that dealt with terrorism, bank robberies, Muslim integration, and violence against women (for example, cases of honor killing, forced marriage, and violence in Afghanistan and Pakistan). However, there were also articles concerned with discrimination or violence against Muslim women who wear the headscarf. Similarly, in order to shape public opinion, *BILD* not only featured editorials like the other newspapers did, but also generated its own news on the issue. For example, a non-Muslim *BILD* journalist, Katharina Nachtsheim, dressed up publicly as a "Muslim woman" and described what it was like to be a "burka woman" for one day.[67]

In addition to reviewing the newspaper data, we also analyzed political discussions in the DIK. We collected all the material available on the headscarf from the DIK website from 2006 through 2013. The DIK is a high-profile government-sponsored forum for the discussion of topics related to Muslims in Germany; it started in 2006 as part of the platform on integration of the then ruling CDU-SPD government, and ended in 2013. The conference was organized by the German Ministry of the Interior and its participants were government representatives as well as experts, individual Muslim citizens, and representatives of Muslim organizations invited by the Ministry of the Interior. During its existence, there were annual meetings and DIK sponsored a website that published both official reports and writings by individual DIK participants.

Yurdakul interviewed three women to hear their thoughts about conflicts of belonging in the headscarf debates in Germany. Dr. Naika Foroutan, an Iranian-German scholar, is the organizer of the Young Islam Conference and leader of the HEYMAT (*Hybride Europäisch-Muslimische Identitätsmodelle* or Hybrid European-Muslim identity models) research project, which explores the hybrid identities and strategies of belonging for young Muslims in Europe. Soraya Hassoun is a headscarf-wearing student with Lebanese and German parents who completed her master's thesis on Islamic feminism in Germany in the Humboldt University's transdisciplinary program on Gender Studies. She works actively in Muslim Voices (*Muslimische Stimmen*), an online platform for Muslim women in Germany. Finally, Yurdakul interviewed Hüda Sağ, a headscarf-wearing Muslim woman of Turkish background who studies at the University of Bielefeld. She attended the Young Islam Conference in Berlin in 2011.

The German National Narrative in Debates on the Headscarf

Schoolteacher Fereshta Ludin's case was the first to be carried to the Constitutional Court and it set the terms of the headscarf debate for the years following 2004. For many, Ludin's headscarf represented a threat to Germany's unifying Judeo-Christian values and to German definitions of state neutrality and gender equality. The issue of state neutrality in religion, buttressed by arguments regarding gender equality, dominated the debate as German states sought to regulate the headscarf in the aftermath of the Ludin decision. Additionally, the issue of the headscarf was taken up by German feminists as a symbol of women's oppression. Subsequent to the Ludin case, the headscarf debate became part of a general debate on Islam and integration, but not necessarily its main focus. However, after 2009, three cases led to another flare-up of the headscarf debate: the murder of headscarf-wearing Marwa el-Sherbini in a German courtroom, the publication of Thilo Sarrazin's controversial anti-immigrant book *Germany Abolishes Itself* (*Deutschland schaft sich ab*), and a discussion of the headscarf in the DIK. After discussing how the Ludin case set the terms of the debate, we analyze the three latter cases to show how a prevalent version of the German national narrative continues to be structured by the desire for homogeneity and its tension with the realities of diversity.

State Neutrality in Religion:
Homogeneity Versus Diversity

During the peak of the Ludin headscarf case in late 2003 and early 2004, German politics was divided in ways that dramatically changed the political climate in Germany. Those who argued that Muslim women should be allowed to wear their headscarves as teachers in public schools attempted to redefine the German national narrative by diminishing the power of homogeneity in favor of recognition of difference and diversity. However, defenders of German homogeneity as the bedrock of German national belonging drew on arguments regarding state neutrality, buttressed by a defense of gender equality, to argue against granting women the right to wear headscarves while being teachers in public schools.

Discussions of the Ludin case often drew simultaneously from arguments about gender equality and those about state neutrality in religion, and it can be difficult to find material that separates these two ideas. For example, when three thousand Muslim women protested on behalf of Ludin in early January 2004, Lale Akgün, Bundestag member for the SPD and the SPD's spokesperson on issues related to Islam, stated:

It is absurd to declare the clear subordination under a symbol of gender separation as emancipation and to see this in principle as the normal case of female Muslim existence. [Those who really want] emancipation in the sense of the Enlightenment and of humanism will critically watch a headscarf discourse that does not concern the individual Muslim woman, but rather the religious-cultural power of interpretation within Islam.[68]

Women like Akgün occupy the position of privileged explainers of Muslim culture to the larger German public. By arguing that the headscarf represents gender oppression while marking Islam itself as undemocratic, Akgün simultaneously supported the protection of the German version of gender equality and of state neutrality in religion (with clear echoes of Turkish pro-secular enlightenment discourse, as discussed in Chapter 3).

Similar arguments were put forth by powerful non-Muslim politicians. Indeed, Angela Merkel, then the newly elected chancellor, argued in a letter to fellow members of the CDU that "the Christian order of values must not be put into opposition to the religious and ideological neutrality of the state."[69] SPD President of the German Parliament Wolfgang Thierse added concerns with gender equality, stating, that the state "fundamentally has the duty to be neutral toward all religions. [However] a cross is not a symbol of oppression, while the headscarf is for many Muslim women."[70] In short, these politicians did not promote the neutrality of strict secularism as did France and Turkey, where religiosity is not supposed to enter the public sphere. Rather, they argued that Christian symbols represent a value orientation that is not only acceptable but also requires protection, while they denied the expression of Islamic symbols on the basis of their purported gender inequality. Thus they protected German homogeneity through appeals to German Christian culture and gender equality.

Such arguments can create the impression that state neutrality in religion has a uniform meaning throughout Germany. However, state neutrality means different things for different social actors operating in the various Länder. For example, German states governed by the CDU (either by itself or in coalition with another party) conceptualize state neutrality as compatible with a celebration of the Judeo-Christian values that have historically permeated Germany's education culture.[71] Many authors—including Mark Siemons, a journalist and frequent contributor to *FAZ* on issues related to German Turks—have argued, however, against this blurry line between "religion" and "culture," citing Angela Merkel's earlier comment:

Angela Merkel writes in her letter to her fellow party members that even the cosmopolitan neutral state has the need "to bear upon the Christian origins of our value order and the boundaries of tolerance." Yet, if we consider this argument seriously, it would concern the religious content pertaining to the articulation of a political position, not to its cultural representation. What exactly does politics expect of crucifixes, chapels, and Christmas trees as a mere commemoration of historical Christianity?[72]

Here Siemons questioned the purported neutrality of religion as cultural expression. Merkel's and other CDU politicians' arguments explicitly referred to the overlaps between German culture and Christian religious symbols. Thus they created an assumed homogeneous society that excluded non-Christians, such as Jews and Muslims.

Other newspaper articles also argued that the blurry line between religion and culture is problematic. Some parents, for example, saw a conflict between their beliefs and the religious symbols allowed in certain schools.[73] They simply found them proselytizing, regardless of whether they were

Islamic or not. These parents would prefer the strict secularism of France or Turkey, but they remained a minority in Germany.

In a similar vein, at the end of the 1990s, a court case put Judeo-Christian symbols and the state neutrality principle to the test. A group of parents in Bavaria complained that their human rights were violated and asked for the prohibition of religious symbols, mainly crucifixes, in schools. In its ruling, the regional court allowed Bavarian schools to keep crucifixes in the classrooms, although this was against the state neutrality principle. Indeed, the Constitutional Court overturned the decision, stating that crucifixes are an infringement on freedom of religion and in contradiction with the constitution.[74] However, despite the Constitutional Court's judgment, the crucifixes remain in Bavarian schools.[75]

Thus, in the German context, state neutrality does not mean that the German states treat all religions equally. On the contrary, by treating Christian symbols as cultural ones, these symbols are declared as simply representing German belonging and thus as having a place in public schools. Because Muslim traditions are considered to be outside traditional German culture, it becomes possible for some German states to argue that state neutrality and, consequently, school peace (*Schulfrieden*) are jeopardized when Muslim teachers are allowed to wear the headscarf, but not when Christian (or in some cases, Jewish) symbols are present. In this line of reasoning, the headscarf's religious meaning is placed in opposition to Christian cultural traditions. State neutrality in religion is maintained by emphasizing the culture rather than the religiosity of Christianity. At the same time, "Judeo-Christian values" and "Muslim values" are placed in opposition to each other, in part by assuming that both are internally homogeneous.

Several of the leading German women in immigration politics, such as Barbara John and Rita Süssmuth of the CDU and Marieluise Beck of the Green Party, countered claims against the headscarf grounded in this interpretation of state neutrality in religion. These women defended the supporters of the headscarf by emphasizing not only the reality of German diversity but also *respect* for diversity. They stated the following in an open letter about restrictions on the headscarf for teachers in public schools:

Whether or not one should opt for a more strictly secular school system, or if one wants to make the religious plurality in our society visible in the schools too, the equal treatment of all religions is mandated by the constitution. A treatment of Islamic symbols different than that of Christian or Jewish ones is extremely problematic from the viewpoint of integration and exacerbates conflicts instead of reducing them. A . . . ban of the headscarf, which also would be gender specific, would be a religiously based discrimination, which amounts in practice to a complete exclusion from a profession.[76]

Thus, even though these women represented quite different political parties, they joined together in their call for recognition of diversity and the application of equal rights in religious expression. Green Party member Marieluise Beck's argument for recognition can be understood through her party's historical support for multiculturalism, and Barbara John and Rita Süssmuth, both CDU members, extended the state's recognition of their religion, Christianity, to other religions practiced by people in Germany. They then linked this to support for the headscarf as expressed in the open letter just quoted. In doing so, they took a very clear stance on principles of equal treatment, denying the distinction between Christianity and Islam drawn by some defenders of restrictions on the headscarf.

Such arguments received heavy criticism, however. In February 2004, close to one hundred women academics, politicians, artists, doctors, and teachers, many of Turkish background, argued that Marieluise Beck and other leading politicians' call against headscarf bans was at best misguided. They accused Beck and others of paternalism and of vastly overestimating the number of women who were truly free in donning the headscarf. They believed instead that many Muslim women in Germany had already taken off the headscarf, and if they still wore it, it was because they felt rejected by society and were "powerless against their instrumentalization by Islamic forces."[77] In their open letter, these women asked Marieluise Beck:

Who within the Muslim population would feel marginalized if the headscarf were prohibited in school? Only those who are under the influence of the Islamists and for whom wearing the headscarf is a *sine qua non* not only in the private sphere but also in the public service. All those for whom religion is a private matter and all those who are indifferent to religious precepts know and accept without problems the constitutional principle of neutrality in the school system.[78]

These opposing voices, some of whom came from German Muslim women and leading members of Turkish immigrant organizations, clearly took a secular perspective that strongly echoed Turkish interpretations of secularism. According to them, Islam is a private matter and the headscarf does not belong in public schools. Their open letter was an attempt to insert their voices into the debate, against those who argued for an interpretation of state neutrality that would allow teachers to wear the headscarf in schools. From their secular perspective, state neutrality meant leaving religious symbols out of state institutions altogether. As such, their position differed substantially from CDU politicians' support for Christian symbols in schools, and by extension from the dominant German interpretation of state neutrality in religion.

Ostensibly the headscarf debate led to a revisiting of the concept of state neutrality. A summary of the discussion that lasted through the early months of 2004, argued that the core of the debate dealt with the question of whether all religious symbols should be banned at public schools or whether this measure should be applied only to the headscarf.[79] On the surface, then, this was a debate about the tension between state schools' obligation to represent state neutrality and teachers' right to religious freedom. Although the tension between homogeneity and diversity continues to play an important part in the underlying debate and in the development of the German national narrative of belonging, as the arguments by Lale Akgün and the open letter by German Muslim women suggest, gender issues are also at the heart of this debate and alert us to the complexity of the overall issue.

Gender Equality, the Headscarf, and Playboy: "Varieties of Feminism"?

Tensions between the longing for homogeneity and the realities of diversity continued in discussions by German feminists.[80] After the direct question about Fereshta Ludin's headscarf had been settled, German feminists used the headscarf as a foil to strengthen their arguments in defense of gender equality. As many commentators have pointed out, anti-Muslim feminists argued that the headscarf is a political symbol of women's oppression that has no place in a German society that supports gender equality.[81]

Necla Kelek, who made her name as a sociologist with intimate knowledge of Turkish communities in Germany through the publication of her 2005 bestseller *The Foreign Bride* (*Die Fremde Braut*), strongly disapproves of young girls wearing a headscarf. Kelek used her status as a public figure to discuss elementary schoolgirls in headscarves. From the platform of the DIK, Kelek argued that the headscarf turns girls into sexual targets and robs them of their childhood, which violates Germany's constitution (the Basic Law):

On this point the Basic Law is very clear. At fourteen, a person reaches the age of discretion in the matter of religion. It is for this reason that I say that the headscarf cannot exist in primary schools. The headscarf turns girls into sexual beings before they reach puberty; their "right to a childhood" is taken away. This is not compatible with our society, which needs equal, self-assertive, and responsible citizens. Whoever forces a headscarf on little girls abuses the principle of freedom of religion.[82]

By focusing on children as persons incapable of consent, Kelek reinforced images of Muslims as backward, with Islam and Muslim men oppressing not only Muslim women but also Muslim girls. In this way, Kelek also brought up the issue of women's agency, in which Muslim women are oppressed while wearing the headscarf, a recurrent theme across the countries analyzed in this book.

Kelek served on various committees for the German government as an expert on issues related to integration, women's rights, and Islam. One of these prestigious appointments was for the DIK, Germany's Islam conference, which gave her a platform to make the argument just presented. Although Kelek, being of Turkish descent, used a stigmatizing discourse that portrayed Muslims as backward, she represented herself as the "authentic" voice of Muslim women who live under Islamic patriarchal rules and are silenced in their own communities. Kelek frequently pointed out that there is a close relationship between gender equality and the integration of Turkish communities into German society. She portrayed Turkish communities as capable of becoming more German. She also conveyed a message compatible with anti-Muslim discourse, specifically, the call for Germany to save Muslim women from Muslim men.[83] For Kelek, Muslim women can be emancipated only if they become Westernized. Her interviews and articles in newspapers imply that she sees herself and other immigrant women leaders as "code breakers" who decipher Muslim culture for a German audience. She becomes the voice for all women rather than reflecting the diverse experiences of Turkish women in Germany. Thus Kelek uses her individual experiences as a woman from a Turkish and Muslim background as proof in public debates that women need to be emancipated by the West, and in this case, in Germany and under Western cultural rules.

Alice Schwarzer, the famous editor of the women's magazine *Emma* and controversial veteran of the German feminist movement, supports Necla Kelek's position.[84] In what were highly provocative statements, Schwarzer intentionally aligned the national narrative of the ethno-racial homogeneity of the Nazi years with contemporary Islam. Drawing parallels between National Socialists and Muslims, Schwarzer compared the headscarf to the *Judenstern* (the yellow star that Jews were forced to wear in

Germany and in countries occupied by Germany during World War II). In her eyes, the headscarf identifies women as Muslim in much the same way that the star identified people as Jews. Her statement, which created a heated debate in the media, was as follows:

The headscarf is the flag of Islamism. The headscarf is a sign that makes women into others, into second-class humans. As a symbol, it is a form of "marking," akin to the yellow star. And the headscarf and the full body coverage are in truth a serious obstacle and constraint for movement and communication. I find it self-evident that we should take countries like France as examples and ban the headscarf from schools and kinder-gartens, for teachers and students alike.[85]

Schwarzer's anti-Muslim tone and her comparison of the headscarf to the yellow star attracted the attention of German newsmakers and political actors, many of whom felt that Schwarzer went too far, that she instru-mentalized the yellow star for her own purposes. However, Schwarzer has continued to make these kinds of arguments in edited books that collec-tively state that the headscarf, as an expression of "Islamism," should not be tolerated in Germany.[86]

Schwarzer's statements were also severely criticized by some Muslim women in Germany. For Schwarzer and Kelek, feminism provides both a clear-cut analysis of the headscarf—it oppresses women—and a clear-cut approach to the issue—it should be banned. However, such clear-cut analyses were challenged by several German Muslim women. For example, *Die Zeit* reported that Saliha Kubilay, a young Muslim woman, confronted Schwarzer during a public discussion at a university: "Where in the femi-nist movement did you stop progressing so as to fail to grasp to this day that Islamic feminism has been long present in Germany?"[87] With her question, Kubilay attempted to show Schwarzer—and by extension the reporter attempted to show the readership of *Die Zeit*—that Schwarzer's brand of feminism fails to acknowledge the diversity of perspectives in Germany. However, for many observers, especially for some German femi-nists, what is at stake is women's free choice. Many doubt that Muslim women would choose to wear the headscarf of their own free will rather than take the opportunity to show their hair as a sign of their integration into German society.[88] For these women, like Alice Schwarzer, belonging to Germany requires advocating against the wearing of the headscarf. In so doing, they again reinforce the homogeneity that continues to struc-ture the German national narrative of belonging. However, women like

Akgün, Kelek, and Schwarzer might argue that what they are up against is not diversity but rather a forced homogeneity on the side of conservative Islam that imposes wearing the headscarf on the majority of the women who wear it in Germany. In such arguments, diversity would result from the freedom of women from different ethnic backgrounds to show their hair and bodies.

Indeed, in media reporting, female nudity is associated with Muslim women's integration, and covering is associated with a failure to integrate into Germany. In May 2011, *Deutsche Welle,* Germany's international broadcaster, reported about Sıla Şahin,[89] the first German-Turkish film actress to pose nude in Playboy, in May 2011.[90] Asking whether posing naked should be seen as the ultimate act of integration, the reporter portrayed Sıla Şahin as a Muslim woman who said she was liberated by posing nude in Playboy. The German weekly *Die Zeit* problematized this understanding of emancipation and questioned the sensational interviews about Şahin's nudity in *Playboy* by asking why she had to discuss her upbringing, ethno-national background, and the pressure she received from her parents as part of her story in order to get attention for her photos, and by boldly titling the newspaper article "Breasts with Migration Background."[91] This reporting, as well as Şahin's posing for *Playboy,* both played into and questioned the cliché of Turkish women being emancipated in the West by uncovering themselves.

Homogeneity in Diversity: Leitkultur or Cultural Diversity?

As the preceding discussion of the German feminist approach to the headscarf suggests, the issue of the headscarf did not go away after the Constitutional Court decided on the Ludin case. The continuing tension between homogeneity and diversity in the German headscarf debates came to the fore in two events that happened in the late 2000s: the July 1, 2009, murder of Marwa el-Sherbini, and the September 6, 2010, publication of a book by Thilo Sarrazin.

With the murder of Marwa el-Sherbini in 2009, the mostly negative discussion of the headscarf in the German media suddenly transformed into a more differentiating and self-critical one. The headscarf-wearing Muslim immigrant Marwa el-Sherbini was murdered by Alex W., an *Aussiedler* (a term for immigrants of German decent from the former Eastern Bloc countries). Earlier in 2009, el-Sherbini had sued Alex W. for calling her a terrorist, a whore, and an Islamist while she was pushing her son on a swing in her neighborhood playground in Dresden. During the court proceedings, Alex W. stabbed el-Sherbini with a knife he had brought into the courtroom. El-Sherbini died on-site; she was three months pregnant and her husband and three-year old son witnessed her murder.

After el-Sherbini's murder, German media and political discourse went through a period of self-reflection, turning to the issue of discrimination against Muslims, especially women with headscarves as targets of anti-Muslim racism. Presenting el-Sherbini as a devout Muslim, a mother, and an educated immigrant (she worked as a pharmacist in Germany in order to obtain a German accreditation in that field), newsmakers and politicians critically discussed the relationship between the headscarf and integration. Initially there was controversy as to whether or not Germans had paid enough attention to this murder. Though it was reported on right away, the spotlight increased after street protests broke out in Germany and Egypt, with people publicly expressing their outrage that this murder had been committed in a German courtroom where el-Sherbini had gone to ask for protection for herself and her family. This led author and journalist Claudius Seidl to ask for a critical reflection on el-Sherbini's murder in particular, and on the headscarf debate in general:

The murder is not an indication that German society is Islamophobic; shameful for this society, however, was the fact that it needed the grief and horror of the Egyptians in order for the German public to realize what took place here in our midst. And to all headscarf prohibitionists and liberators of Muslim women, to all of those who argue that Muslim women's emancipation should begin with the dress order, to all those who do not wish German children to bear the veils of Muslim teachers: Could we maybe stay silent for a year and reflect, out of piety toward the dead headscarf-wearing Marwa el Sherbini?[92]

El-Sherbini's murder showed Germans a different kind of victimhood—she was not the Muslim victim of her religion but rather the Muslim victim of Islamophobia.

The suspicion that Seidl might be too generous in disclaiming German Islamophobia made the discussions of el-Sherbini's murder a major turning point in German mainstream media and politics. In the aftermath of the murder, German media and politicians heatedly started to discuss immigration politics from a more critical point of view, by showing how these politics could themselves be understood as generating inequality and violence. El-Sherbini—as a woman wearing a headscarf—was portrayed as an empowered Muslim woman who took her attacker to court. That the German court system failed to protect her put into question the very notion of adopting German culture and values as the path to emancipation of German Muslim women.

Not long after the murder, Thilo Sarrazin's book *Germany Abolishes Itself: How We Put Our Country at Risk* returned the headscarf debate to more familiar exclusionary political and media discussions.[93] Advocating the restriction of immigration, Sarrazin, a German politician from the SPD, a former minister of finance for the State of Berlin, and a former member of the executive board of the German Federal Bank (*Deutsche Bundesbank*), had already gained notoriety with his anti-Muslim and anti-immigrant writings and interviews since 2009, before el-Sherbini's tragic death. His 2010 book and related expressions dominated the German media for more than a year. One of the most cited parts from his interview, which appeared in the quarterly German intellectual magazine *Lettre International*, is about the "headscarf girls": "A large number of Arabs and Turks in this city [Berlin], whose number has grown through bad policies, have no productive function other than as fruit and vegetable vendors. I don't need to respect anyone who lives off the state, denies the state, doesn't do anything to educate their kids, and just produces more headscarf girls."[94] By ending his litany with the phrase "just produces more headscarf girls," Sarrazin evoked the image of a mass of immigrants in Germany who are unemployable and dependent on welfare. By relying on controversial statistical data, Sarrazin argued that German society would be taken over by Muslims because of their high fertility rate. Comparing Germany to the Balkans, he said that the Turks will conquer Germany just as Kosovars conquered Kosovo, not with arms but with a high birth rate; in this way he reduced Turkish women to their reproductive capacities and blamed them for what he called the "self-abolishment" of Germany.

Germany Abolishes Itself sold more than a million copies. It was on sale in many newspaper stores, gas stations, and supermarkets, often featured in front of the cashiers. In an attempt to analyze the readership of Sarrazin, well-known German politician Daniel Cohn-Bendit, from the Green Party, positioned Sarrazin as the voice of a section of middle-class Germans who have problems with immigration politics in Germany. He argued that Sarrazin's statements on unproductive immigrants who cause social disintegration resembled the Nazi propaganda of pre-World War II, in which Jews became scapegoats for the economic problems of German society.[95]

Sarrazin faced fierce criticism from many prominent members of German society, as well as from the Central Council of Jews and the Turkish Community in Germany, in press releases, books, and media interviews. In the aftermath of el-Sherbini's murder, many critics of Sarrazin challenged the racist discourse he evoked. They simultaneously demanded that German society should be more sensitive to discrimination against Muslims, including women who choose to wear headscarves as an expression of their religiosity.

The highly vocal outrage against Sarrazin's arguments, combined with the popularity of his book, demonstrates the complexity of the debate in Germany. Sarrazin clearly hit a nerve in the German national consciousness. Yet, despite the critiques, people were not able to silence him, because this would be against freedom of speech. For example, as a consequence of his controversial writings, the SPD started arbitration proceedings with the aim to exclude him from membership; however, in the end, the SPD party's arbitration court allowed Sarrazin to remain a party member. Allowing Sarrazin his voice enabled his opponents to make counter claims: whereas Sarrazin echoed arguments from the period immediately preceding World War II, many Germans used the debate about his arguments to say that they were no longer those racist Germans of the Nazi times.

As demonstrated by the Sarrazin debate, media reporting and political discussions oscillate between encounters with the realities of Germany's social, political, and historical diversity, and deeply held desires for an imagined homogeneity, especially around questions of Muslim immigrant integration. Many strong political figures have argued in favor of social and cultural homogeneity, such as in the Leitkultur debate, and have stigmatized Muslims as a threat to this homogeneity.[96] At the same time, Fereshta Ludin, who had become the public symbol of the rejection of the headscarf, also received the prestigious Three Kings Award in 2012, for her contribution to an interreligious project between an Islamic elementary school in Kreuzberg, a predominantly immigrant neighborhood, and the Clemens-Brentano Elementary School in Lichterfelde, a middle-class neighborhood, both in Berlin. This award is given by the Berlin branch of *Dioezesanrat,* a national Catholic organization dedicated to the maintenance of Catholic heritage and the development of interreligious dialogue in Germany. During her short speech at the award ceremony in the Berlin-

Brandenburg Academy of Science, Ludin mentioned the importance of interreligious dialogue in pedagogy, emphasizing her role as a teacher. The seeming irony of positioning Ludin as a contributor to the German society who develops interreligious dialogue shows how some political and religious milieus are transformed through a narrative of diversity, to which we now turn.

"Germanness" Redefined: A National Narrative of Diversity

Since 2004, German politics and the German public have used the headscarf as a starting point for a larger discussion of the integration of Muslim immigrants in Germany. The federal report entitled "Integration Plan of the Federal Government" (*Integrationsplan* of the *Bundesregierung*) identified Muslim communities as "not integrated," in part because they show a lack of political unity and representation. However, at the same time, those communities themselves have actually started to organize. In recent years, we have seen a proliferation of Muslim groups in Germany. No longer are Muslims represented solely by long-established organizations, such as the Turkish Federation of Berlin-Brandenburg (*Türkischer Bund Berlin-Brandenburg*) or the Islamic Community Milli Görüs (*Islamische Gemeinschaft Milli Görüs*). Rather, many small youth organizations, such as Friday (*Juma*), Muslim Voices (*Muslimische Stimmen*), and Muslim Youth in Germany (*Muslimische Jugend in Deutschland*), have been active in claiming their expressions of a specific Muslim identity in belonging to the German public sphere. On the individual level, there has been a generational change, with young Muslims wearing or not wearing headscarves entering universities, nongovernmental organizations, and workplaces.

The headscarf weaves in and out of these articulations of what it means to be German and Muslim at the same time. To understand how German Muslims interpret the headscarf, we situate their arguments in broader debates on integration and belonging. Nina Mühe, an anthropologist at European University Viadrina in Frankfurt (Oder), published a report in 2010, "At Home in Europe: Muslims in Berlin," for the Open Society Foundations. Mühe, herself a German Muslim, argues that being perceived as "German" is a part of identity-building processes that enable self-identification with Germanness. In her interviews with Muslims in Berlin, Mühe found that although 40 percent of interviewed Muslims say they belong to Germany, only 25 percent define themselves as Germans, and an even lower percentage (11 percent) believe that others perceive them as Germans.[97]

As Islamic studies scholar Riem Spielhaus also argues, female activists from within Islamic organizations and communities are still rarely acknowledged as representatives of Muslim women in public debates, while female critics of Islam and male functionaries dominate the discourse.[98] Yet young Muslim women, who are becoming more active and prominent in debates on belonging, suggest that it is indeed possible to be German *and* wear the headscarf. The DIK website has provided a platform for women to be active in the headscarf debates. For example, Ayten Kılıçarslan, the first woman chair of the DITIB, a mainstream Turkish religious organization with strong ties to Turkey, argued on the DIK website that German politicians, including feminists, misunderstand the meaning of the headscarf:

It is completely wrong to deduce a specific symbolism from a religiously motivated style of clothing, especially if human rights—in this case women's rights—are considered to be violated as a result. From a theological perspective the headscarf is a religious symbol. It is taken as a political symbol only by means of the bans and the reasoning behind the bans, which is not consistent by itself. No woman who wears the headscarf out of her own free will sees it as a symbol of oppression. Politics should distance itself from the so-called "headscarf coercion" (the headscarf ban as a *Diktat*) and see headscarf-wearing women from a secular perspective as individuals rather than excluding them from the public sphere and the society.[99]

Similarly, in an interview on the DIK site, Hasibe Özaslan, project leader at the Intercultural Council (*Interkulturellen Rat*), argued that the headscarf debates have done Muslim women in Germany a great disservice: "The reduction of her identity to a piece of clothing does not do justice to the Muslim women in Germany. It is much more important what Muslim women have in their brain, what performance they can deliver, than what they wear on their head."[100]

Prominent Muslim women like Kılıçarslan and Özaslan attempt to bring in a greater diversity of Muslim women's perspectives to discussions on the headscarf, by trying to be interpreters for German society. In the German media, the interpreter role is largely given to women who are critical about Islam and the headscarf, such as Necla Kelek, and rarely to women who actually wear or support the right to wear it.

Thus, the DIK website, as a hybrid of German state and Muslim voices, could serve as a platform for arguments against the dominant interpretation of the meaning of the headscarf and the meaning of German belonging. By giving voice to the women who are actually wearing headscarves, the DIK website attempts to show the multiple definitions of belonging to the German national identity.[101]

In an interview, Naika Foroutan, a political scientist in Berlin, attempted to answer the question of belonging from a more independent position than the German state-supported arguments placed on the DIK website. Foroutan was born to German and Iranian parents and lived in Iran during her childhood. She has been interested in immigration-related issues, and more recently in discrimination against Muslims. Foroutan attempted to determine the factors that define hybrid identities and their associated lifestyles with a focus on code-switching[102] between two languages. She told us that code-switching proves an individual's belonging to more than one culture and to a hybrid identity. In her view, this was currently the norm in Muslim communities in Germany.[103] Considering that the German state has emphasized the importance of learning the German language in order to be fully integrated into German society, Foroutan's perspective on the significance of code-switching between two languages (for example, German and Farsi) can be considered a break from homogeneous identity construction through compulsory language classes for immigrants. For Foroutan, code-switching is a sign of belonging to a "hybrid identity" on which German state authorities put little emphasis.[104]

Foroutan became a strong critic of Thilo Sarrazin and she publicly argued with him on the Beckmann Show, a popular and critically acclaimed talk show on German TV. According to Foroutan, Sarrazin attempted to create a model of Germanness that excludes Muslims. In her article "Who Is Us?" (*Wer ist wir?*) she self-reflexively analyzed her experience of being on the show to make clear what it meant to be simultaneously Muslim and German: "Whom did I actually have in mind when I said 'we' again and again? Until three weeks ago, my 'we' was a German 'we.' One in which, naturally, several systems of reference resonated, even the Iranian origin-we of my father. Then suddenly my 'we' was a migrant, Muslim 'we' in which my being German [*Deutschsein*] seemed to be entirely faded out."[105] Foroutan makes it clear that from her view Sarrazin's arguments take something away from German Muslims, undermining their sense of belonging, even though many prominent members of German society have critiqued Sarrazin for his utterances.

Similar to Foroutan, well-known journalist Hilal Sezgin argued that Sarrazin's emphasis on being Muslim in Germany is problematic. In her article "Germany Is Abolishing Me" (*Deutschland schafft mich ab*), she responded to Sarrazin's discourse by arguing that no one sees a need to differentiate between German Protestants and German Catholics. She therefore questioned the reasons for differentiating between Muslim and non-Muslim identities in Germany. Calling this process "Muslimification," she argued that "I 'am' ultimately a Muslim woman. Although I was born and grew up here, I 'am' a Muslim immigrant. I ask myself at what point things started to go wrong and how they can be worked out."[106] Sezgin protests that she was labeled "Muslim," and finds it problematic to reduce people to their religious background. People like Sezgin have diverse identities; many of them were born and grew up in Germany, but that part of their identity is not recognized by the general public. As demonstrated in Foroutan's and Sezgin's statements, many Muslims have engaged in efforts to change the national narrative of belonging as a reaction to the Sarrazin debate in Germany. These reactions have either tended to follow the lines of Muslimification, or been an invention of a hybrid German Muslim identity.

In response to Sarrazin's problematic reference to the "girls with headscarves" as evidence of a failure of the integration process in Germany, the role of gender in constructing a German Muslim identity has also been discussed. The main question was, "What does it mean to wear the headscarf?"

In her article "Muslimification of Muslims," Katajun Amirpur, a well-known journalist and a professor of Islamic Studies, attempts to answer this question: "What does the headscarf mean to Muslims when the headscarf, at this point at least, is always taken as an indication of Muslims' lacking will to integrate? . . . Wearing the headscarf is often only the expression of the search for one's own identity. For many Muslims, religion is simply a personal form of making sense of the foreign."[107] As Amirpur articulated in this quote, confusion over the meaning of the headscarf has in different ways generated a social burden that many Muslim women have to confront. In making such arguments, Amirpur also tries to interpret the role of the headscarf for a German audience, but unlike interpreters such as Necla Kelek, she does so in a way that shows a pathway to belonging for headscarf-wearing women in Germany.

The social burden of the headscarf's imputed meaning sometimes falls onto the shoulders of women who don't wear headscarves, who are frequently asked, "Why don't you wear a headscarf?" as though wearing a headscarf is an assumed aspect of Muslim identity in Germany. Although Naika Foroutan, Hilal Sezgin, and Katajun Amirpur are all women who identify as Muslim and are recognized as public intellectuals in German society, they themselves do not wear the headscarf.

In order to learn more about the perspectives of young women with headscarves, Yurdakul conducted two interviews, one with Soraya Hassoun, a student in the Gender Studies Master's Program at Humboldt University of Berlin, and another with Hüda Sağ, a student in the Department of Education at the University of Bielefeld.

Yurdakul met with Soraya Hassoun in her office at the university. She was wearing a white headscarf embellished with lace and *paillettes* on one side and falling over one of her shoulders. Soraya, who grew up with German-Lebanese parents and is married to a Lebanese man, identifies herself as German and her socialization was in a German-Christian culture because she was raised by her German-Christian mother. In the interview with Hassoun on June 22, 2011, she said she feels excluded from being considered German: "I feel German, but excluded because I wear a headscarf. Religion has nothing to do with my own nationality. I can equally be a German woman as a Christian one. But others do not see it that way. If your name is not Hans-Peter then you are not German." Although she says "I feel German," Hassoun echoes Mühe's argument that the identification of others affects the identification of self. In addition, Hassoun's use of Hans-Peter rather than Beate-Christina implies that Germanness for her is also associated with a certain masculinity.

Hassoun is active in a Muslim group, Muslim Voices (*Muslimische Stimmen*), which uses social media to attract attention to Muslim issues and events in Germany. One of her biggest worries is that she will not be able to find a job after finishing her studies because she wears a headscarf. She says her exclusion may be aggravated if she is also excluded from the job market: "In a cook, a cleaning lady, in cheap labor . . . they do accept the headscarf . . . but not in teachers. It is a lie that the school is to stay neutral. Why must I work as a cook, why can't I [work] as a teacher?"[108] Hassoun echoes Merve Kavakçı-Islam's argument that one becomes noticeable as a headscarf-wearing woman in Turkish parliament, whereas the headscarf-wearing cleaning lady is rendered invisible. Such class divisions based on the headscarf clearly structure German discourses and experiences as well.

Hüda Sağ, who was born in Germany and raised by her Turkish parents, has similar observations. She says she wanted to be a schoolteacher; however, she had to give up her dreams because a Muslim woman with a headscarf cannot work as a teacher in some states in Germany.[109] Now she wants to stay in academia and become a professor. Sağ argues that immigrants should not just be "tolerated" by Germans; she wants instead to be politically involved, socially recognized with her headscarf, and given equal opportunities in German society. She has already been involved in various research projects and groups, such as the Action Committee of Muslim Women (*Aktionsbündnis Muslimische Frauen*), an organization that aims to give voices to Muslim women and encourages them to participate in political processes.

In Yurdakul's phone interview with Sağ on June 16, 2011, Sağ said that in contemporary German society, the meaning of being German is changing: "Being German is no longer biological. We are always plural, always heterogeneous. . . . For me being German is not related to German blood or to being Christian. Unfortunately, I cannot say that I am German like everybody else because I am a Muslim woman. But being German is a part of my identity and being Muslim and being German do not represent a contradiction to me." Sağ takes the argument of the journalists, researchers, and activists quoted earlier to its logical conclusion: by participating in German debates, and by doing so as a Muslim woman with strong ties to German society, she is enacting an emerging German Muslim identity. The dominant national German narrative of belonging might not recognize these women's existence as German Muslims, but their everyday practices demonstrate the possibility of a far more cosmopolitan understanding of belonging. This belonging is no longer rooted in the homogeneity of a perceived shared culture: for Sağ, to be Muslim and German is no longer a contradiction in terms.

Sağ is not alone in such articulations. German Turkish author Zafer Şenocak eloquently claims the possibilities of such diversity: "Since I am German, I am much more concerned with my Turkish potential and I have stopped seeing a contradiction there. . . . The penchant for monoculturalism, which always culminates in the flat [same old] speech 'diversity has failed,' in the meantime impedes the future of Germany."[110]

As members of German society, Soraya Hassoun, Hüda Sağ, and Zafer Şenocak define diversity as the new German national narrative.[111]

However, this national narrative is constructed not only by people who immigrated to Germany, but the version of the German national narrative that is centered on diversity rather than homogeneity is also used by Germans who are themselves transformed as a result of the immigration process. In a personal conversation, anthropologist Nina Mühe, who wears a headscarf, says she feels most comfortable walking in the streets of Berlin, where all kinds of people mix with each other. Within this display of diversity, she feels safe and accepted by other people. She feels unwelcome in some areas of Berlin that have been referred to as "white ghettos."[112] For Mühe, it is not about the headscarf only; it is about acceptance of difference. In a 2013 newspaper interview about the fifteenth anniversary of the Baden Württemberg court's decision on the wearing of headscarves in schools, Fereshta Ludin made a similar point: "I did not fight for the headscarf, I fought for the right to self-determination.[112]" Yet the forms that such self-determination can take continue to generate conflicts of belonging in the German national narrative.

6

Retelling National Narratives

IN HIS BOOK *IDENTITY,* Milan Kundera writes, "Remembering our past, carrying it around with us always, may be the necessary requirement for maintaining, as they say, the wholeness of the self."[1] Analogously, national narratives form a collective memory that maintains the national self, a sense of wholeness with many internal contradictions. As political actors engage in debates that mark only certain parts of the population as belonging to a given nation-state, they revisit, reaffirm, rearticulate and at times transform this national narrative. Sometimes some elements of a national narrative might seem forgotten, but then we see them pop up again in a different form or context, reinvigorated by new political actors who creatively reassemble already existing elements. By doing so, these political actors continuously revitalize the meaning of national belonging.

National narratives are to some degree latent and made explicit by political actors only when they experience a sense of threat to national belonging.[2] In the countries discussed in this book, the headscarf has at times come to represent such a threat and is thus an ideal case for studying how political actors draw on existing national narratives to define belonging. By challenging established national narratives, the headscarf as a symbol of "otherness" generates conflicts over definitions of national belonging. These conflicts reveal the continued salience of old narratives of belonging while delineating the parameters of inclusion and exclusion in contemporary nation-states.

In all four of the countries we have looked at, a vast array of political actors have channeled the divergent meanings attached to the headscarf through the public sphere, communicating with each other in multiple institutional and organizational venues, including news media, parliaments, nongovernmental organizations, legal institutions, and activist organizations. By approaching the national narrative of each country as revolving around a core that can change in the retelling, from minor shifts to the invention of an entirely different narrative, we were able to investigate the extent to which the interpretations of narrative elements are reaffirmed, reinterpreted, or altogether rejected in favor of a different narrative in the headscarf debates. Ultimately, the very debates over whether the countries discussed in this book can or cannot include women who wear headscarves motivate changes in the national narratives that shape belonging in these European nation-states as well as in Turkey, the nation-state that straddles East and West.

The book's chapters have illustrated how newsmakers, political actors, and social activists generated boundaries of inclusion and exclusion by (re)articulating national narratives. Sharply delineated exclusionary arguments came to the fore when the French Conseil d'Etat affirmed a lower court's decision to deny a burka-wearing woman French citizenship for not conforming to French values.[3] Similarly, Turkish newspapers and television channels prominently featured the popular secular opinion that those who wear the headscarf belong to Iran or Saudi Arabia, and therefore should go there.[4] In the Netherlands, the parliament and media debated a proposal by right-wing politician Geert Wilders to levy a "headrag tax" on women who wear the headscarf; Wilders argued that women who wear headscarves should pay for a license to pollute the public sphere. In Germany, "headscarf girls" were represented through the neologism integration-refusers (*Integrationsverweigerer*). All these examples depict women who wear the headscarf as not belonging to the established nation-state, be it a Muslim majority country or a country of immigration.

At the same time, headscarf-wearing women represented in the media explicitly claimed belonging to a nation by drawing on already established discursive elements that structure each country's national narrative. French reporting on the headscarf ban in elementary and secondary schools that was passed in 2004 showed young headscarf-wearing women enacting their citizenship rights through public protest, with the country's most influential newspaper, *Le Monde,* interviewing young women who brandished French revolutionary slogans of *egalité* and *liberté* on their cheeks as they wore headscarves in the colors of the French tricolor. Similarly, Turkish women with headscarves ran a campaign during the 2011 national elections challenging the ruling party to appoint headscarf-wearing women as candidates for parliament. Though neither secular nor religious men were sympathetic to their campaign, they were able to gain media attention and thus laid claim to taking part in the creation of an emerging Turkish national narrative. In the Netherlands, an association of young Muslim women launched an ad campaign showing posters of "Real Dutch" (*Echt Nederlands*) that depicted young Muslim women engaged in the "typically" Dutch activities of drinking tea and eating herring in a direct challenge to the controversial anti-Muslim statements made by right-wing politician Geert Wilders. In Germany, a group of Muslim women with and without headscarves who called themselves "neighborhood mothers" (*Stadtteilmütter*) visited the Auschwitz Nazi-era concentration camp in a gesture designed to connect with the past of the country in which they live. Right after the visit, they prepared a documentary film and a brochure on national belonging to Germany that included headscarf-wearing women. These examples of women's attempts to counter exclusionary definitions of national belonging garnered extensive media attention in ways that ultimately reimagined or rearticulated narratives of national belonging.

Applying the Analytical Framework to Other Countries and Cases

Our analytical approach to the headscarf debates in these four countries can be extended both to headscarf debates elsewhere and to other issues that generate conflicts of belonging. Our starting point was to move beyond focusing on a perceived crisis: rather than assessing the potential disruptions that religiosity or immigration posed to secularism, democracy, or gender equality, we instead analyzed the opportunities provided by headscarf debates for revisiting the meaning of national belonging. From this perspective, garments like the headscarf became a metonym for religion's place in the public sphere, and a style of clothing that can challenge existing national narratives. We argue that national debates remain relevant even in a world where supranational governing bodies are gaining increasing importance in determining the meaning of citizenship. We therefore focused on national debates in order to analyze the conflicts within discourses of national belonging.

The analytical framework used in this book can be fruitfully applied to studying the same issue across several countries. From France, Turkey, the Netherlands, and Germany, we now briefly turn to three English-speaking countries—Britain, Canada, and the United States—to illustrate this point. For each country, we did an analysis of major national newspapers between 2004 and 2011.[5] This cross-national comparison shows how different historical contexts and political structures lead to specific conflicts of national belonging.

Currently, 5 percent of the British population identifies as Muslim.[6] In Britain, the national narrative of multiculturalism is informed by a history of colonialism in which former colonial subjects now live in what was once the heart of the Empire. British colonial rule was to a large degree predicated on leaving intact "native" cultural and legal customs pertaining to private life. This approach fed into a British multiculturalism that granted significant cultural rights to immigrant groups when the former colonial subjects came "home." Some writers, like Steven Vertovec, have argued that multiculturalism has been influential in the "enclavization" of immigrant communities by essentializing and homogenizing them and their "cultures" through state-affirmed rules and regulations.[7] Others, however, have claimed that the integration and participation of diverse immigrant groups necessitates a form of multicultural recognition. They have developed the notion of "mature multiculturalism" to recognize that multicultural policy and practice requires acknowledging both the good and the bad that community life offers.[8]

Citing ongoing conflicts around racial, ethnic, and religious differences, public debates in Britain have lately turned away from multiculturalism toward a focus on social cohesion.[9] In this changed perspective, conformity to more distinctly British practices and values, rather than recognition of group-based differences, has become the orienting point for British politics of integration.[10]

Diverging from the binary opposition of multiculturalism and social cohesion, Steven Vertovec in his later work coins the term *super-diversity* to describe the British population's increasing complexity in terms of country of origin, migration channel, and legal status. Disagreeing with those who argue that immigrant integration depends on fostering social cohesion across differences in ways that emphasize similarity, Vertovec suggests that cultural differentiation and full participation in a society are not incompatible.[11] However, although British politicians and newsmakers are undoubtedly aware of this super-diversity, when they discuss the issues of headscarf-wearing women they are not always capable of holding onto the idea that new immigrants have multiple and complex definitions of belonging to Britain.

Historically, much of British headscarf regulation has reflected multiculturalism. Ever since a court case in 1998, the headscarf has largely become an accepted part of school uniforms, though the details of regulation are left up to schools, which are expected to act in accordance with the British Race Relations Act and the Human Rights Act.[12] Similarly, the Metropolitan Police have uniform-specific headscarves for Muslim street officers, which shows how a multicultural national narrative structures the relationship between state authority and religious expression.[13] However, as the case of Shabina Begum and the Jack Straw debate shows, garments such as the *jilbab* (a long garment worn over women's clothes) and niqab are much more controversial than the headscarf.[14] In 2003, sixteen-year-old Shabina Begum came to school wearing a jilbab. Interpreting the garment as potentially divisive for its largely Muslim population (reiterating the argument about peer pressure that is so important in the French headscarf ban), the school tried to prohibit Begum from wearing it.[15] The ensuing legal case lasted three years and ended in 2006 with a Court of Appeals decision in favor of the school.[16] In that same year, foreign minister Jack Straw initiated a heated public debate when he publicly voiced his discomfort with the niqab.[17] Echoing the German debates, Straw argued that the headscarf is a "visible demonstration of separateness that is driving white and Asian communities into 'parallel lives,'"[18] and suggested that he would like the face veil to be abolished in Britain.

As this court case and the Straw debate suggest, British forms of multiculturalism have come under increasing pressure during the past decade as debates have increasingly emphasized social cohesion and a far more assimilationist form of integration. Although social cohesion policies are supposed to support the equality of citizens regardless of their racial, ethnic, and class background, the public discussion often focuses on how to get Muslims out of their ghettos.[19]

As Muslims do in other countries, British Muslims actively participate in such debates. On the question of whether to allow the full veil in public schools, some Muslim political actors in Britain called for a ban of the niqab. Dr. Taj Hargey, an imam and chairman of the Muslim Educational Centre of Oxford, focused on social cohesion when he argued that "Muslim children are being brainwashed into thinking they must segregate and separate themselves from mainstream society."[20] However, others, such as Baroness Uddin, member of the House of Lords for the Labour Party, objected to the anti-Muslim undertones of the Straw debate and argued for the multicultural recognition of Muslim differences. She justified her objections by echoing French discussions of stigmatization, and linking stigmatization to radicalization: "We have attacked those who would be our greatest allies in meeting the current challenges of terrorism and radicalisation." Baroness Uddin warned that the debate had caused "havoc" in the Muslim community and created "a feeling of vulnerability and demonisation of Muslim women."[21] Thus, both Muslim and non-Muslim interlocutors defined belonging in Britain through the juxtaposition of multiculturalism and social cohesion as they debated the place of the headscarf in British society.

Canada's national narrative centers on multiculturalism even more strongly than the British case. Unlike the countries we focused on in the main part of this book, Canada has never defined itself as a homogeneous nation. Rather, Canada's national narrative of belonging is rooted in diversity, with multiculturalism becoming a way to deal with ongoing tensions between the original Francophone and Anglophone settlers. At the same time, the continuing severe poverty and structural disadvantages of Canada's indigenous peoples undermine the rhetorical multiculturalism displayed in street festivals and food fairs.

When it comes to legal and policy regulation of the headscarf, Canada combines a multicultural approach with Dutch-style neutrality in regard to religion. Furthermore, contrary to the other countries analyzed in this book, Canadian interlocutors defended burka and niqab wearers through the discourse of multiculturalism, even as they stated their personal aversion to seeing women in those garments. Discussing the niqab, columnist Sheema Khan argued, "Hate the niqab all you want. But banning it is not a Canadian value."[22] A number of other columnists joined Khan in her defense of multiculturalism as the quintessential Canadian value. One argued, "If the niqab makes us uncomfortable, that's our problem, not theirs."[23] Another columnist wrote that "a veil is only a veil; bare breasts are only bare breasts. If either makes you uncomfortable, tough. That's what a multicultural society is all about."[24]

Muslims have been in Canada for more than a century, but in recent decades the Muslim population has steadily increased, making up an estimated 2.8 percent of the Canadian population in 2010 (estimated to rise to 6.6 percent by 2030).[25] Despite ongoing public support, Canadian multiculturalism has come under pressure as this population has increased in size. As of 2006, the newly elected Conservative government has worked to rewrite Canada's national narrative in an attempt to dismantle the country's multicultural legacy. They have done so by problematizing the integration of recent immigrants, particularly those hailing from Muslim-majority countries, even as they have successfully courted the votes of established immigrant communities.[26]

As in other countries, in Canada the perceived gender inequalities among Muslims have become a focal point in the ongoing politics of nation-building, with multiculturalism seen as standing in tension with gender equality. For example, Tarek Fatah, the founder of the small but vocal Muslim Canadian Congress, a secular Muslim organization, argued that the burka and niqab are "a very clear sign that women are the possessions of men, and it's being thrust on North America and Europe. Most Muslims are fed up with the niqab and burka."[27] Influential *Globe and Mail* columnist Margaret Wente drew on such accounts to argue that "my open-minded tolerance deserts me when I see women completely covered up. In every culture where this is the norm, women are oppressed."[28] According to Wente, the niqab and burka have crossed the limits of Canadian multiculturalism and should be banned. Indeed, in 2011 the Conservative government prohibited niqab-wearing women from taking the oath of citizenship, a largely symbolic policy that nonetheless led to a profound sense of unease among Canadian Muslims.[29]

Despite these efforts of the Conservative government, a national narrative of multiculturalism continues to structure Canadian debates over belonging. It does so in part by drawing on a contrast between Quebec, which does not subscribe to a multicultural philosophy, and the rest of Canada. Indeed, when the provincial government of Quebec proposed an extremely restrictive ban on the niqab, the editorial board of the *Globe and Mail* wrote, "Quebec is surely big enough, and resilient enough, to withstand some religious dissenters. . . . Mr. Charest [Quebec's Liberal Prime Minister] said he was acting to defend 'our values.' But surely one of 'our values' is the right to dissent from 'our values.'"[30] This quote illustrates how Quebec's repeated attempts to curtail the wearing of the headscarf, and now the niqab, inform how belonging to Canada is defined by marking the distinction between the rest of Canada and the minority nation of Quebec.[31]

In August 2013, the division between Quebec and the rest of Canada was front-page news again when it became clear that Quebec's minority

Parti Québécois government was planning to propose a "charter of Que-bec values" that would emphasize the secular character of Quebec society and prohibit government employees (including those in hospitals, schools, day-care facilities, and universities) from wearing conspicuous religious symbols. Polls suggested that the majority of Francophone Quebecois were in favor of such a charter, whereas the rest of Canada was largely appalled at this infringement on freedom of religion.[32] The responses in the anglo-phone media outside of Quebec suggest that, as in prior discussions of the differences between Quebec and the rest of Canada, articulations of belonging portray Quebec as failing to be multiculturalist while the rest of Canada is. Furthermore, not only multiculturalism but also pluralism anchors belonging in Canada; "our values" are ones you can dissent from and still belong. Such accounts have bolstered arguments for freedom of religion regarding the wearing of the headscarf and the niqab, even in the face of the aversion that the niqab inspired in Canada, as it did elsewhere.

The United States, like Canada, is a country rooted in migration. Unlike in Canada, however, in the United States multiculturalism has not historically been the dominant element in the national narrative of belonging. Rather, the idea of the "melting pot," a fusion of cultures, ethnicities, and religions, combines with a strong notion of "personal free-dom" to generate the American national narrative. Though largely cliché, the idea of the melting pot nonetheless reflects a strong assimilationist tendency in American society—an assimilationism, however, that is ul-timately "not opposed to difference, but to *segregation, ghettoization* and *marginalization.*"[33] This assimilationism can in turn be countered by the notion of personal freedom.

U.S. Muslims accounted for 1.7 percent of the population in 2010. They have had a long-standing presence in the United States and are an in-ternally highly diverse group, with the majority being African American.[34] Within the United States, wearing a headscarf is to a large degree pro-tected under the right to freedom of religion.[35] However, the U.S. debates focus outward when it comes to questioning whether public expressions of Islam in the form of specific clothing for women can be a tolerable dif-ference. The social and emotional impact of 9/11, the terrorism discourse of the Bush administration, and the military interventions in Iraq and Afghanistan led to a reconstitution of the national narrative through a juxtaposition of "American" and "Muslim" in which "Muslim" came to signify "foreign."

As elsewhere, gender equality plays a key role in this articulation of the U.S. national narrative. The invasion of Afghanistan was justified by a desire to "save brown women from brown men,"[36] with Laura Bush's radio address on American Thanksgiving 2001 arguing that "the fight against terrorism is also a fight for the rights and dignity of women."[37] Nine years later, the woman commander of a women's Marine unit fighting in Afghanistan argued that the presence of women fighters is important because "if [our participation in the fighting] means that someday women don't have to wear a burka, great."[38] Such quotes suggest a national narrative in which Americans are the saviors of the vulnerable, as an odd notion of gendered chivalry combines with a particular understanding of gender equality as individual freedom.

In the U.S. case, media debates about the headscarf and burka focused largely on spaces of invasion abroad. When newspaper discussions turned to issues within the United States, some of these reports showed the country as a multiethnic, tolerant nation in which the presence of women's headscarves posed no threat to national belonging but rather reflected an American capacity to build cohesiveness out of difference. Journalists reinforced this image of American open-mindedness and tolerance through positive contrasts between the United States and the negative judgments and stereotypes they attributed to European countries. Accounts of the burka, however, extended the portrayal of oppressed Muslim women abroad to Muslim women in America by describing angry brothers hitting women who had taken off the burka and gone out to work.[39]

The experiences of American Muslims suggest that, as in the other countries discussed in this book, Muslim women's belonging is far more threatened by structural discrimination than by such family dynamics. In a 2011 report,[40] the Pew Research Center showed that discrimination against Muslims in the United States is the biggest fear of American Muslims. This fear is warranted by concrete cases of labor market discrimination that have been discussed in the media. For example, the *New York Times* reported on the case of Imane Boudlal, a twenty-six-year-old from Casablanca, Morocco, who was forced to leave her job at Disneyland in California when she decided to wear the headscarf at work.[41] In 2012, Boudlal sued Disneyland for workplace discrimination. This case generated media reports that portrayed a Muslim woman fully conversant in American discourses of individual rights protection in her confrontation with the all-American Walt Disney Company. Thus we see a tension in American national narratives both at home and abroad—with narratives of the American national home more likely to integrate Muslim women into narratives of belonging, whereas stories of Muslims abroad, particularly in the Middle East or Asia, generate an image of Islam as fully contradictory to American values.

In sum, these brief analyses of media discussions of the headscarf in three English-speaking countries show how these debates can be analyzed through the framework developed in this book. In all these countries, analysis of headscarf debates as conflicts over belonging shows how such debates can lead to the (re)articulation of national narratives.

One can also analyze debates about honor killing, circumcision, ritual slaughter, polygamous marriage (both Muslim and Mormon), and gay marriage as conflicts of national belonging. Each of these debates revolves around particular issues related to bodily harm, morality, justice, and fairness; from the resulting discussions we can see the shifting contours of national belonging. We do not argue that the headscarf debates in different countries raise the same substantive issues (for example, the headscarf debates discussed in this book raise issues about gender equality, secularism, modernity, tolerance, and democratic principles). Rather, all of these debates raise different salient issues that challenge established national narratives. By analyzing them, we see how they become conflicts of belonging and opportunities to (re)articulate national narratives.

Rethinking National Belonging and Transnationalism

In all of the countries discussed in this book the notion of wearing the headscarf becomes a metonym for a difference that threatens the established national narrative. Rather than looking at general immigrant integration politics or questions of secularism in liberal democracies, we have shown that an analysis of a single, concrete conflict reveals how such perceived threats factor into the ongoing production of national narratives of belonging.

Yet, though we can trace the important discursive elements of a national narrative by analyzing media and parliamentary debates, we cannot assess which of these elements are particularly salient for those who are encountering them in everyday situations. Reports from women in Internet forums that they are being yelled at on the street to stop wearing their headscarves suggest how the negotiation of conflicts over belonging also happens in everyday life. Similarly, the stories of the difficulties that Turkish, German, and Dutch headscarf-wearing women encounter in the labor market that we heard while researching this book mark the importance of the interactional level at which these conflicts over national belonging are worked out. These stories also suggest future directions for research.

First, it would be useful to study the ethnographic and interactional level at which belonging is produced. This would mean a move beyond newspapers, parliaments, and courts and toward a focus on how national narratives give meaning to belonging as people engage with each other in the public sphere, through an analysis of how inclusions and exclusions are experienced in everyday interactions. In their edited volume on everyday practices of multiculturalism, Amanda Wise and Selvaraj Velayutham provide evidence that such encounters become moments in the negotiations surrounding cultural difference, creating particular ethnic and racial boundaries.[42] Such an approach can be extended to ethnographic work on how conflicts of belonging produce national narratives at the level of interaction. As Liisa Malki suggests in her analysis of the discursive production of Hutu national identity in exile, the physical location of Hutu refugees, either in segregated camps or mingled in local communities, profoundly affects their narrative of belonging.[43] Conducting research on the localized experiences of headscarf-wearing women could illustrate the everyday construction of national belonging.

Second, and related, in this book we treated belonging largely metaphorically rather than experientially, which leaves room for ethnographic research with a focus on participation as an expression of belonging. In a sense, our present analysis is informed by a trend in immigrant-receiving countries to focus on culture in integration debates. The shift away from analyzing immigrants' socioeconomic status has meant that issues like the headscarf are discussed in terms of beliefs and values as opposed to their material impact.[44] However, our findings indicate that labor market discrimination and the socioeconomic impact of headscarf discourses have a tremendous effect on Muslim women and, by extension, on the Muslim communities in these countries. It is certainly worthwhile to investigate whether other women have encountered situations like the one experienced in the Netherlands by Nora el-Jebli, who suspected that she failed to obtain an accountant position after showing up to sign her contract wearing a headscarf. Similarly, as Annelies Moors in her analysis of the proposed Dutch "burka ban" argues, passing a ban excludes these women

ing basic services and from participating in society.[45] To date, little work has been done to map how these exclusionary politics affect Muslim headscarf- or niqab-wearing women's capacity to enact belonging in the various domains of the public sphere.

The effect of religious practice on participation in the public sphere remains similarly understudied.[46] As Carl-Ulrik Schierup, Peo Hansen, and Stephen Castles emphasize in their analysis of the linkages between immigrant integration and ongoing welfare state formation, such research into the impact of religious practices on various forms of participation would focus on the processes of exclusion and inclusion in the broad conception of citizenship and social welfare.[47] Although women's participation in the labor market is important, we need to be careful not to reduce the notion of citizenship to this sole aspect.[48] Rather, we should research how headscarf-wearing women participate in formal politics and other aspects of everyday life that directly shape their experience of inclusion and exclusion.

Finally, much of our argument has focused on showing the specificities of the national narrative of each country we studied, including the three cases briefly discussed in this concluding chapter. However, our data clearly suggest strong transnational currents in these debates, with themes such as gender equality, liberalism, multiculturalism, secularism, and democratic participation recurring in all of the countries under study. Although we have shown how these themes are given specific meanings within the various national contexts, the question remains, how are these concepts reflected and treated across national borders? For example, research into how the European Court of Human Rights' decision not to grant Leyla Şahin the right to wear her headscarf in a Turkish university affects different national public debates can show how supranational discourses and practices impact national conflicts over belonging. Clearly the production of national narratives does not happen in isolation. Rather, transnational conduits of people, media, and law affect the ways in which these conflicts are initiated and interpreted. One aspect of this global conduit could be Olivier Roy's conceptualization of "globalized Islam" in the form of an *ummah,* a global Muslim community.[49] Looking at shared discursive formations, Nilüfer Göle argues that a transnational image of Islam is prevalent in Western European countries, an image of a "feminine" Islam, with its headscarf and its demand for belonging.[50] Along these lines, we argue that future research on issues of Muslim integration and identity should also pay attention to the transnational dimension and focus on the movement of discourses and practices across and beyond nation-states. However, rather than get mired in arguments regarding the decline of the nation-state or the decreasing importance of the national in conflicts over belonging, such research should produce a dialogue between all these levels.

In sum, although we have focused on nation-states in our analysis of headscarf debates, we have also shown that national belonging is shaped in a globalized context. This context is informed by anxieties regarding the place of religion in the public sphere, especially following—but also preceding—the terrorist attacks of 9/11. As Seyla Benhabib, in her analysis of the French 2004 headscarf ban in schools, argues, "the headscarf affair" (*l'affaire du foulard*) eventually came to stand for all dilemmas of national identity in the age of globalization and multiculturalism. She summarized these dilemmas in this question: "How is it possible to retain French traditions of *laïcité*, republican equality, and democratic citizenship in view of France's integration into the European Union, on the one hand, and the pressures of multiculturalism generated through the presence of second- and third-generation immigrants from Muslim countries on French soil, on the other hand?"[51] Variations of these dilemmas inform the headscarf debates in all four countries analyzed in this book. Transnational ties, global movements, diversity of populations, and multicultural policies suggest not just similarity but also convergence across nation-states. However, by dissecting the apparent universals of gender equality, religious neutrality, and liberal democratic or republican values that recur in headscarf debates, we can see the continuing particularities in national narratives. The headscarf debates reflected new challenges to the nation-state and reproduced national narratives through conflicts of belonging.

Appendix

IN THIS BOOK, we have mapped how newsmakers, politicians, and civil society activists, Muslims and non-Muslims alike, articulate national narratives as they debate the headscarf. Here we give a detailed overview of our research methods and processes of data collection and analysis.

In many studies of national identity formation, politicians and newsmakers are the sources of sociological and political analysis.[1] Following this strategy, we collected newspaper articles—from three newspapers in France and Turkey and four in the Netherlands and Germany—that spanned the political spectrum in those countries. We then supplemented the newspaper data with parliamentary documents, including transcripts of parliamentary discussions, government reports, and proposed and passed laws. However, although national belonging is deeply intertwined with ongoing projects of nation-state formation in which politicians and newsmakers play a key role, they are not the only actors in this arena.[2] Therefore, we also explored sources of alternative discourses on the Internet, and conducted interviews with key informants engaged in articulating inclusionary discourses of belonging. We were thus able to map the institutionalized power relations in each country, including who engages in headscarf debates, who has the power to define who belongs and who does not, and how the headscarf is embedded in discourses of inclusion and exclusion.

We are critical of objectifying techniques, such as methods that categorize people as Muslim without paying attention to the criteria that define Muslims.[3] Similarly, we focus on nation-states but are wary of methodological nationalism, a reductionist methodological approach that renders transnational linkages invisible. Methodological nationalism presumes the nation-state as the sole point of reference in social and political processes and fails to interrogate their coherence across state boundaries.[4] To avoid both of these pitfalls (homogenizing social groups into single categories and methodological nationalism), using a cross-country analysis, we looked at how the headscarf has come to signify conflicting meanings of belonging in national narratives. Similarly, we did not reduce media coverage to mere numbers. Although we do not deny that peaks in media coverage are important indicators of how heated a debate is, we focused our analysis not on how often the headscarf was discussed in the news but rather on the meanings attached to the headscarf in those reports.

In his extended case method, Michael Burawoy emphasizes the extension of theory by integrating outlier cases and showing how these unusual cases allow for the building of new theories.[5] Our aim in drawing on Burawoy's analytical approach was to contribute to existing theories on national belonging by turning the headscarf debates into an exemplary case. In line with the extended case method, we did not rely on an inductive analysis of our data. Rather, we identified key elements in the historical development of the national narrative in each country and then analyzed the ways in which they were referenced in the debates. Here we have drawn on Rudolf De Cillia and colleagues' distinctions among what they call "constructive, perpetuating, transformational, and destructive macro-strategies of discourse" in their analysis of everyday definitions of national identities.[6] We paid particular attention to discourses that provide radically different accounts of national belonging in order to gauge the potential for even more radical transformations. Such discourses can critique prevalent accounts of the national narrative, for example, by claiming that exclusion is nondemocratic. Alternatively, they offer new representations of what is at stake in these debates, for example, by claiming that the headscarf debates take attention away from socioeconomic problems that affect minority communities. Such discourses often appear as blips in the news media—blips that we further investigated through Internet searches and, where possible, interviews with key figures in these discourses. Alternative discourses often are produced by headscarf-wearing women or by Muslim women who do not wear the scarf but engage in headscarf politics. These women's political activism shows the possibilities for alternative articulations of national belonging in the context of country-specific national narratives. Often these women embody the boundaries of belonging, giving new meaning to belonging to the nation.[7]

Our data were collected specifically for each country and then analyzed comparatively. We paid attention to the sociopolitical and historical contexts in each country in order to reflect how conflicts of belonging come to the surface of national narratives. This contextual focus helped us to see the national specificities in each country, such as variations in their histories of migration and streams of Muslim migrants, and differences in political institutions and media trajectories, as well as linguistic differences.

Taking sociopolitical and historical differences into account meant that we collected slightly different material for each country. We analyzed three to four newspapers from each country that reflect the range of commonly articulated views in dealing with headscarf and burka/niqab debates. We complemented the newspaper data with parliamentary discussions that took place during the same periods as the media debates. In some countries (France, Germany, and the Netherlands) we also looked at policy reports, and in Germany we considered a government-initiated conference for Muslims. The data we collected covered slightly different ranges of years in each country, starting at different times but selectively updating the data through the final edits in late 2013. The French data from *Le Figaro* starts in 1996, the earliest year it was available online, in order to capture the interlude between the first flare-up of the headscarf debate in 1989 and the headscarf ban of 2004. We then focused in-depth on the newspaper of record, *Le Monde,* starting in 2003 when Sarkozy reignited a debate that ultimately led to the headscarf ban in French schools. In Turkey, 2002 was the most important year, because it is when the Ak Party came to power. The Dutch data start in 2004, when the debate on immigrant integration reached its peak. In Germany, 2004 was also a significant starting point, because it is when Fereshta Ludin's case came to the Constitutional Court. By paying attention to these slight variations in years during which the headscarf and burka/niqab were salient in national political organization, we were able to capture the conflicts of belonging in national narratives rather than be bounded by the objectivist but ultimately arbitrary rules of a methodology that would dictate the gathering of artificially similar data.

Overview of the Data by Country
France

For our analysis of the French headscarf debates, we turned to *Le Monde* and *Le Figaro*. We added *Libération* for our analysis of the burka ban. These three newspapers have different political perspectives. *Le Monde,* generally somewhat left-learning, attempts to represent as wide a range of positions as possible through a diverse set of authors and informants, including intellectuals, philosophers, public figures, and politicians. *Le Figaro* is a more lowbrow, politically right-wing newspaper. *Libération* represents the left of the French political spectrum, and often provides the most in-depth analyses. *Le Monde* and *Le Figaro* have estimated daily circulation rates of more than 300,000 whereas *Libération* has a circulation of 134,000 thousand. All of these papers have online editions that were launched mostly in the mid-1990s. We used Factiva, which has archived records of these newspapers, as our search platform to collect all of the articles.

As we show in Chapter 2, the French media debate on the headscarf started much earlier than the debates in other countries—in 1989, when three schoolgirls in Creil were expelled from their middle school for not removing their headscarves. We collected newspaper data from *Le Figaro* from October 1996 (the earliest year available through Factiva) through September 2009 to gauge these early discussions. This background information helped us to see the roots of the current debates. We searched the news from each day of the week using *voile islamique* (Islamic veil) and *foulard islamique* (Islamic scarf) as search words, gathering a total of 607 articles for this period.

On the basis of our reading of existing scholarly work on the French headscarf debates, as well as the understandings we gleaned from *Le Figaro,* we then turned to *Le Monde,* the French newspaper of record, as our primary source of newspaper analysis for the headscarf debates. We started by collecting *Le Monde* articles from April 2003, when Nicolas Sarkozy inadvertently ignited the 2003 headscarf debate, ending the first round of data gathering with articles from November 3, 2009. To manage the amount of data, we limited our search by adding the key words *femme* (woman) and *fille* (girl) to *voile integral, foulard islamique, voile islamique,* and burqa or burka. We collected 404 articles from this first period.

To capture the burka/niqab debates, we identified 1,003 articles from three newspapers for the period of June 1, 2009, to June 1, 2010, that used the term *burka, burqa,* or *voile integral* (315 articles from *Le Monde,* 413 articles from *Le Figaro,* and 274 articles from *Libération*). To manage the amount of data, and given our interest in the gender dimension of the debates, we analyzed the articles that also referenced *femme* or *fille* in order to capture the gender dimension of the debate (291 articles from *Le Monde,* 385 articles from *Le Figaro,* and 245 articles from *Libération*). This resulted, however, in only a small reduction in the total number of articles (945), suggesting that gendered concerns have indeed become a core aspect of these debates.

To capture formal political discussions, we looked at the major reports prepared by the Stasi and Gerin Commissions. We did not conduct interviews with Muslim women in France. Instead, we conducted an extensive Internet search to map Muslim women's groups and women's groups that advocate on behalf of Muslim women's rights in order to identify the kinds of claims they made regarding the headscarf and burka. We found that these groups were few and far between.

The French data were collected and analyzed with the help of a native French-speaking research assistant, Inder Marwah, then a PhD candidate in the University of Toronto's Department of Political Science. We asked him to create a chronology of the headscarf debate in France from the collected data and to complement it with detailed memos of the most significant events, such as the Stasi law, Sarkozy's speech to the UOIF in 2003, and others. We mapped this data by using a more open-ended inductive coding method to identify the main themes in the reporting. Then the newspaper articles were coded according to the categories that historically formed the French national narrative. Inductive coding helped us to go through the data without being restricted by already decided categories, and to see the development of historical events. It provided us with a bird's-eye view of the data. In the next round of coding, we combined inductive coding with deductive coding, this time with set categories in mind, which allowed us to identify the transformation of existing categories in each national narrative. The combination of inductive and deductive coding allowed us to identify whether new categories had developed in each national narrative. We also identified all the main actors (persons as well as organizations) represented in the debates. In addition, we identified the main Muslim actors to see if they were positioned as making communalist demands or if their participation in the debates instead represented the integration of French Muslims. Here we found that these interlocutors by and large represented the same spectrum of argument and opinion voiced by non-Muslim actors.

Turkey

The Turkish newspaper data were collected from three major national newspapers—*Hürriyet, Zaman,* and *Cumhuriyet.* We chose these newspapers in order to reflect the political spectrum, from mainstream liberal (*Hürriyet*) to religious (*Zaman*) to far left (*Cumhuriyet*). These articles were identified by searching on the terms *başörtüsü* and *türban,* both of which refer to the headscarf but the first is nonpoliticized whereas the second reflects an understanding of the headscarf as a political statement. For specific reporting on events we also checked the religious newspapers, *Yeni Şafak* and *Vakit,* as well as other major daily newspapers, such as the mainstream liberal *Milliyet* and *Radikal.*

Hürriyet and *Zaman* are the highest-circulating newspapers in Turkey. *Hürriyet* has an estimated circulation of half a million and *Zaman* has eight hundred thousand readers. *Cumhuriyet* has a significantly lower circulation compared to the other two, estimated at about fifty thousand. Our newspaper data from *Hürriyet* and *Zaman* starts in 2002, when the Ak Party came to power for the first time, and finishes after the national elections in July 2011, when the Ak Party came to power for the third time. The data from *Cumhuriyet* focuses on 2008, when Ak Party leaders attempted to lift the headscarf ban in Turkish universities by changing the constitution. Due to the high volume of data available in Turkey, only each Thursday's editions were analyzed. In this way, we analyzed approximately three thousand newspaper articles from Turkey.

Turkey's rapid sociopolitical transformation was reflected in the media and its discourses. For example, during our data collection and analysis period, the owner of *Hürriyet,* Aydın Doğan, dramatically changed his opposing stance toward the Ak Party. As a result, in 2009, *Hürriyet's* critical line toward the headscarf disappeared in just a few months. We observed in many media outlets numerous court cases against journalists who criticized the Ak Party, and specifically the prime minister. This threat to freedom of speech in the media, especially after 2009, made the Turkish newspaper data opaque.[8] Compared to the data obtained from other countries, such as Germany, the Turkish newspaper data directly reflected these dramatic government influences. To remedy this effect, for this later period we gave some weight to other data sources that are independent of the government's influence, such as bianet.org, Facebook, and Twitter.

We also collected data from the parliamentary discussions that took place during two governing periods of the Ak Party from 2002 to 2010, with a specific focus on two issues: Leyla Şahin's appeal to the European Court of Human Rights in 1998 and the attempt to lift the headscarf ban in higher education in 2008. Relevant discussions were examined from the 22nd Legislation Period (November 19, 2002, to June 3, 2007) and from the 23rd Legislation Period (August 4, 2007, to June 12, 2011), which coincided with the Ak Party's first and second governing periods.

The Turkish newspaper and parliamentary data were downloaded with the help of our research assistants, who were native Turkish speakers: Selin Çağatay was a doctoral student in the Department of Gender Studies at Central European University, Budapest; and Özlem Kaya was a doctoral student in the Atatürk Institute of Modern Turkish History at Boğaziçi University. A chronology of the headscarf debate in Turkey was created from the collected data, complemented with detailed memos about the most significant events, such as the case of Leyla Şahin, the 2008 attempts to change the constitution, and others. After mapping this data, we used inductive and deductive coding to ensure that our coding was in alignment with the other countries' cases; however, we also paid special attention to the categories that historically formed the Turkish national narrative.

Gökçe Yurdakul collected interview data in Istanbul and Ankara, Turkey. Together with research assistant Özlem Kaya, she conducted face-to-face interviews using open-ended questions with journalist and documentary filmmaker Ayşe Böhürler, as well as with Zeynep Göknil Şanal and Berrin Sönmez, two members of the Başkent Women's Platform, and Atilla Yayla, professor of political science at a new private polytechnic school in Balat, Istanbul. These interviewees were chosen because of their prominent roles in the media debates. Given that they are public figures, they did not request confidentiality or anonymity and we did not give them pseudonyms. Each interview lasted about two hours and was conducted in the interviewee's office.

The Netherlands

We looked at four national Dutch newspapers that together cover the range of political stances and class positions in Dutch public debate. We collected all articles—news as well as opinion pieces—on the headscarf and burka/niqab for the period beginning January 1, 2004, when the culturalization of the integration debate was a *fait accompli,* and ending February 15, 2011; we selectively updated until 2013. The most elite paper, *NRC,* published 172 articles; the more lowbrow *Telegraaf* published 132; the paper most interested in religious issues, *Trouw,* published 177; and the left-of-center, social democratic *Volkskrant* published 131 articles during this period. In addition, we conducted a targeted search for the Don Bosco College case (the last flare-up of the headscarf controversy while we were writing the book). Between January 2011 and April 2012 we gathered 15 articles from the *NRC,* 16 from the *Telegraaf,* 35 from *Trouw,* and 21 from the *Volkskrant.* We also gathered 120 documents containing parliamentary discussions and parliamentary questions, as well as other documents sent to parliament, from January 1995 (when the archive became available online) through May 12, 2011. Finally, we looked at the Equal Treatment Commission (ETC) database and identified the number of decisions made in headscarf and burka cases in order to assess the proportion of positive and negative decisions (which showed that the ETC decided overwhelmingly in favor of headscarf- and niqab-wearing women).

A chronology of the headscarf debate in the Netherlands was created from the collected data, then complemented with detailed memos about the most significant events, such as Ayaan Hirsi Ali's statements prior to her departure from the Netherlands in 2006, and Wilders' proposal to introduce a "headrag tax" in 2009. Next, the newspaper data were printed and coded, first inductively, to identify main themes, then deductively, according to the multiple categories that historically formed the Dutch national narrative. The data were collected and analyzed with the help of a native Dutch speaker, research assistant Lars Nickolson, a policy researcher in the field of immigrant integration in the Netherlands.

The interview data from the Netherlands was collected by Anna Korteweg. She interviewed three Dutch Muslim women who are active in headscarf politics: Leyla Çakir of Al Nisa (an advocacy organization for Dutch Muslim women), Nora el-Jebli of the Dutch Polder Moslima Headscarf Brigade, and Fatima Elatik, a headscarf-wearing Labor Party politician who is mayor of one of the Amsterdam boroughs. As in Turkey, the women we interviewed in the Netherlands are public figures and they spoke to us without requesting confidentiality or anonymity. The interviews lasted between one to one and a half hours. The interview with Elatik took place in her office, the other two interviews were conducted in public places. The interviews were analyzed in a way similar to how we analyzed the other data.

Germany

The German newspaper data were collected from four major sources: *taz, Süddeutsche Zeitung (SZ)*, *Frankfurter Allgemeine (FAZ)*, and *BILD*. Similar to our choices in the other countries, we chose these newspapers in order to cover the political spectrum in German media. *SZ* appeals to a left-liberal readership, *FAZ* is a conservative newspaper, and *taz* is a left-wing newspaper that reflects the political perspective of the Green Party. Among these highbrow newspapers, *SZ* has the highest circulation, at 1.1 million per day. *FAZ* has an estimated circulation of almost four hundred thousand, and *taz* has the lowest circulation of all three, with about sixty thousand. Finally, *BILD*, a tabloid, was added because it is the newspaper with the highest circulation in Germany, with about three million copies sold daily. Our German newspaper data cover the period from 2004 to 2011 (with selective updates until 2013). We started from Fereshta Ludin's case in the Constitutional Court, using the word *Kopftuch* (headscarf) as the search term. We collected 393 articles from *FAZ*, 415 from *taz*, and 104 from *SZ*. From *BILD* we collected 169 articles, starting from 2006 (because previous data were not available from the online archive) and ending in 2010. Because these papers are regionally published and nationally distributed (*FAZ* is published in Frankfurt, *SZ* in Munich, and *taz* and *BILD* in Berlin), each newspaper combines a focus on its region with a national perspective. The regional differences in media reporting are reflective of the German federal governmental structure and attendant political and cultural differences.

We also turned to the German Islam Conference, or DIK (*Deutsche Islam Konferenz*), in order to reflect the government's view on the headscarf debates. The DIK started in 2006 and ended in 2013 as part of the platform on integration of the Christian Democratic Union/Social Democratic Party government, in power at that time. The DIK was organized annually by the German Ministry of the Interior. The participants were government representatives as well as experts, individual Muslim citizens, and representatives of Muslim organizations, all of whom who were invited by the Ministry of the Interior. The DIK's website publishes both official reports and writings by individual participants. We collected all material on the headscarf in Germany from 2008 through 2013 from this website. We also gathered data on headscarf debates in the German federal parliament, which suggested that the issue was not heavily discussed outside the Fereshta Ludin debate.[9]

The German data were downloaded from the relevant online archives of the newspapers and the DIK website with the help of two research assistants: Natalie Lohmann, then a PhD student at the Humboldt University of Berlin's Graduate School of Social Sciences; and Paulina Garcia del Moral, a PhD candidate at the University of Toronto's Department of Sociology, who also updated the initial database and conducted preliminary data analysis. Newspaper reports and parliamentary discussions that contained the keyword *Kopftuch* or *Burka* were saved as Word files. As with the other cases, a chronology of the headscarf debate in Germany was created from the collected data, complemented with detailed memos about the most significant events, such as Fereshta Ludin's court case, the Sarrazin debate, the murder of Marwa el-Sherbini, and others. After this mapping was completed, the data were first coded in line using the inductive open coding procedure used in the other cases. Then deductive coding was used to code the data according to the categories that historically formed the German national narrative.

Yurdakul interviewed three women to hear their thoughts about conflicts of belonging that arose in the headscarf debates in Germany. These women were selected because of their strong engagement in these debates as well as in debates about related issues concerning Muslims in Germany. Again, as public figures, they did not request anonymity. Naika Foroutan, an Iranian-German scholar, is the organizer of the Young Islam Conference and leader of the HEYMAT project, which explores the hybrid identities and strategies of belonging of young Muslims in Europe. She has been active in debating against Thilo Sarrazin in the German media. Soraya Hassoun is a headscarf-wearing student with Lebanese and German parents who is writing her master's thesis on Islamic feminism in Germany. She is active in Muslim Voices (*Muslimische Stimmen*), an online platform for Muslim women in Germany. Finally, Hüda Sağ, a headscarf-wearing Muslim woman of Turkish background, is studying at the University of Bielefeld. She attended the Young Islam Conference in Berlin in 2011. By interviewing these women, we gained insight into the lives of Muslim women who are active in the Muslim communities in Germany. Each interview lasted between one and two hours and was conducted at the Humboldt University. The interview with Hüda Sağ was conducted on the phone. An attempt to interview Fereshta Ludin was not realized.

Final Remarks on the Data Sources

In addition to examining the four countries discussed in the main chapters of this book, we also analyzed the headscarf debates in Britain, Canada, and the United States, in order to employ our analytical framework in countries that have significantly different immigration and integration politics. In Britain we looked at the *Daily Telegraph* and the *Guardian*, in Canada we looked at the *Globe and Mail* and the *Toronto Star*, and in the United States we looked at the *New York Times*. We used the same data collection and analysis methods as we used for the other cases in the book, albeit in a smaller scope. The outcome of this brief analysis is reflected in the book's concluding chapter. The British newspaper data were collected by Bingül Durbaş in 2011, when she was a doctoral candidate at the University of Sussex; the Canadian and American newspaper data were collected by Angelica Rao in 2011 and 2012, when she was a master's student in the sociology department at the University of Toronto.

For the four countries covered in the book's central chapters, we also collected transnational newspaper data, that is, reports in their newspapers on headscarf debates in other countries. For example, from the German newspapers we collected articles on the Turkish headscarf debates, and vice versa. French newspaper discussions made repeated reference to the Leyla Şahin case, but also discussed the shortcomings of Dutch multiculturalism that French representatives from the Stasi Commission saw reflected in Dutch approaches to the headscarf. Turkey saw significant reporting on the European debates, such as a reflection on Leyla Şahin's case in the European Court of Human Rights, and articles on French secularism in both the headscarf and burka/niqab debates, seeing them as reference points for Turkish secularism. German newspapers reported on the lifting of the headscarf ban in Turkish universities as a process of democratization whereas, ironically, the headscarf is banned for teachers working in German schools. The Dutch were appalled to learn that the French advocated their headscarf ban in schools by pointing to the Dutch "failed multicultural experiment." Newspaper reports called to task the Dutch politicians who had talked to the representatives of the Stasi Committee when they visited the Netherlands. Collecting such transnational data helped us to see the perspective of each country's media on other countries' headscarf debates, and alerted us to the potential impact of transnational linkages, as discussed in our concluding chapter, even as these data confirmed the continuing significance of the nation in these conflicts over belonging.

Notes

Chapter 1

1. There are many types of headscarves, each with multiple names and appearing in numerous styles. For the purposes of this book, we use the names most common in each country under discussion. At a minimum, the headscarf covers a woman's hair, but it can also cover her neck and shoulders, with the niqab also covering her face, and the burka covering even her eyes. For a detailed analysis of the cultural and political significance of headscarves and styles, please see Tarlo (2010) and Moors and Tarlo (2013).

2. Cindoğlu and Zencirci, 2008; Vertovec, 2011.

3. Anderson, 1991; Calhoun, 1997; Malkki, 1992.

4. Bowen, 2008; Scott, 2007.

5. See also Killian, 2003; Laborde, 2008; Winter, 2008.

6. Joppke, 2009.

7. Yuval-Davis, 2011.

8. Rosenberger and Sauer, 2012.

9. See also Elver, 2012; and Kuru, 2009.

10. Yuval-Davis, 2011.

11. Analogous to Barth, 1969.

12. Anderson, 1991.

13. Eder, 2006; Wodak, de Cillia, and Reisigl, 2009.

14. Wimmer, 2013, Brubaker, 1996.

15. Yuval-Davis, 1997, 2006.

16. Calhoun, 1997; Wodak, de Cillia, and Reisigl, 2009.

17. Renan, 1882.

18. Appiah, 2007.

19. Gilroy, 1993.

20. Mühe, 2010; Bucerius, 2007.

21. Özyürek, 2011.

22. Anderson, 1991; see also Bhabha, 1990; Hall and du Gay, 1996; Wodak, de Cillia, and Reisigl, 2009.

23. Frosh and Wolfsfeld, 2006, 106.

24. Vertovec, 2011; Wodak, de Cillia, and Reisigl, 2009, 156.

25. See for example, British Labour Party politician Trevor Phillips, cited in Joppke, 2009, 83; and German Social-Democratic Party politician Erhardt Körting, cited in Yurdakul and Korteweg, 2013.

26. Wodak, de Cillia, and Reisigl, 2009; Malkki, 1992.

27. Haritaworn, Tauqir, and Erdem, 2008; Yurdakul, 2010; Shooman, 2011.

28. Göle, 1996.

29. Phalet, Baysu, and Verkuyten, 2010.

30. Hoodfar, 2003.

31. Atasoy, 2006.

32. Mushaben, 2005. In a story relayed in the NRC (July 26, 2004), one of the Dutch newspapers, a teacher asked a girl who always wore a headscarf to class why she had not worn one to the school dance the night before. The girl's response: "Miss, I don't have time to fix my hair up in the morning." (See also Chapter 4, p. 117.)

33. Göcek, 1999; Saktanber, 2002; Seggie, 2011.

34. Cindoğlu, 2011.

35. Bouteldja, 2011; Moors, 2009a.

36. Yurdakul, 2006.

37. Moors, 2009b.

38. This resemblance between Âlâ and Elle was brought up in a conversation with Nilüfer Göle.

39. See also Moors, 2009b; Scott, 2007.

40. Scott, 2007.

41. MacLeod, 1992. Analyses of the headscarf-wearing practices of European Muslims generated similar arguments, with Gaspard and Khosrokhavar (1995), Killian (2003), Saktanber (2002), and Van Nieuwkerk (2004) and others showing that headscarf-wearers are not forced but rather choose to don their scarfs, albeit for a wide variety of reasons.

42. Mahmood 2001, 2005.

43. Elver, 2012.

44. Lettinga and Saharso, 2012; Berghahn and Rostock, 2009.

45. Brubaker, 1992; Duyvendak, 2011; Prins, 2004; Triadafilopoulos, 2012.

46. Bjornson. 2007; Entzinger, 2006; Koopmans, Statham, Giugni, and Passy, 2005.

47. Germany had colonies only for a relatively short period of time, roughly from 1890 to 1918.

48. Wodak, de Cillia, and Reisigl, 2009.

49. Bowen, 2008; Scott, 2007.

50. Nieuwenhuis, 2005.

51. Korteweg, forthcoming.

52. Sezgin, 2011.

Chapter 2

1. *Le Monde,* November 2, 2003.
2. Laborde, 2008, 7.
3. "Integrating Minorities: The War of the Headscarves," *The Economist,* February 5, 2004, at http://www.economist.com/node/2404691, last accessed July 2, 2013.
4. *Le Monde,* June 19, 2009. All translations are by Inder Marwah, Emily Laxer or Anna Korteweg.
5. *Le Monde,* June 19, 2009.
6. Steven Erlanger, "Parliament Moves France Closer to a Ban on Facial Veils," *New York Times,* July 14, 2010, page 6.
7. Note that the Conseil constitutionel differs from, for example, the US Supreme Court. Appointments are political and time-limited, and until recently the Conseil constitutionel served largely in an advisory capacity to the government.
8. Prior to the headscarf ban, only 14 percent of all Muslim women in France wore a headscarf; this means that the headscarf was worn by fewer than a third of Muslim women who proclaimed to be actively religious (Scott, 2007, 3). Only an estimated two thousand women wore the niqab (the burka is rarely worn) when the ban on face coverings was debated.
9. See also Laborde, 2008.
10. Bowen, 2008, 51.
11. Scott 2007, 17; Bowen 2008, 51; Kastoryano, 2002.
12. See also el-Tayeb, 2011.
13. Silberman, Alba, and Fournier, 2007.
14. For example, Portes and Zhou, 1993; Zhou, 1997.
15. Freedman, 2004; Silberman, Alba, and Fournier, 2007; Scott, 2007.
16. See Bowen, 2008; also Scott, 2007.
17. Brubaker, 1992; Weber, 1976.
18. Laborde, 2008; Pocock, 1995.
19. Laborde, 2008; as opposed to the Athenian republicanism described by Pocock, 1995.
20. Scott, 2007.
21. Laborde, 2008; Scott, 2007.
22. Laborde, 2008, 7.
23. Laborde, 2008, 7–8.
24. Bowen, 2008, 12; see also Brubaker, 1992; Weil, 2008.
25. Bowen, 2008, 26; see also Weil, 2008.
26. Bowen, 2008, 26.
27. Bowen, 2008, 29.
28. Bowen, 2007.
29. Scott, 2007, 12, emphasis in original.
30. Weil, 2008; Weill, 2006.
31. Laborde, 2008, 8–9.
32. Bowen, 2008, 17.

33. Bowen, 2007, 2008.

34. "France Boosts Women Politicians," *BBC News,* at http://www.news.bbc.co.uk/2/hi/europe/6192864.stm, last accessed August 15, 2012.

35. Scott, 2005a; see also Göle and Billaud 2011.

36. Scott, 2005b, 2007.

37. Scott, 2005b.

38. Scott, 2005b, 2007.

39. Bowen, 2008, 83–86.

40. Bowen, 2008, 86–87.

41. Bowen, 2008, 87.

42. Freedman, 2004.

43. Scott, 2007, 27.

44. Bowen, 2008, 89.

45. Bowen, 2008; Scott, 2007.

46. Bowen, 2008; Weil, 2008; Weill, 2006.

47. *Le Figaro,* April 24, 2003.

48. *Le Figaro,* May 12, 2003.

49. *Le Monde,* May 10, 2003.

50. Laborde, 2008.

51. *Le Monde,* May 6, 2003.

52. *Le Figaro,* April 30, 2003.

53. *Le Monde,* November 25, 2003.

54. Bowen 2008, 121.

55. *Le Monde,* May 22, 2003.

56. *Le Monde,* June 18, 2003.

57. *Le Monde,* November 15, 2003.

58. Weil, 2008.

59. *Le Monde,* February 4, 2004.

60. *Le Monde,* June 18, 2003.

61. Bowen 2008, 48–62; Freedman, 2004, 17–18.

62. See, for example, Weil, 2008.

63. *Le Figaro,* May 6, 2003.

64. *Le Figaro,* May 6, 2003.

65. *Le Figaro,* May 6, 2003.

66. *Le Figaro,* April 21, 2003.

67. *Le Figaro,* May 6, 2003.

68. *Le Monde,* May 10, 2003.

69. *Le Monde,* October 14, 2003.

70. Billaud and Castro, 2013.

71. "La Présidente—maître Gisèle Halimi," at http://www.choisirlacausedesfemmes.org/qui-sommes-nous/la-presidente.html, last accessed May 8, 2012.

72. *Le Monde,* October 24, 2003.

73. *Le Monde,* May 30, 2003.

74. Killian, 2003, 2006; Gaspard and Khosrokhavar, 1995; Göle, 1996.

75. *Le Monde*, December 7, 2003.

76. Billaud and Castro, 2013.

77. In 2003, NPNS conducted a series of marches across France to raise awareness regarding the issues faced by immigrant women and girls in the *banlieues*. Thirty thousand participated in the concluding march in Paris. Prime Minister Raffarin received NPNS, recognized them in the Bastille Day celebrations of 2003, and heard their demands for publishing a guide on respect to be distributed in schools and housing projects, for establishing safe houses for women, for developing pilot sites to make women's voices heard, for establishing training seminars for women, and for creating spaces for female victims of violence in police stations.

78. Bellil, 2003; Amara, 2007.

79. See also Weil, 2008.

80. *Le Monde*, March 8, 2005.

81. Glenn, 1999, 2002; Davis, 2008; Knapp, 2005; Yuval-Davis, 1997, 2006.

82. Scott, 2007.

83. *Le Monde*, May 10, 2003.

84. *Le Monde*, November 2, 2003.

85. Weil, 2008, 2707.

86. Bowen, 2008, 137.

87. *Le Monde*, November 16, 2003.

88. Korteweg and Triadafilopoulos, 2013; see also Yuval-Davis, 1997.

89. Spivak, 1994; Abu-Lughod, 2002.

90. McClintock, 1995.

91. See also Freedman, 2004.

92. *Le Monde*, June 24, 2009.

93. Mullally, 2011.

94. *Le Monde*, July 12, 2008. The journalist is directly quoting the Conseil d'État.

95. Parvez, 2011.

96. *Le Monde*, July 3, 2009.

97. *Le Monde*, October 25, 2009; ellipsis in original.

98. *Le Monde*, October 28, 2009.

99. *Le Monde*, January 31, 2010.

100. *Le Monde*, March 31, 2010.

101. *Le Monde*, April 29, 2010.

102. Angelique Chrisafis, "France's Burqa Ban: Women Are 'Effectively Under House Arrest,'" *Guardian*, September 19, 2011, at http://www.guardian.co.uk/world/2011/sep/19/battle-for-the-burqa/print, last accessed November 13, 2011.

103. Pauline Mevel, "French Court Hands Down First 'Burqa Ban' Fines," Reuters, September 22, 2011, at http://af.reuters.com/article/worldNews/idAFTRE78L2QK20110 922?pageNumber=2&virtualBrandChannel=0&sp=true, last accessed November 13, 2011.

104. Hammarberg, 2011. In a blog post, Hammarberg said, "Much deeper problems of intercultural tensions and gaps have been sidetracked by the burka and niqab discus-

sions. Instead of encouraging this unfortunate discourse, political leaders and governments should take more resolute action against hate crimes and discrimination against minorities," at http://commissioner.cws.coe.int/tiki-view_blog_post.php?postId=157, last accessed November 13, 2011.

105. Bouteldja, 2011.

106. See, for example, "Trappes: A aucun moment je n'ai porté atteinte à un des policiers" [Trappes: At no point did I violate the authority of one of the officers]. *Le Monde*, July 24, 2013, at http://abonnes.lemonde.fr/societe/article/2013/07/24/trappes-a-aucun -moment-je-n-ai-porte-atteinte-a-un-des-policiers_3452674_3224.html, last accessed December 3, 2013.

107. Selby, 2011.

108. Özyürek, 2014; Yükleyen, 2011.

109. *Le Monde*, July 12, 2008.

110. *Le Monde*, July 4, 2009. These comments were made by Jacques Guillemain and were included in *Le Monde*'s "Debates" section, which airs different perspectives on a given issue.

111. *Le Monde*, September 26, 2009.

112. *Le Monde*, October 15, 2009, emphasis added.

113. *Libération*, July 6, 2010.

114. *Le Figaro*, May 12, 2010.

115. *Le Monde*, June 23, 2009.

116. *Le Monde*, June 19, 2009. The journalist is quoting directly from the proposal for a commission of inquiry on the burka.

117. *Le Monde*, December 27, 2009.

118. *Libération*, July 13, 2010.

119. See Scott, 2007.

120. Scott, 2007.

121. *Le Monde*, June 24, 2009.

122. *Libération*, January 13, 2010.

123. *Libération*, April 22, 2010.

124. *Le Monde*, June 27, 2009.

125. *Libération*, October 28, 2010.

126. Scott, 2007, 13.

127. *Le* Monde, January 11, 2010.

128. *Libération*, February 8, 2010.

129. *Le Monde*, February 11, 2010.

130. *Le Monde*, February 11, 2010; emphasis in original.

131. See, for example, the video at http://www.dailymotion.com/video/xc3jrf_video -ilham-moussaid-25-ans-et-voil_news, last accessed March 14, 2011.

132. *The Guardian*, February 10, 2010.

133. *Le Monde*, February 11, 2010.

134. "L'affaire Baby Loup en quatre questions" [The Baby Loup affaire in four questions]. *Le Monde*, November 27, 2013, at http://abonnes.lemonde.fr/societe/article/2013/11/27/ l-affaire-baby-loup-en-quatre-questions_3520954_3224.html, last accessed December 2, 2013.

135. Stephanie le Bars, "Baby Loup: la bataille politico-judicaire sur le voile s'amplifie" [Baby Loup: The political-juridical battle concerning the veil intensifies], *Le Monde,* October 17, 2013; Abedennour Bidar, "La laïcité ne doit pas devenir un tabou" [Laicite should not become a taboo], *Le Monde,* October 23, 2013.

136. This account of the Trappes riots and their aftermath is based on reporting in *Le Monde* from July 19–26, when multiple articles on this event and its related issues appeared every day. Articles on file with authors.

137. "Trappes: A aucun moment je n'ai porté atteinte à un des policiers" [Trappes: At no point did I assault any of the police officers"], *Le Monde,* July 24, 2013, at http://abonnes.lemonde.fr/societe/article/2013/07/24/trappes-a-aucun-moment-je-n-ai-porte -atteinte-a-un-des-policiers_3452674_3224.html, last accessed December 3, 2013.

138. "Femmes voilee de Trappes: 3 mois de prison avec sursis pour le mari" [Veiled women of Trappes: 3 months in prison for the husband], *Le Monde,* November 8, 2013, at http://abonnes.lemonde.fr/societe/article/2013/11/08/femme-voilee-de-trappes-3-mois-de -prison-avec-sursis-pour-le-mari_3510465_3224.html, last accessed December 1, 2013.

139. Hugues LaGrange, "Il faut reconnaître la diversité religieuse" [We must recognize religious diversity], *Le Monde,* July 25 2013, at http://abonnes.lemonde.fr/idees/article/2013/07/25/ il-faut-reconnaitre-la-diversite-religieuse_3453843_3232.html, last accessed December 1, 2013; Jacques Maillard, "Le voile révèle les failles du pacte républicain" [The veil reveals the failings of the Republican pact], *Le Monde,* July 23, 2013, at http://abonnes.lemonde.fr/idees/ article/2013/07/23/le-voile-revele-les-failles-du-pacte-republicain_3452498_3232.html, last accessed December 1, 2013.

140. Pew Global Attitudes Project, 2010.

141. Bouzar in *Libération,* February 8, 2010.

142. "Trappes: un jeune blessé à l'oeil, six arrestations" [Trappes: One youth's eye is hurt, six arrests], *Le Monde,* July 19, 2013.

Chapter 3

1. Aktaş, 2006; Aybars, 1975.

2. Since 2011, these files are being translated from Ottoman into contemporary Turkish. They are expected to be digitally available to the public in a few years.

3. *Yeni Şafak,* November 26, 2011. The story about her execution is also narrated by other journalists and authors, such as Cihan Aktaş and Çetin Altan. However, since the Independence Court archives are not yet available to the public, the historical details of this execution has not yet been analyzed by historians. All translations from Turkish are by Selin Çağatay and Gökce Yurdakul.

4. Kuru, 2009, 187–188.

5. Kuru, 2009, 187–193.

6. Seggie, 2011.

7. We intentionally use "some pro-seculars" in order to emphasize the heterogeneity of pro-secular people in Turkey. As mentioned in the text, some pro-seculars are strictly against religion, considering themselves atheists, while others actively practice Islam but are against its presence in the public sphere.

8. Kavakçı-İslam, 2010, 22.

9. Özyürek, 2006.

10. Religious and ethnic minorities, such as Jews and Kurds, as well as anyone with a different opinion, are excluded from being considered fully "Turkish." Jews are excluded on the basis of religion—because they are not Muslims—and Kurds are excluded on the basis of ethnicity—because they are seen as refusing assimilation. In the Turkish context, secularism excludes people from accessing the state sphere on the basis of religion and ethnicity, which also intersect in some cases (such as with Alevi and Sunni Kurds).

11. See also Göle, 2002.

12. Tugal, 2009.

13. Although the Ak Party has this discourse of inclusiveness, it only targets certain groups to be included in the Turkish Sunni Muslim polity. For example, there have been very limited attempts to improve the rights of Alevis in Turkey (for details, please see Zırh, 2012). Similarly, the Greek Orthodox (Halki) Seminary in Heybeliada in Istanbul, remains closed, despite international interventions. The Greek Orthodox seminary was closed in 1971 under a law that put religious and military training under state control (*Today's Zaman*, June 30, 2009).

14. Hale and Özbudun, 2009.

15. In a Twitter message, internationally renowned music composer Say questioned the Islamic depiction of paradise. Upon complaint, he was sentenced to jail for ten months for "publicly insulting religious values that are adopted by a part of the nation" (*Hürriyet*, April 15, 2013).

16. The Democratization Package of the AK Party, which was officially announced by Erdoğan on 30 September 2013, deals with discrimination against minorities, especially introducing some rights for the Kurdish minority in Turkey in addition to lifting the headscarf ban. The rights of some minorities, such as Alevis, are ignored, however. For example, the reopening of the Greek Orthodox Aya Triada Seminary in Heybeliada, which was closed to the public in 1971, was not realized.

17. A multiethnic and multireligious empire with borders from southeastern Europe to North Africa, the Ottoman Empire was ruled by the Sultan, who was also the Caliph, the ruler of the Islamic *ummah*.

18. Karpat, 2001, 353.

19. Kuru, 2009.

20. İmam Hatip schools are vocational schools for educating imams. They are state-run schools and the imams are civil servants.

21. These are the major principles that Kemal Atatürk used in founding the Turkish state.

22. Though Independence courts were reduced in number and abolished between 1921 and 1927 (Aybars 1975), the mentality of protecting the government and Kemalist principles continued. Not only was opposition to the Republic punished, but any kind of diversity from the homogeneous national narratives was similarly targeted.

23. This military coup was motivated by both left- and right-wing political conflict, which became violent, including massacres in Bahçelievler, Ankara; Kahramanmaraş; and

Taksim Square, Istanbul. As a result of countrywide political instability, General Kenan Evren announced a military coup on September 12, 1980.

24. Hale and Özbudun, 2009.

25. Şen, 2004.

26. Azak, 2010.

27. Personal correspondence with Ahmet Yükleyen, 2011.

28. Yavuz, 2009.

29. Both religious women and religious men were opposed to the university regulations regarding their religious and political beliefs; as a result, many chose to study abroad or drop out of university.

30. The religious clergy schools were exempted from this regulation.

31. Cindoğlu, 2011.

32. Cindoğlu, 2011, 33–34.

33. Çağatay, 2009.

34. Çağatay, 2009, 5.

35. Çağatay, 2009.

36. Kavakçı-İslam, 2010, 58.

37. Turgut Özal was prime minister and then president of Turkey until 1993. He was known for his politics "against the current" in religious and international affairs as well as in financial matters. Özal tremendously changed Turkish politics and economics by arguing for freedoms at all levels, including the removal of the headscarf ban.

38. Under Turgut Özal's leadership, the Motherland Party introduced into Turkish politics important debates about topics ranging from neoliberal economics to human rights.

39. Çağatay, 2009.

40. Kavakçı-İslam, 2010, 58.

41. Leyla Şahin was not the only student who took her case to the ECtHR.

42. Elver, 2012.

43. ECtHR, Fourth Section, The Case Of Leyla Sahin v. Turkey, Application No. 44774/98, Judgment, Strasbourg Para. 99.

44. Nieuwenhuis, 2005; Koenig, 2009.

45. *Hürriyet*, November 16, 2005.

46. *Zaman*, February 7, 2008.

47. Mehmet Ali Şahin, former Vice Prime Minister, shows the Ak Party's ambivalent attitude to the headscarf in his interview in *Milliyet* (May 24, 2006). For a sociological account of this ambivalence, see Çağatay (2009).

48. For detailed discussions, see http://www.tbmm.gov.tr/tutanak/donem23/yil2/bas/b059m.htm and http://www.tbmm.gov.tr/tutanak/donem23/yil2/bas/b062m.htm.

49. The first three articles of the Constitution are about the unity of the Turkish Republic: that it is a secular and democratic state, that its geographical borders were determined in 1923, that its language is Turkish, and that the Turkish flag is the crescent and the star on a red background.

50. *Radikal*, October 5, 2010; *Hürriyet*, February 25, 2008.

51. *Zaman*, October 7, 2010.

52. See also Seggie, 2011.

53. Because the protests are continuing as we are writing this book, it is too early to say that the emerging narrative is a new or an alternative national narrative to the pro-religious and pro-secular ones.

54. Turam, 2007; Yavuz and Esposito, 2003; Yükleyen and Yurdakul, 2011.

55. Yavuz, 2013.

56. Newspapers such as *Hürriyet* and *Milliyet* have been critical of the Ak Party government. Aydın Doğan, as well as the journalists he employed, made critical comments against the Ak Party in these newspapers. In 2009, companies that belonged to Aydın Doğan were charged with a tax fine of approximately 2.53 billion USD. To pay this fine in full, Doğan had to sell some of his companies, including his newspapers. He retired in 2010.

57. *Cumhuriyet*, January 31, 2008.

58. Benhabib, 2011.

59. Even in its earlier decision in 1998, the Court said, "The sovereign and effective power of the state is not religious principles but science and reason. . . . To allow the headscarf because of religious beliefs violates the principle of secularism by basing a regulation in the field of public law on religious principles. . . . In a secular state, the legal system cannot embrace religious necessities. . . . Regardless of their status, people who participate in the universities, which are bound to work within the framework of the secularism principle of the Turkish constitution, should not be shaped according to the rules of religion" (Constitutional Court Decision on the Headscarf, 1998).

60. *Hürriyet*, July 10, 2003.

61. This quote is a translation from Turkish to English that is mistranslated in the newspaper. The correct translation should be "rule of law" and not "social state of law."

62. *Hürriyet*, October 30, 2003.

63. For the discussion, see http://www.tbmm.gov.tr/tutanak/donem22/yil3/bas/b005m .htm.

64. *Cumhuriyet*, February 7, 2008.

65. Saktanber and Çorbacıoğlu, 2008; Özdalga, 2007.

66. *Cumhuriyet*, February 7, 2008.

67. Wiltse, 2008.

68. Arat, 2005, 18.

69. *Cumhuriyet*, February 7, 2008.

70. *Cumhuriyet*, January 31, 2008.

71. *Hürriyet*, November 16, 2005.

72. The concept of honor is rarely mentioned by Ak Party politicians in headscarf debates; it is therefore difficult to find other connections between honor and the headscarf in the election rallies or political discussions that have taken place through the years. The term *honor* is commonly used by nationalists in Turkey. It may be argued that in this specific instance Arınç connected honor and the headscarf in an election rally in order to appeal to Nationalist Movement Party (*Milliyetçi Hareket Partisi*) voters in Kahramanmaraş. (We are grateful to Gökhan Tuncer for pointing this out.)

73. Election rally in Kahramanmaraş, October 18, 2002.

74. *Zaman*, January 15, 2008.

75. Boucher, 2012; Maclure and Taylor, 2011.

76. The period in which these discussions occurred was the 22nd Legislation Period, from November 14, 2002, to June 3, 2007.

77. In the same session, Abdullah Gül was asked whether or not he would consider withdrawing his wife Hayrünnisa Gül's application to the ECtHR against Turkey (for the same reasons as Leyla Şahin). Although Abdullah Gül defended his wife's right to apply to the ECtHR as a citizen, Hayrünnisa Gül later withdrew from the case without providing the reason why.

78. The poll was conducted by MetroPOLL Strategic and Social Research Center (*Stratejik ve Sosyal Araştırmalar Merkezi*).

79. *Zaman*, January 10, 2008.

80. *Cumhuriyet*, October 13, 2011.

81. Kader.org, accessed July 8, 2012.

82. Stated at the International Meeting on Gender Equality co-organized by the Turkish parliament's Gender Equality Commission and the United Nations Development Program, March 24, 2011.

83. *Zaman*, October 16, 2008.

84. *Milliyet*, October 23, 2010.

85. *Zaman*, March 10, 2005.

86. See also Çağatay, 2009.

87. Aslan-Akman, 2011.

88. *Zaman*, October 30, 2003.

89. Ünal and Cindoğlu, 2013. Currently, in Turkey abortion is legally permitted up to the tenth week of pregnancy. In special cases, abortion later than the tenth week is also permitted.

90. May 31, 2012.

91. *Hürriyet*, May 30, 2012.

92. Marshall-Aldıkaçtı, 2008.

93. Bianet.org, 2012, at http://bianet.org/bianet/insan-haklari/138741-1930lardan-2012ye-nufus-muhendisligi, last accessed on November 27, 2013.

94. Böhürler, 2006.

95. *Zaman*, October 23, 2003.

96. *Yeni Şafak*, October 30, 2010.

97. December 22, 2010.

98. *Yeni Şafak*, January 30, 2010.

99. *Haber Vitrini*, online news portal, June 13, 2004.

100. Kavakçı-İslam 2010, 78.

Chapter 4

1. Wilders, quoted in the *Volkskrant*, December 21, 2005.

2. Centraal Bureau voor de Statistiek (CBS), 2010, 170; Duyvendak, 2011.

3. El-Tayeb, 2011.

4. Gijsberts, Huijnk, and Dagevos, 2011, 40.

5. CBS, 2012.

6. Dagevos and Gijsberts, 2007, 20.

7. Gijsberts and Dagevos, 2009, 273.

8. Lettinga, 2011, 40.

9. Moors, 2009a.

10. CBS, 2012, 87.

11. Bjornson, 2007; Duyvendak and Scholten, 2012; Entzinger, 2003, 2006; Prins, 2004.

12. ETC number 1997-149. See http://www.cgb.nl/oordelen/oordeel/217307/volledig, last accessed August 9, 2012.

13. As of October 2012, the work of the ETC was taken over by the Dutch College for Human Rights, which has the same mandate as the ETC when it comes to headscarf cases.

14. *NRC,* January 27, 2012.

15. Moors, 2009b.

16. Brown, 2006.

17. Prins, 2004, 32; see also Bracke, 2011; Lettinga and Saharso, 2012.

18. Van Bijsterveld, 2005; van der Burg, 2009.

19. Bruinsma and de Blois, 2007.

20. Buruma, 2007, 79.

21. Buruma, 2007, 80; Lijphart, 1989.

22. Buruma, 2007, 80.

23. Wouters, 1987; de Swaan, 1996.

24. Buruma, 2007, 80.

25. See also Wetenschappelijke Raad voor het Regeringsbeleid (WRR), 2007, chapter 3; Bryant, 1997, 158.

26. Buruma, 2007, 78.

27. Van der Veer, 2006, 118.

28. Duyvendak, 2006, 2011; Mepschen, Duyvendak, and Tonkens, 2010.

29. For an etymology of this phrase, see http://weblogs.nrc.nl/woordhoek/2008/10/01/doe-maar-gewoon-dan-doe-je-al-gek-genoeg, accessed April 27, 2012.

30. All translations from the Dutch are by Anna Korteweg.

31. Bracke, 2011; see also Haritaworn, Tauqir, and Erdem, 2008.

32. Korteweg and Yurdakul, 2009; Yurdakul and Korteweg, 2013.

33. Mepschen, Duyvendak, and Tonkens, 2010.

34. Mepschen, Duyvendak, and Tonkens, 2010, 967.

35. Van der Veer, 2006, 118, 119.

36. But see Haritaworn, Tauqir, and Erdem, 2008.

37. Haritaworn, Tauqir, and Erdem; see also Bracke, 2011.

38. Bussemaker, 1993; Korteweg, 2006a.

39. Van Bijsterveld, 2005.

40. Bruinsma and De Blois, 2007; see also Verhaar and Saharso, 2004.

41. Nickolson, 2010; see also Akkerman, 2005; Maussen, 2012.

42. *NRC,* April 13, 2004.

43. Tahir, *NRC,* January 24, 2004.

44. *NRC,* January 24, 2004.

45. *NRC,* January 24, 2004.

46. Bruinsma and De Blois, 2007, 120; see also Akkerman, 2005.

47. *Trouw,* February 26, 2011.

48. All in *Trouw*, April 8, 2011.

49. Van der Veer, 2006, 119.

50. http://www.wijblijvenhier.nl.

51. http://www.wijblijvenhier.nl/?p=4254, accessed April 6, 2011.

52. http://zoeken.rechtspraak.nl/ResultPage.aspx, italics added, last accessed June 21, 2012.

53. Lettinga and Saharso, 2012.

54. Kustaw Bessems, *De Pers,* at http://www.deondernemer.nl/binnenland/335365/Ik-raak -niet-verwoest-door-verlies.html, September 8, 2009, updated August 27, 2010, last accessed June 22, 2013.

55. *NRC,* September 22, 2009.

56. *NRC,* July 26, 2004.

57. *Volkskrant,* January 12, 2012.

58. TK h-33229, September 16, 2009, 2–69.

59. Theo van Gogh was murdered by a young Dutch Muslim man, Mohammed Bouyeri, who was deeply offended by the movie *Submission,* which Van Gogh had helped Ayaan Hirsi Ali to make. In the movie, women had Koranic texts written on their naked bodies. For further analysis, see Korteweg 2006b.

60. Bat Ye'or, 2005.

61. TK h-33229, September 16, 2009, 2-68-9, at https://zoek.officielebekendmakingen .nl/h-33229.pdf, last accessed August 16, 2012.

62. TK h-33229, September 16, 2009, 2-69.

63. TK h-33229, September 16, 2009, 2-69.

64. TK h-33229, September 16, 2009, 2-70.

65. TK h-33229, September 16, 2009, 2-70.

66. TK h-33229, September 16, 2009, 2-71.

67. TK h-33229, September 16, 2009, 2-71.

68. Korteweg, 2013.

69. Moors, 2009a.

70. Moors 2009a.

71. Moors 2009a, 13–16.

72. Donner press conference, September 16, 2011, reported in *Volkskrant*, September 16, 2011.

73. Moors, 2009a, 17.

74. Moors 2009a, 17.

75. Moors 2009a, 18.

76. *NRC,* April 25, 2008.

77. *Trouw,* September 28, 2009.

78. *NRC,* February 9, 2008.

79. *NRC,* April 25, 2008.

80. *NRC,* April 25, 2008.
81. *NRC,* April 25, 2008.
82. *Volkskrant,* December 22, 2005.
83. http://www.winterboerka.nl/faq.html, last accessed July 23, 2012.
84. *Trouw,* May 29, 2010.
85. See Moors 2009a.
86. See also Mahmood, 2005; Korteweg, 2008.
87. Interview with Leyla Çakir, January 22, 2012.
88. Interview with Leyla Çakir, January 22, 2012.
89. Interview with Leyla Çakir, January 22, 2012.
90. Interview with Leyla Çakir, January 22, 2012.
91. Interview with Nora el-Jebli, January 25, 2012.

Chapter 5

1. BVerfGe, 2BvR, Supra, note 24; see Fournier and Yurdakul, 2006, 172.
2. Since 2011, another lawsuit has been under way in the Constitutional Court, and a ruling is expected; for more information, see http://www.zeit.de/gesellschaft/zeitges chehen/2011-08/kopftuch-klage-verfassungsgericht.
3. Amir-Moazami, 2007; Berghahn and Rostock, 2009; Sauer and Rosenberg, 2012; Yurdakul, 2006; Fournier and Yurdakul, 2006.
4. Özyürek, 2011a; Yurdakul, 2009.
5. Plessner, 1974.
6. *Deutsche Islam Konferenz Bericht* [German Islam Conference Report], 2010, at http:// www.deutsche-islam-konferenz.de, last accessed November 26, 2013.
7. Statistisches Bundesamt, 2013.
8. Diefenbach, 2007.
9. Kirsten, Reimer, and Kogan, 2008.
10. We use the term integration in quotation marks, in order to show that this term is used by politicians, and not by us. In addition, we find the current use of this term problematic. See also Spielhaus, 2012a.
11. Spielhaus, 2012a.
12. *Der Spiegel,* September 5, 2010.
13. *Deutsche Welle,* October 17, 2010.
14. Christian Democratic Union, "Arbeitsgrundlage für die Zuwanderungs-Kommission der CDU Deutschlands" [Working principles for CDU Germany's Immigration Commission], November 6, 2000, at http://www.cdu.de. All translations from German are by Hartmut Könitz, Paulina Garcia del Moral and Gökçe Yurdakul.
15. The new CDU-SPD government decided in early 2014 to continue the DIK in a narrower format. See http://www.faz.net/aktuell/politik/inland/islamkonferenz-weiter-in -verschlankter-form-12771638.html, last accessed March 4, 2014.
16. Amir-Moazami, 2009.
17. Plessner, 1974.
18. For some historians and political observers, Bismarck failed to consolidate the whole

cultural nation into the new nation-state, a discourse taken up by the Nazis and used as justification for occupying and adding Austria and the western part of Czechoslovakia to the German Reich.

19. *Kulturkampf* is the historical name of the 1871–1878 conflict between the Roman Catholic Church and the Prussian government led by Otto von Bismarck. See also Chin, Fehrenbach, Eley, and Grossmann, 2009, 16.

20. Aschheim, 1983; Klusmeyer and Aleinikoff, 2001.

21. Arendt, 1973; Bodemann, 2010; Chin, Fehrenbach, Eley, and Grossmann, 2009.

22. Arendt, 1973.

23. This happened to the point where it can be very difficult to publish analyses of "race" in the contemporary German context; see Chin, Fehrenbach, Eley, and Grossmann, 2009.

24. Chin, Fehrenbach, Eley, and Grossmann, 2009, 22.

25. Yurdakul and Bodemann, 2006.

26. Kohl's speech at the Knesset in Israel on January 24, 1984. The original speech is not available online, but for a follow-up on the use of this term, please see *der Spiegel* at http://www.spiegel.de/spiegel/print/d-13519977.html.

27. The perspective on and language in reference to East Germany also depended on the political leaning of the speaker; the left-leaning media tended to accept the existence of East Germany as a state and used the official term *DDR* (Deutsche Demokratische Republik, or German Democratic Republic), while the right-leaning press talked about the "Zone" or put the official name in quotation marks.

28. *FAZ*, March 14, 2009.

29. *Wirtschaftswunder* (economic miracle) refers to the rebuilding of West German industry and the subsequent regrowth of its economy after the Second World War.

30. Herbert, 1990.

31. The German authorities issued numerous invitations to guest workers after large-scale worker agreements with countries such as Turkey, Yugoslavia, Italy, Algeria, and Morocco, among others. For more information on this theme, see Herbert 1990 and Yurdakul 2009.

32. Dale and Ruspini, 2002.

33. *Die Tagesschau*, November 24, 2012.

34. *Berliner Morgenpost*, June 12, 1993; *Milliyet*, June 19, 1993.

35. Chin, Fehrenbach, Eley, and Grossmann, 2009, 13.

36. Brubaker, 1992, 51.

37. Brubaker, 1992; Hansen and Koehler, 2005; Schönwälder and Triadafilopoulos, 2012.

38. This information can be found at the Federal Government's website at http://www.bundesregierung.de/Webs/Breg/DE/Bundesregierung/BeauftragtefuerIntegration/Staatsangehoerigkeit/_node.html, last accessed November 26, 2013.

39. Korteweg and Yurdakul, 2010; Yurdakul and Korteweg, 2013.

40. Ferree, 2012, 2.

41. Klusmeyer and Aleinikoff, 2001, 521; see also Mushaben, 2005; Pautz, 2005.

42. Sarrazin, 2010.

43. *Die Welt*, November 17, 2010.

44. *Die Welt*, November 17, 2010.

45. *Die Welt,* November 17, 2010.

46. And it probably never was, as we have argued earlier; see also Mushaben, 2005.

47. Von Blumenthal, 2009.

48. Von Blumenthal, 2009.

49. See Landeszentrale der politische Bildung, Baden-Württemberg [Federal state center of political education: Baden-Württemberg], "Verfassung des Landes Baden-Württemberg" [Constitution of Baden-Württemberg State], from November 11, 1953 (GBl. S. 173), specifically articles 15 and 16, at http://www.lpb-bw.de/bwverf/bwverf.htm, last accessed November 27, 2013.

50. Von Blumenthal, 2009.

51. Ast and Spielhaus, 2012; Frings, 2010; Peucker, 2010.

52. Berghahn, 2009.

53. *Bundesarbeitsgericht* (BAG), 10.10.2002 –2 AZR 472/01.

54. Berghahn, 2009.

55. Rottmann and Ferree, 2008.

56. Ferree, 2012; Howard, 2012.

57. Spielhaus, 2012b.

58. Spielhaus, 2012b, 249–250.

59. Jonker, 2000, 313.

60. AMJ, which has a large number of followers, received this status in 2013. The organization claims no political affiliation with Islamic movements. For an in-depth legal explanation in German, see http://www.lto.de/recht/hintergruende/h/diskussion-um-anerkennung-der-islam-und-das-grundgesetz.

61. See also Azzaoui, 2012.

62. Fournier and Yurdakul, 2006.

63. As mentioned in Chapter 3, Alevis are a religious minority in Turkey.

64. Vertrag zwischen der Freien und Hansestadt Hamburg, dem DITIB-Landesverband Hamburg, SCHURA—Rat der Islamischen Gemeinschaften in Hamburg und Verband der Islamischen Kulturzentren [Agreement between the Free and Hanseatic City of Hamburg, the DITIB Association at the Federal State of Hamburg, SCHURA—Council of Islamic Communities in Hamburg, and the Islamic Cultural Centers Association], 2012, at http://www.hamburg.de/contentblob/3551370/data, last accessed July 3, 2013. Different from public law corporation status (which Ahmadiyya Muslim Jamaat received in Hesse in 2013), this agreement in Hamburg does not include receiving taxes from organizational members. When a religious organization is entitled to be designated a public law corporation, it can then collect taxes from its members, which can be used for developing social facilities such as educational institutions, senior homes, and others.

65. In German, *das Bild* has two meanings: both "picture" and "to form."

66. The online archive was not available before 2006.

67. *BILD,* May 8, 2010; *BILD,* May 9, 2010.

68. *taz,* January 26, 2004; originally published as a position paper on December 17, 2003, at http://www.lale-akguen.de.

69. *FAZ,* January 3, 2004.

70. *FAZ*, January 4, 2004.

71. *SZ*, July 26, 2007; *taz*, January 12, 2004.

72. *FAZ*, January 7, 2004.

73. *SZ*, June 26, 2008.

74. BVerfGE 93, 1 1 BvR 1087/91.

75. Schaal, 2006. Similarly, in the Italian Lautsi case, Italy appealed the ECtHR's initial rejection of crucifixes as religiously neutral cultural symbols. When Italy appealed, the ECtHR argued that crucifixes can remain in the schools because they are "essentially passive symbols" (*Guardian*, March 18, 2011; see also Michl, 2010). This statement, which solved the Italian court case, also made many CSU politicians in Bavaria who wanted to retain crucifixes in schools happy.

76. Press release available online, December 1, 2003, http://www.bpb.de/politik/innenpolitik/konfliktstoff-kopftuch/63284/offener-brief-position.

77. *taz*, February 14–15, 2004.

78. *taz*, February 14–15, 2004.

79. *taz*, January 5, 2004; *taz*, January 8, 2004.

80. The subtitle of this section is from Ferree, 2012.

81. Beck-Gernsheim, 2006; Lutz, 2009; Rommelspacher, 2010; Yurdakul, 2010. See also Sara Lennox (1995) for an analysis of earlier debates. For the Central Council of Ex-Muslims (*Zentralrat der Ex-Muslime*), and for several feminists such as Seyran Ates, Serap Cileli, Necla Kelek, Alice Schwarzer, and Viola Roggenkamp, the headscarf represents an unambiguous symbol of women's oppression (*FAZ*, February 2, 2006; *FAZ*, February 11, 2006; *FAZ*, December 15, 2007; *FAZ*, September 12, 2008; *taz*, February 11, 2004).

82. *DIK*, April 14, 2009.

83. Yurdakul, 2010.

84. Ferree, 2012, 74–76.

85. *FAZ*, July 4, 2006.

86. Schwarzer, 2002, 2011.

87. *Die Zeit*, January 26, 2011.

88. *taz*, July 23, 2004; *taz*, October 19, 2006; *taz*, August 20, 2009.

89. See note 11.

90. Interview with Gökçe Yurdakul in *Deutsche Welle*, at http://www.dw.de/turkish-german-womans-playboy-cover-stirs-controversy/a-15021188-1, last accessed November 26, 2013.

91. "Brüste mit Migrationshintergrund," April 19, 2011.

92. *FAZ*, July 12, 2009.

93. Sarrazin, 2010.

94. Sarrazin, 2009, 200–201.

95. *Der Spiegel online*, September 18, 2010.

96. In her book *Stolen Honor: Stigmatizing Muslim Men in Berlin*, anthropologist Katherine P. Ewing argues that Leitkultur is beyond a threat to homogeneity. In fact, Muslim men are usually perceived as a threat to the German constitution, which portrays this minority population as being outside the perceived German polity. Drawing on Habermas's

notion of constitutional patriotism, Ewing argues that the stigmatization of Muslim men within a debate of constitutional patriotism is a paradox, because people become a part of a polity through their allegiance to the constitution and not by virtue of their ethnic or religious background. We are grateful to Ewing for bringing the relationship between Leitkultur and constitutional patriotism to our attention during a workshop in Paris. For more on this issue, please see Ewing, 2008.

97. Mühe, 2010, 60.

98. Spielhaus, 2009.

99. *DIK,* April 27, 2009.

100. *DIK,* August 6, 2012.

101. What was discussed in the DIK during the actual conference was very different from what is represented on the website, however. The actual conference focused more on integration and security issues, whereas the website was designed to discuss the diversity of perspectives of Muslim women.

102. *Code-switching* means to alternate between two or more languages while speaking or writing in order to draw from different contexts. Many bilingual and multilingual people in Germany use code-switching between their native language and German. Colloquially, code-switching is referred to as *Kanaksprak.*

103. Foroutan, 2011.

104. Foroutan and Schäfer, 2009.

105. *Die Zeit,* September 23, 2010.

106. *Die Zeit,* September 3, 2010.

107. *Taz,* January 25, 2011.

108. Interview, June 22, 2011.

109. For an argument on the intersection of gender and religion in job market discrimination, see Ast and Spielhaus (2012).

110. Şenocak, 2011, 91.

111. O'Brien, 2009.

112. Kanak Attak, 2001. See also interview with Gökçe Yurdakul, "Germans Need to Come Out of Their White Ghettos," *Hürriyet Daily News,* May 12, 2012.

113. In *tagesspiegel,* August 7, 2013.

Chapter 6

1. Kundera, 1999.

2. Eder, 2006.

3. Mullally, 2011.

4. April 30, 2006, Habertürk, at http://www.youtube.com/watch?v=unTLJskQALQ.

5. For Britain we collected 107 newspaper articles from the *Guardian,* 94 from the *Independent,* and 76 from the *Daily Telegraph,* without letters to the editor. We turned to the newspaper of record for both the United States and Canada: we collected and analyzed 140 articles from the *New York Times (NYT)* and 214 from the *Globe and Mail* published between January 1, 2006, and December 31, 2011, including letters to the editor.

6. Office for National Statistics, "What does the Census tell us about religion in 2011?"

at http://www.ons.gov.uk/ons/rel/census/2011-census/detailed-characteristics-for-local
-authorities-in-england-and-wales/sty-religion.html, last accessed November 29, 2013.

7. Vertovec, 1996.

8. Phillips, 2007; see also Modood, 2005; Parekh, 2000.

9. Yuval-Davis, Anthias, and Kofmann, 2005; Crowley and Hickman, 2008.

10. Dustin and Phillips, 2008.

11. Vertovec, 2007.

12. Kiliç, 2008.

13. BBC News, April 24, 2001.

14. BBC News, March 2, 2005.

15. Kiliç, 2008, 445.

16. House of Lords, 2006, at http://www.publications.parliament.uk/pa/ld200506/ld
judgmt/jd060322/begum-1.htm, last accessed July 7, 2013. See also BBC News, March 22,
2006, at http://news.bbc.co.uk/2/hi/uk_news/education/4832072.stm, last accessed July 7,
2013.

17. *Daily Mail*, October 7, 2006.

18. Kiliç, 2008.

19. See, for example, Thompson in *Telegraph*, March 1, 2009.

20. *Telegraph*, October 2, 2010.

21. *Independent*, October 17, 2006.

22. *Globe and Mail*, December 14, 2012.

23. Norman Spector in the *Globe and Mail*, October 23, 2006.

24. John Ibbitson, *Globe and Mail*, October 25, 2006.

25. See Pew Research Center, "Muslim Population by Country," at http://features.pew
forum.org/muslim-population/?sort=Country, last accessed August 14, 2012.

26. Inder Marwah and Phil Triadafilopoulos, "How Quebec's Charter Turned the Tories
into Ethnic Champions," *Globe and Mail*, November 28, 2013, at http://www.theglobeand
mail.com/globe-debate/how-quebecs-charter-turned-the-tories-into-ethnic-champions/
article15649296, last accessed December 2, 2013.

27. *Globe and Mail*, March 10, 2010.

28. *Globe and Mail*, March 18, 2006.

29. *Globe and Mail*, December 12, 2011.

30. *Globe and Mail*, March 26, 2010.

31. See also Juteau, 2003.

32. Ingrid Peritz, "Opposition Party Says PQ Secular Charter 'Too Radical,' but Supports Some Bans; Charter of Quebec Values Popular with Francophones, Not Supported
by Minorities," *Globe and Mail*, August 26, 2013.

33. Brubaker, 2001, 543, emphasis in original; see also DeWind and Kasinitz, 1997;
Zolberg and Long, 1999.

34. Pew Research Center, 2011.

35. Elver, 2012.

36. Spivak, 1994.

37. November 17, 2001; Abu-Lughod, 2002.

38. *NYT,* November 3, 2010.
39. *NYT,* December 27, 2010.
40. Pew Research Center, 2011.
41. *NYT,* September 24, 2010.
42. Wise and Velayutham, 2009.
43. Malkki, 1992; see also Gupta and Aradhana, 2007, for general ideas on studying ethnographies of the state than can translate into ethnographies of national narratives.
44. But see Fournier and Yurdakul, 2006.
45. Moors, 2011.
46. Spielhaus, 2011; Brubaker, 2013.
47. Schierup, Hansen, and Castles, 2006.
48. Schierup, Hansen and Castles, 2006, 16–17.
49. Roy, 2004.
50. Göle, 2011.
51. Benhabib, 2006, 71.

Appendix
1. Joppke, 2009; Koopmans and Statham, 2010.
2. Bowen, 2008; Klausen, 2006; Laurence, 2011.
3. Spielhaus, 2012a.
4. Wimmer and Glick Schiller, 2002.
5. Burawoy, 1998.
6. De Cillia, Reisigl, and Wodak, 1999, 157; see also Wodak, de Cillia, and Reisigl, 2009.
7. Şenocak, 2011.
8. Kurban and Sözeri, 2013.
9. See also Joppke, 2009.

Bibliography

Abu-Lughod, Lila. 2002. "Do Muslim Women Really Need Saving? Anthropological Reflections on Cultural Relativism and Its Others." *American Anthropologist* 104(3):783–90.

Akkerman, Tjitske. 2005. "Anti-immigration Parties and the Defence of Liberal Values: The Exceptional Case of the List Pim Fortuyn." *Journal of Political Ideologies* 10(3):337–354.

Aktaş, Cihan. 2006. *Türbanın Yeniden İcadı* [Reinvention of the turban]. Istanbul: Kapı Yayınları.

Amara, Fadela. 2003. *Ni Putes Ni Soumises* [Neither whores nor submissives]. Paris: Éditions la découverte.

Amir-Moazami, Schirin. 2007. *Politisierte Religion: Der Kopftuchstreit in Deutschland und Frankreich* [Politicized religion: The headscarf conflict in Germany and France]. Bielefeld: Transcript Verlag.

Amir-Moazami, Schirin. 2009. "Islam und Geschlecht unter liberal-säkularer Regierungsführung: Die Deutsche Islam Konferenz" [Islam and gender under liberal-secular governing: The German Islam Conference]. In *Tel Aviver Jahrbuch für deutsche Geschichte— Juden und Muslime in Deutschland: Rechts Religion, Identität* [Tel Aviv yearbook for German history—Jews and Muslims in Germany: Law, religion, identity], edited by José Brunner and Shai Lavi, 185–205. Göttingen: Wallstein.

Anderson, Benedict. 1991 (1983). *Imagined Communities: Reflections on the Origin and Spread of Nationalism*. London: Verso.

Appiah, Anthony. 2007. *Cosmopolitanism: Ethics in a World of Strangers*. New York: Norton.

Arat, Yeşim. 2005. *Rethinking Islam and Liberal Democracy: Islamist Women in Turkish Politics*. Albany, NY: SUNY Press.

Arendt, Hannah. 1973. *The Origins of Totalitarianism*. New York: Harcourt, Brace.

Aschheim, Steven. 1983. *Brothers and Strangers: The East European Jews in Germany and German Jewish Consciousness, 1800–1923*. Madison: University of Wisconsin Press.

Aslan-Akman, Canan. 2011. "Challenging Religious and Secularist Patriarchy: Islamist Women's New Activism in Turkey." *Journal of Levantine Studies* 1(2):103–124.

Ast, Fréderique, and Riem Spielhaus. 2012. "Tackling Double Victimization of Muslim Women in Europe: The Intersectional Response." *Mediterranean Journal of Human Rights* 16:357–382.

Atasoy, Yıldız. 2006. "Governing Women's Morality: A Study of Islamic Veiling in Canada." *European Journal of Cultural Studies* 9(2):203–221.

Aybars, Ergün. 1975. *İstiklal Mahkemeleri* [Independence courts]. Ankara: Bilgi Yayınevi.

Azak, Umut. 2010. *Islam and Secularism in Turkey: Kemalism, Religion and the Nation State.* London: I. B. Tauris.

Azzaoui, Mounir. 2012. "Auf dem Weg zur Anerkennung muslimischer Religionsgemeinschaften: Der religionspolitische Kompromiss in NRW zum Islamischen Religionsunterrich" [Toward recognizing Muslim religious communities: The political compromise in Northern Westfalia in Islamic religious courses]. *AMOS International* 6(1):18.

Barth, Frederich. 1969. "Introduction." In *Ethnic Groups and Boundaries: The Social Study of Cultural Difference,* edited by Frederich Barth, 9–38. Boston: Little, Brown.

Beck-Gernsheim, Elisabeth. 2006. "Turkish Brides: A Look at the Immigration Debate in Germany." In *Migration, Citizenship, Ethnos,* edited by Y. Michal Bodemann and Gökçe Yurdakul, 158–185. New York: Palgrave Macmillan.

Bellil, Samira. 2003. *Dans l'enfer de Tournantes* [In the hell of gang rapes]. Paris: Gallimard.

Benhabib, Seyla. 2006. *Another Cosmopolitanism.* Oxford, UK: Oxford University Press.

Benhabib, Seyla. 2011. *Dignity in Adversity: Human Rights in Troubled Times.* Cambridge, UK: Polity Press.

Berghahn, Sabine. 2009. "Ein Quadratmeter Stoff als Projektionsfläche. Gesetzliche Kopftuchverbote in Deutschland und anderen europäischen Ländern" [One square meter cloth as projection site: Legal headscarf ban in Germany and other European countries]. At http://www.fu-berlin.de/sites/gpo/pol_sys/politikfelder/Ein_Quadratmeter _Stoff_als _Projektionsflaeche/index.html. Last accessed July 12, 2013.

Berghahn, Sabine, and Petra Rostock, eds. 2009. *Der Stoff, aus dem Konflikte sind: Debatten um das Kopftuch in Deutschland, Österreich und der Schweiz* [The cloth that is in conflict: Debates about the headscarf in Germany, Austria and Switzerland]. Bielefeld: Transcript Verlag.

Bhabha, Homi K., ed. 1990. *Nation and Narration.* London: Routledge.

Billaud, Julie, and Julie Castro. 2013. "Whores and Niqabees: The Sexual Boundaries of French Nationalism." *French Politics, Culture, and Society,* 31(2):81–101.

Bjornson, Marnie. 2007. "Speaking of Citizenship: Language Ideologies in Dutch Citizenship Regimes." *Focaal: European Journal of Anthropology* 49:65–80.

Bodemann, Y. Michal. 2010. "Deutschland und die orientalische Welt: Der Jude/Fremde in der klassischen deutschen Soziologie" [Germany and the oriental world: Jew/stranger in classical German sociology]. In *Staatsbürgerschaft, Migration und Minderheiten: Inklusion und Ausgrenzungsstrategien im Vergleich* [Citizenship, migration and minorities: Inclusion and exclusion strategies in comparison], edited by Gökçe Yurdakul and Michal Y. Bodemann, 47–70. Wiesbaden: Verlag Sozialwissenschaften.

Böhürler, Ayşe. 2006. *Duvarların Arkasında: Müslüman Ülkelerde Kadın* [Behind the walls: Women in Muslim countries]. Istanbul: Timaş Yayınları.

Boucher, Francois. 2012. *Open Secularism and the New Pluralism*. PhD thesis submitted to Queen's University, Kingston, Canada, Department of Philosophy. At http://qspace .library.queensu.ca/bitstream/1974/7532/1/Boucher_François_201209_PhD.pdf. Last accessed July 12, 2013.

Bouteldja, Naima. 2011. *Unveiling the Truth: Why 32 Muslim Women Wear the Full-Face Veil in France*. New York: Open Society Foundations. At http://www.opensocietyfoundations .org/publications/unveiling-truth-why-32-muslim-women-wear-full-face-veil-france. Last accessed July 12, 2013.

Bowen, John. 2007. "A View from France on the Internal Complexity of National Models." *Journal of Ethnic and Migration Studies* 33(6):1003–1016.

Bowen, John R. 2008. *Why the French Don't Like Headscarves: Islam, the State, and Public Space*. Princeton, NJ: Princeton University Press.

Bracke, Sarah. 2011. "Subjects of Debate: Secular and Sexual Exceptionalism, and Muslim Women in the Netherlands." *Feminist Review* 98:28–46.

Brown, Wendy. 2006. *Regulating Aversion: Tolerance in the Age of Identity and Empire*. Princeton, NJ: Princeton University Press.

Brubaker, Rogers. 1992. *Citizenship and Nationhood in France and Germany*. Cambridge, MA: Harvard University Press.

Brubaker, Rogers. 1996. *Nationalism Reframed: Nationhood and the National Question in the New Europe*. Cambridge, UK: Cambridge University Press.

Brubaker, Rogers. 2001. "The Return of Assimilation? Changing Perspectives on Immigration and Its Sequels in France, Germany, and the United States." *Ethnic and Racial Studies* 24(4):531–548.

Brubaker, Rogers. 2013. "Categories of Analysis and Categories of Practice: A Note on the Study of Muslims in European Countries of Immigration." *Ethnic and Racial Studies* 36(1):1–8.

Bruinsma, Fred, and Matthijs de Blois. 2007. "Pluralism in the Netherlands and *Laïcité* in France: The Islamic Challenge at a Symbolic Level." In *Explorations of Legal Cultures*, edited by Fred Bruinsma and David Nelken, 113–132. The Hague: Reed BV.

Bryant, Christopher G. A. 1997. "Citizenship, National Identity and the Accommodation of Difference: Reflections on the German, French, Dutch and British Cases." *Journal of Ethnic and Migration Studies* 23(2):157–172.

Bucerius, Sandra. 2007. "What Else Should I Do—Cultural Influences on the Drug Trade of Young Migrants in Germany." *Journal of Drug Issues* 37(3):673–698.

Bundesarbeitsgericht (BAG) [Federal Labor Court]. 2002. *Kündigung einer Verkäuferin wegen Tragens eines—islamischen—Kopftuchs* [Dismissal of a saleswomen due to wearing of Islamic headscarf]. Urteil vom 10.10.2002—2 AZR 472/01 [Judgment from 10.10.2002]. At http://lexetius.com/2002,3160. Last accessed December 2, 2013.

Bundesregierung [Federal Government]. No date. Staatsbürgerschaft [Citizenship]. At http://www.bundesregierung.de/Webs/Breg/DE/Bundesregierung/Beauftragtefuer Integration/Staatsangehoerigkeit/_node.html. Last accessed November 26, 2013.

Burawoy, Michael. 1998. "Extended Case Method." *Sociological Theory* 16(1):4–33.

Buruma, Ybo. 2007. "Dutch Tolerance: On Drugs, Prostitution, and Euthanasia." *Crime and Justice* 35:73–113.

Bussemaker, Jet. 1993. *Betwiste Zelfstandigheid: individualisering, sekse en verzorgingsstaat* [Contested independence: Individualization, gender and the welfare state]. Amsterdam: Uitgeverij SUA.

Çağatay, Selin. 2009. *An Overview of the "Headscarf Issue" in Turkey: Kemalism, Islamism and the Women's Movement.* Istanbul: Friedrich-Ebert-Stiftung.

Calhoun, Craig. 1997. *Nationalism.* Minneapolis: Minnesota University Press.

Centraal Bureau voor de Statistiek (CBS). 2010. *Jaarrapport Integratie.* Den Haag. At http://www.cbs.nl/NR/rdonlyres/E564B557-93DC-492E-8EBD-00B3ECA10FA3/0/2010b61pub.pdf. Last accessed August 9, 2012.

Centraal Bureau voor de Statistiek (CBS). 2012. *Jaarraport Integratie.* At http://www.cbs.nl/NR/rdonlyres/A1B765EE-5130-481A-A826-2DCCD89F81C9/0/2012b61pub.pdf and http://www.cbs.nl/NR/rdonlyres/3E1D543F-B1A9-4B6A-BCB3-92FA3B0D97B9/0/pb13n007.pdf. Last accessed June 17, 2013.

Chin, Rita, Heide Fehrenbach, Geoff Eley, and Atina Grossmann, eds. 2009. *After the Nazi Racial State: Difference and Democracy in Germany and Europe.* Ann Arbor: University of Michigan Press.

Cindoğlu, Dilek. 2011. *Headscarf Ban and Discrimination: Professional Headscarved Women in the Labor Market.* Istanbul: TESEV Yayinlari.

Cindoğlu, Dilek, and Gizem Zencirci. 2008. "Withering the Counter Hegemonic Potential of the Headscarf: Public Sphere, State Sphere and the Headscarf Question in Turkey." *Middle Eastern Studies* 44(5):791–806.

Crowley, Helen, and Mary Hickman. 2008. "Migration, Post-industrialism and the Globalized Nation State: Social Capital and Social Cohesion Re-examined." *Ethnic and Racial Studies* 31(7):1222–1244.

Dagevos, Jaco, and Mérove Gijsberts, eds. 2007. *Jaarraport Integratie 2007* [Annual Integration Report 2007], November 13. The Hague: Sociaal en Cultureel Planbureau (SCP). At http://www.scp.nl/english/Publications/Summaries_by_year/Summaries_2007/Integration_Report_2007.

Dale, Angela, and Elsabetta Ruspini, eds. 2002. *The Gender Dimension of Social Change: The Contribution of Dynamic Research to the Study of Women's Life Courses.* London: Polity Press.

Davis, Kathy. (2008). "Intersectionality as Buzzword: A Sociology of Science Perspective on What Makes Feminist Theory Successful." *Feminist Theory* 9(1):67–85.

de Cillia, Rudolf, Martin Reisigl, and Ruth Wodak. 1999. "The Discursive Construction of National Identities. *Discourse & Society* 10(2):149–173.

de Swaan, Abram. 1996. *Zorg en de staat. Welzijn, onderwijs en gezondheidszorg in Europa en de Verenigde Staten in de nieuwe tijd* [Care and the state: Well-being, education and healthcare in Europe and the United States in the new era]. Amsterdam: Bert Bakker.

Deutsche Islam Konferenz Bericht [German Islam Conference Report], 2010. At http://www.deutsche-islam-konferenz.de. Last accessed November 26, 2013.

DeWind, Josh, and Paul Kasinitz. 1997. "Everything Old Is New Again? Processes and Theories of Immigrant Incorporation." *International Migration Review* 31(4):1096–1111.

Diefenbach, Heike. 2007. *Kinder und Jugendliche aus Migrantenfamilien im deutschen Bildungssystem. Erklärungen und empirische Befunde* [Children and youth from migrant families in the German education system: Explanations and empirical findings]. Wiesbaden: VS Verlag für Sozialwissenschaften.

Dustin, Moira, and Phillips, Anna. 2008. "Whose Agenda Is It? Abuses of Women and Abuses of 'Culture' in Britain." *Ethnicities* 8(3):405–424.

Duyvendak, Jan Willem. 2006. *De Staat en de Straat: Beleid, Wetenschap, en de Multiculturele Samenleving* [The state and the street: Policy, science, and the multicultural society]. Amsterdam: Boom Uitgevers.

Duyvendak, Jan Willem. 2011. *The Politics of Home: Belonging and Nostalgia in Europe and the United States.* New York: Palgrave Macmillan.

Duyvendak, Jan Willem, and Peter Scholten. 2012. "Deconstructing the Dutch Multicultural Model: A Frame Perspective on Dutch Immigrant Integration Policymaking." *Comparative European Politics* 10(3):266–282.

Eder, Klaus. 2006. "Europe's Borders: The Narrative Construction of the Boundaries of Europe." *European Journal of Social Theory* (9):255–271.

El-Tayeb, Fatima. 2011. *European Others: Queering Ethnicity in Postnational Europe.* Minneapolis: University of Minnesota Press.

Elver, Hilal. 2012. *The Headscarf Controversy: Secularism and Freedom of Religion.* Oxford, UK: Oxford University Press.

Entzinger, Han. 2003. "The Rise and Fall of Multiculturalism: The Case of the Netherlands." In *Toward Assimilation and Citizenship: Immigrants in Liberal Nation-States,* edited by Christian Joppke and Ewa Morawska, 59–86. New York: Palgrave Macmillan.

Entzinger, Han. 2006. "Changing the Rules While the Game Is On: From Multiculturalism to Assimilation in the Netherlands." In *Migration, Citizenship, Ethnos,* edited by Y. Michal Bodemann and Gökçe Yurdakul, 121–146. New York: Palgrave Macmillan.

Ewing, Katherine P. 2008. *Stolen Honor: Stigmatizing Muslim Men in Berlin.* Palo Alto, CA: Stanford University Press.

Ferree, Myra Marx. 2012. *Varieties of Feminism: German Gender Politics in Global Perspective.* Stanford, CA: Stanford University Press.

Foroutan, Naika. 2011. "Heymat." *Humboldt Spektrum,* June 8. At http://www.heymat.hu -berlin.de. Last accessed December 2, 2013.

Foroutan, Naika, and Isabel Schäfer. 2009. "Hybride Identitäten—Muslimische Migranten und Migrantinnen in Deutschland und Europa." [Hybrid identities—Muslim men and women migrants in Germany and Europe]. *APuZ* 5:11–18. At http://www.bpb.de/publikationen/KTORL9,0,0,Lebenswelten_von_Migrantinnen_und_Migranten.html. Last accessed July 12, 2013.

Fournier, Pascale, and Gökçe Yurdakul. 2006. "Unveiling Distribution: Muslim Women with Headscarves in France and Germany." In *Migration, Citizenship, Ethnos,* edited by Y. Michal Bodemann and Gökçe Yurdakul, 167–184. New York: Palgrave Macmillan.

Freedman, Jane. 2004. Secularism as a Barrier to Integration? The French Dilemma. *International Migration*, 42(3):5–27.

Frings, Dorothee. 2010. *Diskriminierung aufgrund der islamischen Religionszugehörigkeit im Kontext Arbeitsleben—Erkenntnisse, Fragen und Handlungsempfehlungen. Diskriminierungen von Musliminnen und Muslimen im Arbeitsleben und das AGG* [Discrimination on the basis of belonging to Islamic religion in the context of work life—Knowledge, questions and recommendations for action: Discrimination against Muslim people in work life and the AGG]. Berlin: Antidiskriminierungsstelle des Bundes.

Frosh, Paul, and Gadi Wolfsfeld. 2006. "*ImagiNation*: News Discourse, Nationhood and Civil Society." *Media, Culture & Society* 29(1):105–129.

Gaspard, Françoise, and Farhad Khosrokhavar. 1995. *Le Foulard et la République* [The scarf and the republic]. Paris: La Découverte.

Gijsberts, Mérove, and Jaco Dagevos, eds. 2009. *Jaarraport Integratie 2009* [Annual Integration Report 2009]. The Hague: Sociaal en Cultureel Planbureau (SCP). At http://www.scp.nl/Publicaties/Alle_publicaties/Publicaties_2009/Jaarrapport_integratie_2009.

Gijsberts, Merove, Willem Huijnk and Jaco Dagevos, eds. 2011. *Jaarraport Integratie 2011* [Annual Integration Report 2011]. The Hague: Sociaal en Cultureel Planbureau (SCP). At http://www.scp.nl/Publicaties/Alle_publicaties/Publicaties_2012/Jaarrapport_integratie_2011.

Gilroy, Paul. 1993. *The Black Atlantic: Modernity and Double Consciousness*. Cambridge, MA: Harvard University Press.

Glenn, Evelyn Nakano. 1999. "The Social Construction and Institutionalization of Gender and Race." In *Revisioning Gender*, edited by Myra Marx Ferree, Judith Lorber, and Beth B. Hess, 3–43. Thousand Oaks, CA: Sage.

Glenn, Evelyn Nakano. 2002. *Unequal Freedom: How Race and Gender Shaped American Citizenship and Labor*. Cambridge, MA: Harvard University Press.

Göcek, Fatma. 1999. "To Veil or Not to Veil: The Contested Location of Gender in Contemporary Turkey." *Interventions: International Journal of Postcolonial Studies* 1(4):521–535.

Göle, Nilüfer. 1996. *The Forbidden Modern: Civilization and Veiling*. Ann Arbor: University of Michigan Press.

Göle, Nilüfer. 2002. "Islam in Public: New Visibilities and New Imaginaries." *Public Culture* 14(1):173–191.

Göle, Nilüfer. 2011. *Islam in Europe: The Lure of Fundamentalism and the Allure of Cosmopolitanism*. Princeton, NJ: Marcus Wiener.

Göle, Nilüfer, and Julie Billaud. 2011. "Islamic Difference and the Return of Feminist Universalism." In *European Multiculturalism(s): Cultural, Religious and Ethnic Challenges*, edited by Anna Tryandafillidou, Tariq Modood, and Nasar Meer, 116–143. Edinburgh: University of Edinburgh Press.

Gupta, Akhil, and Sharma Aradhana. 2007. *The Anthropology of the State: A Reader*. Malden, MA: Wiley-Blackwell.

Hale, William, and Ergun Özbudun. 2009. *Islamism, Democracy, and Liberalism in Turkey: The Case of the AKP*. New York: Routledge.

Hall, Stuart, and Paul du Gay, eds. 1996. *Questions of Cultural Identity*. Thousand Oaks, CA: Sage.

Hammarberg, Thomas. 2011. "Penalizing Women Who Wear the Burqa Does Not Liberate Them." Council of Europe Commissioner's Human Rights Comment, July 20. At http://commissioner.cws.coe.int/tiki-view_blog_post.php?postId=157. Last accessed November 13, 2011.

Hansen, Randall, and Jobst Koehler. 2005. "Issue Definition, Political Discourse and the Politics of Nationality Reform in France and Germany." *European Journal of Political Research* 44(5):623–644.

Haritaworn, Jin, Tamsila Tauqir, and Esra Erdem. 2008. "Gay Imperialism: Gender and Sexuality Discourse in the 'War on Terror.'" In *Out of Place: Interrogating Silences in Queerness/Raciality*, edited by Adi Kuntsman and Esperanza Miyake, 71–95. York, UK: Raw Nerve Books.

Herbert, Ulrich. 1990. *A History of Foreign Labor in Germany, 1880–1980: Seasonal Workers/ Forced Laborers/Guest Workers*. Ann Arbor: University of Michigan Press.

Hoodfar, Homa. 2003. "More Than Clothing: Veiling as an Adaptive Strategy." In *The Muslim Veil in North America: Issues and Debates,* edited by Sajida Alvi, Homa Hoodfar, and Sheila McDonough, 3–39. Toronto: Canadian Scholars' Press.

Howard, Erica. 2012. "Banning Islamic Veils: Is Gender Equality a Valid Argument?" *International Journal of Discrimination and the Law* 12(3):147–165.

Jonker, Gerdien. 2000. "What Is Other About Other Religions? The Islamic Communities in Berlin Between Integration and Segregation." *Cultural Dynamics* 12(3):311–329.

Joppke, Christian. 2009. *Veil: Mirror of Identity*. Cambridge, UK: Polity.

Juteau, Danielle. 2003. "Canada: A Pluralist Perspective." In *The Social Construction of Diversity: Recasting the Master Narrative of Industrial Nations,* edited by Danielle Juteau and Christiane Harzig, 249–261. New York: Berghahn Press.

Kanak Attak. 2001. "Weißes Ghetto." At http://www.kanak-tv.de./volume_1.shtml. Last accessed December 2, 2013.

Karpat, Kemal. 2001. *The Politicization of Islam: Reconstructing Identity, State, Faith, and Community in the Late Ottoman State*. Oxford, UK: Oxford University Press.

Kastoryano, Riva. 2002. *Negotiating Identities: States and Immigrants in France and Germany*. Princeton, NJ: Princeton University Press.

Kavakçı-İslam, Merve. 2010. *Headscarf Politics in Turkey: A Postcolonial Reading*. Basingstoke, UK: Palgrave Macmillan.

Kelek, Necla. 2005. *Die Fremde Braut. Ein Bericht aus dem Inneren des türkischen Lebens in Deutschland* [The foreign bride: A report from the inside of Turkish life in Germany]. Köln: Kiepenheuer und Witsch Verlag.

Kiliç, Sevgi. 2008. "The British Veil Wars." *Social Politics* 15(4):433–454.

Killian, Caitlin 2003. "The Other Side of the Veil: North African Women in France Respond to the Headscarf Affair." *Gender and Society* 17(4):567–590.

Killian, Caitlin. 2006. *North African Women in France: Gender, Culture, and Identity*. Stanford, CA: Stanford University Press.

Kirsten, Cornelia, David Reimer, and Irena Kogan. 2008. "Higher Education Entry of

Turkish Immigrant Youth in Germany." *International Journal of Comparative Sociology* 49(2–3):127–151.

Klausen, Jytte. 2006. *The Islamic Challenge: Politics and Religion in Western Europe.* New York: Oxford University Press.

Klusmeyer, Douglas, and T. A. Aleinikoff, eds. 2001. *Citizenship Today: Global Perspectives and Practices.* Washington, DC: Brookings Institute and Carnegie Endowment for International Peace.

Knapp, Gudrun A. 2005. "Race, Class, Gender: Reclaiming Baggage in Fast-Traveling Theories." *European Journal of Women Studies* 12(3):249–265.

Koenig, Matthias. 2009. "How Nation-States Respond to Religious Diversity." In *International Migration and the Governance of Religious Diversity,* edited by Paul Bramadat and Matthias Koenig, 293–322. Montreal: McGill-Queen's University Press.

Koopmans, Ruud, Paul Statham, Marco Giugni, and Florence Passy. 2005. *Contested Citizenship: Immigration and Cultural Diversity in Europe.* Minneapolis: University of Minnesota Press.

Koopmans, Ruud, and Paul Statham. 2010. *The Making of a European Public Sphere: Media Discourse and Political Contention.* Cambridge, UK: Cambridge University Press.

Korteweg, Anna C. 2006a. "The Construction of Gendered Citizenship at the Welfare Office: An Ethnographic Comparison of Welfare-to-Work Workshops in the United States and the Netherlands." *Social Politics,* 13(3):313–340.

Korteweg, Anna C. 2006b. "The Murder of Theo Van Gogh: Gender, Religion, and the Struggle over Immigrant Integration in the Netherlands." In *Migration, Citizenship, Ethnos,* edited by Y. Michal Bodemann and Gökçe Yurdakul, 147–166. New York: Palgrave Macmillan.

Korteweg, Anna C. 2008. "The Sharia Debate in Ontario: Gender, Islam, and Representations of Muslim Women's Agency." *Gender and Society* 22(4):434–454.

Korteweg, Anna. 2013. "The Dutch 'Headrag Tax' Proposal: The Symbolic and Material Consequences of Impossible Laws." *Social Identities,* 19(6):759–774.

Korteweg, Anna C., and Phil Triadafilopoulos. 2013. "Gender, Religion, and Ethnicity: Intersections and Boundaries in Immigrant Integration Policy Debates." *Social Politics* 20(1):109–136.

Korteweg, Anna, and Gökçe Yurdakul. 2009. "Gender Islam and Immigrant Integration: Boundary Drawing on Honour Killing in the Netherlands and Germany." *Ethnic and Racial Studies* 32(2):218–238.

Korteweg, Anna, and Gökçe Yurdakul. 2010. "Religion, Culture and the Politicization of Honour-Related Violence: A Critical Analysis of Media and Policy Debates in Western Europe and North America." Research Institute for Social Development Paper 12. Geneva: UN Research Institute for Social Development.

Kundera, Milan. 1999. *Identity: A Novel.* New York: Harper Perennial.

Kurban, Dilek, and Ceren Sözeri. 2013. *Policy Suggestions for Free and Independent Media in Turkey.* TESEV. http://www.tesev.org.tr/Upload/Publication/72edd039-df64-40c6-8 daf-d5bd23ff047d/13095ENG_Medya4makale11_03_130nay.pdf. Last accessed July 12, 2013.

Kuru, Ahmet. 2009. *Secularism and State Policies Toward Religion: The United States, France, and Turkey.* Cambridge, UK: Cambridge University Press.

Laborde, Cecile. 2002. "On Republican Toleration." *Constellations* 9(2):167–183.

Laborde, Cecile. 2008. *Critical Republicanism: The Hijab Controversy and Political Philosophy*. New York: Oxford University Press.

Laurence, Jonathan. 2011. *The Emancipation of Europe's Muslims: The State's Role in Minority Integration*. Princeton, NJ: Princeton University Press.

Lennox, Sara. 1995. "Divided Feminism: Women, Racism, and German National Identity." *German Studies Review* 18(3):481–502.

Lettinga, Doutje N. 2011. *Framing the Hijab: The Governance of Intersecting Religious, Ethnic and Gender Differences in France, the Netherlands and Germany*. PhD Dissertation. Amsterdam: Free University. http://dare.ubvu.vu.nl/bitstream/handle/1871/19815/dissertation.pdf?sequence=1, last accessed December 2, 2013.

Lettinga, Doutje, and Sawitri Saharso. 2012. "The Political Debates on the Veil in France and the Netherlands: Reflecting National Integration Models?" *Comparative European Politics* 10(3):319–336.

Lijphart, Arend. 1989. "From the Politics of Accommodation to Adversarial Politics in the Netherlands: A Reassessment." *West European Politics*, 12(1):139–153.

Lutz, Helma, ed. 2009. *Gender-Mobil? Geschlecht und Migration in transnationalen Räumen* [Gender-mobile? Gender and migration in transnational space]. Münster: Verlag Westfälisches Dampfboot.

MacLeod, Arlene Elowe. 1992. "Hegemonic Relations and Gender Resistance: The New Veiling as Accommodating Protest in Cairo." *Signs: Journal of Women in Culture and Society* 17(3):533–557.

Maclure, Jocelyn, and Charles Taylor. 2011. *Secularism and Freedom of Conscience*. Cambridge, MA: Harvard University Press.

Mahmood, Saba. 2001. "Feminist Theory, Embodiment, and the Docile Agent: Some Reflections on the Egyptian Islamic Revival." *Cultural Anthropology* 16(2):202–236.

Mahmood, Saba. 2005. *Politics of Piety: The Islamic Revival and the Feminist Subject*. Princeton, NJ: Princeton University Press.

Malkki, Liisa. 1992. "National Geographic: The Rooting of Peoples and the Territorialization of National Identity Among Scholars and Refugees." *Cultural Anthropology* 7(1):24–44.

Marshall-Aldıkaçtı, Gül. 2008. "A Question of Compatibility: Feminism and Islam in Turkey." *Critical Middle Eastern Journal* 17(3):223–238.

Maussen, Marcel. 2012. "Pillarization and Islam: Church-State Traditions and Muslim Claims for Recognition in the Netherlands." *Comparative European Politics* 10(3):337–353.

McClintock, Anne. 1995. *Imperial Leather: Race, Gender, and Sexuality in the Colonial Contest*. New York: Routledge.

Mepschen, Paul, Jan Willem Duyvendak, and Evelien H. Tonkens. 2010. "Sexual Politics, Orientalism and Multicultural Citizenship in the Netherlands." *Sociology* 44(5):962–979.

Michl, Fabian. 2010. "Die aktuelle Entscheidung Cadit crux?—Das Kruzifix-Urteil des Europäischen Gerichtshofs für Menschenrechte" [The recent decison of the Cadit crux?—The crucifix-judgment of the European Court of Human Rights]. *JURA* 9 (32):690–694.

Modood, Tariq. 2005. *Multicultural Politics: Racism, Ethnicity, and Muslims in Britain*. Minneapolis: University of Minnesota Press.

Moors, Annelies. 2009a. *Gezichtssluiers: Draagsters en Debatten* [Face veils: Wearers and debates]. Research report. Amsterdam School for Social Science Research, Universiteit van Amsterdam, January 31.

Moors, Annelies, 2009b. "The Dutch and the Face-Veil: The Politics of Discomfort." *Social Anthropology/Anthropologie Sociale* 17(4):393–408.

Moors, Annelies. 2011. "Minister Donner as Mufti: New developments in the Dutch 'burqa debates.'" CLOSER, http://religionresearch.org/martijn. Last accessed September 21, 2011.

Moors, Annelies, and Emma Tarlo. 2013. *Islamic Fashion and Anti-fashion: New Perspectives from Europe and North America.* Oxford, UK: Berg.

Mühe, Nina. 2010. *Muslims in Berlin.* London: Open Society Foundations, At Home in Europe Project. At http://www.opensocietyfoundations.org/reports/muslims-berlin. Last accessed December 2, 2013.

Mullally, Siobhan. 2011. "Civic Integration, Migrant Women and the Veil: At the Limits of Rights?" *Modern Law Review* 74(1):27–56.

Mushaben, Joyce Marie. 2005. "More Than Just a Bad Hair Day: The Muslim Head-Scarf Debate as a Challenge to European Identities." In *Crossing Over: Comparing Recent Migration in The United States and Europe,* edited by Holger Henke, 182–220. Idaho Falls, ID: Lexington Books.

Nickolson, Lars. 2010. *Met Recht Geloven: Religie en Maatschappij in Wet en Debat* [The right to believe: Religion and society in law and debate]. Amsterdam: Aksant.

Nieuwenhuis, Aernaut. 2005. "An Analysis of the Margin of Appreciation as Used in the Case of Leyla Şahin v. Turkey." *European Constitutional Law Review* 1:495–510.

O'Brien, Peter. 2009. "Making (Normative) Sense of the Headscarf Debate in Europe." *German Politics and Society* 27(3):66–92.

Özyürek, Esra. 2006. *Nostalgia for the Modern: State Secularism and Everyday Politics in Turkey.* Durham, NC: Duke University Press.

Özyürek, Esra. 2011. "Making Germans out of Muslims: Holocaust Education and Anti-Semitism Trainings for Immigrants." Presentation at Zentrum fur Antisemitismus Forschung, Technical University, Berlin, November 1.

Özyürek, Esra. 2014. *Being German, Becoming Muslim: Race, Religion and Conversion in the New Europe.* Princeton, NJ: Princeton University Press.

Parekh, Bhikhu. 2000. *Rethinking Multiculturalism: Cultural Diversity and Political Theory.* Cambridge, MA: Harvard University Press.

Parvez, Z. Fareen. 2011. "Debating the Burqa in France: The Antipolitics of Islamic Revival." *Qualitative Sociology* 34(2):287–312.

Pautz, Hartwig. 2005. *Die Deutsche Leitkultur: Eine Identitätsdebatte, neue Rechte, Neorassismus und Normalisierungsbemühungen* [The German leading culture: An identity debate, new rights, neoracism and efforts for normalization]. Stuttgart: Ibidem.

Peucker, Mario. 2010. *Diskriminierung aufgrund der islamischen Religionszugehörigkeit im Kontext Arbeitsleben—Erkenntnisse, Fragen und Handlungsempfehlungen Erkenntnisse der sozialwissenschaftlichen Forschung* [Discrimination on the basis of belonging to Islamic religion in the context of work life—Social science research's findings, questions and recommendations for action]. Berlin: Antidiskriminierungsstelle des Bundes.

Pew Global Attitudes Project, 2010. "Widespread Support for Banning Full Islamic Veil in Western Europe." Washington, DC: Pew Research Center, July 8. At http://www.pew global.org/2010/07/08/widespread-support-for-banning-full-islamic-veil-in-western -europe. Last accessed December 2, 2013.

Pew Research Center. 2010. "The Future of the Global Muslim Population." At http:// www.pewforum.org/future-of-the-global-muslim-population-regional-europe.aspx. Last accessed December 19, 2012.

Pew Research Center. 2011. "Muslim Americans: No Signs of Growth in Alienation or Support for Extremism. At http://www.people-press.org/files/2011/08/muslim-american -report.pdf. Last accessed December 2, 2013.

Phalet, Karen, Gülseli Baysu, and Maikel Verkuyten. 2010. "Political Mobilization of Dutch Muslims: Effects of Religious Identity Salience, Goal Framing and Normative Constraints." *Journal of Social Issues* 66(4):759–779.

Phillips, Anne. 2007. *Multiculturalism Without Culture*. Princeton, NJ: Princeton University Press.

Plessner, Helmuth. 1974. *Die Verspätete Nation* [Belated nation]. Berlin: Suhrkamp.

Pocock, J.G.A. 1995. "The Ideal of Citizenship Since Classical Times." In *Theorizing Citizenship*, edited by Ronald Beiner, 29–52. Albany: SUNY Press.

Portes, Alejandro, and Min Zhou. 1993. "The New Second Generation: Segmented Assimilation and Its Variants." *Annals of the American Academy of Political and Social Sciences* 530:74–96.

Prins, Baukje. 2004. *Voorbij de Onschuld: Het Debat over de Multiculturele Samenleving* [After innocence: The debate on multicultural society]. Amsterdam: Van Gennep.

Renan, Ernst. 1882. "Qu'est-ce qu'une nation?" [What is a nation?] Lecture at the Sorbonne, March 11. At http://ig.cs.tu-berlin.de/oldstatic/w2001/eu1/dokumente/Basistexte /Renan1882EN-Nation.pdf. Last accessed December 2, 2013.

Rommelspacher, Birgit 2010. "Emancipation as a Conversion: The Image of Muslim Women in the Christian-Secular Discourse." In *Ethics and Society: Ecumenical Journal of Social Ethics* 2. At http://www.ethik-und-gesellschaft.de/dynasite.cfm?dsmid=107215, last accessed December 2, 2013.

Rosenberger, Sieglinde, and Birgit Sauer, eds. 2012. *Politics, Religion and Gender: Framing and Regulating the Veil*. London: Routledge.

Rottmann Susan B., and Myra Marx Ferree. 2008. "Citizenship and Intersectionality: German Feminist Debates About Headscarf and Anti-discrimination Laws." *Social Politics* 15(4):481–513.

Roy, Olivier. 2004. *Globalized Islam: The Search for a New Ummah*. New York: Columbia University Press.

Saktanber, Ayşe. 2002. "We Pray Like You Have Fun: New Islamic Youth in Turkey Between Intellectualism and Popular Culture." In *Living Islam: Women, Religion and the Politicization of Culture in Turkey*, edited by Deniz Kandiyoti and Ayşe Saktanber, 254–272. New York: I. B. Tauris.

Saktanber, Ayşe, and Gül Çorbacıoğlu. 2008. "Veiling and Headscarf-Skepticism in Turkey." *Social Politics* 15(4):514–538.

Sarrazin, Thilo. 2009. "Klasse statt Masse" [Classes instead of masses]. *Lettre International* 86:197–201.

Sarrazin, Thilo. 2010. *Deutschland Schafft Sich ab: Wie wir unser Land aufs Spiel Setzen* [Germany is abolishing itself: How we put our country at risk]. München: Deutsche Verlags-Anstalt.

Schaal, Gary S. 2006. "Kris des Bundesverfassungs-gerichts? Die 'Kruzifix-Entscheidung' und die Folgen." [Crisis of the Federal Constitutional Court? The crucifix ruling and its outcome]. In *Das Bundesverfassungsgericht im politischen System* [The Constitutional Court in the political system], edited by Robert Chr. van Ooyen and Martin Möllers. Wiesbaden: VS Verlag für Sozialwissenschaften.

Schierup, Carl-Ulrik, Peo Hansen, and Stephen Castles. 2006. *Migration, Citizenship, and the European Welfare State*. Oxford, UK: Oxford University Press.

Schönwälder, Karen, and Phil Triadafilopoulos. 2012. "A Bridge or Barrier to Integration? Germany's 1999 Citizenship Reform in Critical Perspective." *German Politics and Society* 30(1):52–70.

Schwarzer, Alice. 2002. *Die Gotteskrieger und die falsche Toleranz* [God's fighters and false tolerance]. Köln: Kiepenheuer & Witsch.

Schwarzer, Alice. 2011. *Die große Verschleierung: Für Integration, Gegen Islamismus* [The big deception: For integration, against Islamization]. Köln: Kiepenheuer & Witsch.

Scott, Joan Wallach. 2005a. *Parité! Sexual Equality and the Crisis of French Universalism*. Chicago: University of Chicago Press.

Scott, Joan Wallach. 2005b. "Symptomatic Politics: The Banning of Islamic Head Scarves in French Public Schools." *French Politics, Culture & Society* 23(3):106–127.

Scott, Joan W. 2007. *The Politics of the Veil*. Princeton, NJ: Princeton University Press.

Seggie, Fatma Nevra. 2011. *Religion and the State in Turkish Universities: The Headscarf Ban*. New York: Palgrave Macmillan.

Selby, Jennifer. 2011. "Islam in France Reconfigured: Republican Islam in the 2010 Gerin Report." *Journal of Muslim Minority Affairs* 31(3):383–398.

Şen, Serdar. 2004. *AKP Milli Görüşçü mü?* Istanbul: Nokta Yayınları.

Şenocak, Zafer. 2011. *Deutschsein: Eine Aufklärungsschrift* [Being German: A writing of clarification]. Hamburg: Edition Körber Stiftung.

Sezgin, Hilal, ed. 2011. *Manifest der Vielen: Deutschland erfindet sich neu* [Manifesto of the many: Germany finds itself (a)new]. Berlin: Blumenbar Verlag.

Shooman, Yasemin. 2011. "Kronzeuginnen der Anklage? Zur Rolle muslimischer Sprecherinnen in aktuellen Islam-Debatten" [Chief witnesses of the complaint? About the role of Muslim speakers in the contemporary Islam debates]. In *Politik der Zeugenschaft: Zur Kritik einer Wissenspraxis* [The politics of witnesshood: Critique of a knowledge practice], edited by Sibylle Schmidt, Sybille Krämer, and Ramon Voges, 331–352. Bielefeld: Transcript Verlag.

Silberman, Roxane, Richard Alba, and Irene Fournier. 2007. "Segmented Assimilation in

France? Discrimination in the Labour Market Against the Second Generation." *Ethnic and Racial Studies* 30(1):1–27.

Spielhaus, Riem. 2009. "Interessen Vertreten mit vereinter Stimme: Der Kopftuchstreit als Impuls für die Institutionalisierung des Islams in Deutschland" [Interests with a united voice: The headscarf conflict as an impulse for the institutionalization of Islam in Germany]. In *Der Stoff, aus dem Konflikte sind. Debatten um das Kopftuch in Deutschland, Österreich und der Schweiz* [The cloth that gives rise to conflicts: Headscarf debates in Germany, Austria, and Switzerland], edited by Sabine Berghahn and Petra Rostock, 413–437. Bielefeld: Transcript Verlag.

Spielhaus, Riem. 2011. *Wer ist hier Muslim? Die Entwicklung eines Islamischen Bewusstseins in Deutschland Zwischen Selbsidentifikation und Fremzubeschreibung.* [Who is Muslim here? The development of Islamic consciousness between self-identification and ascription to foreignness.] Würzberg: Ergon Verlag.

Spielhaus, Riem. 2012a. *Studien in der postmigrantischen Gesellschaft—eine kritische Auseinandersetzung* [Studies in the postmigrant society—A critical discussion]. Paper presented at the Bundesfachkongress Interkultur, October 26, Hamburg.

Spielhaus, Riem. 2012b. "Counter-Measures to Religious Discrimination: The Example of a Local Initiative in Berlin." In *Les discriminations religieuses en Europe: Droit et pratiques* [Religious discriminations in Europe: Rights and practices], edited by Frédérique Ast and Bernadette Duarte, 239–254. Paris: L'Harmattan.

Spivak, Gayatri Chakravorty. 1994. *Can the Subaltern Speak?* In *Colonial Discourse and Post-Colonial Theory,* edited by Patrick Williams and Laura Chrisman, 66–111. New York: Columbia University Press.

Statistisches Bundesamt. 2013. Bildungsstand der Bevölkerung [Educational status of the population]. At https://www.destatis.de/DE/Publikationen/Thematisch/BildungForsc hungKultur/Bildungsstand/BildungsstandBevoelkerung.html. Last accessed November 27, 2013.

Tarlo, Emma. 2010. *Visibly Muslim: Fashion, Politics, Faith.* Oxford, UK: Berg.

Triadafilopoulos, Triadafilos. 2012. *Becoming Multicultural: Immigration and the Politics of Membership in Canada and Germany.* Vancouver: University of British Columbia Press.

Tugal, Cihan. 2009. *Passive Revolution. Absorbing the Islamic Challenge to Capitalism.* Stanford, CA: Stanford University Press.

Turam, Berna. 2007. *Between Islam and the State: The Politics of Engagement.* Stanford, CA: Stanford University Press.

Ünal, Didem, and Dilek Cindoğlu. 2013. "Reproductive Citizenship in Turkey: Abortion Chronicles." *Women's Studies International Forum* 38:21–31.

van Bijsterveld, Sophie C. 2005. "Permissible Scope of Legal Limitations on the Freedom of Religion or Belief in the Netherlands." *Emory International Law Review* 19:929–987.

Van der Burg, Wibren. 2009. *Het ideaal van de neutrale staat: Inclusieve, exclusieve, and compenserende visies of godsdienst en cultuur* [The ideal of the neutral state: Inclusive, exclusive and compensatory visions of religion and culture]. The Hague: Boom Juridische Uitgevers.

van der Veer, Peter. 2006. "Pim Fortuyn, Theo van Gogh, and the Politics of Tolerance in the Netherlands." *Public Culture* 18(1):111–124.

van Nieuwkerk, Karen. 2004. "Veils and Wooden Clogs Don't Go Together." *Ethnos* 69(2):229–246.

Verhaar, Odile, and Sawitri Saharso. 2004. "The Weight of Context: Headscarves in Holland." *Ethical Theory and Moral Practice* 7(2):179–195.

Vertovec, Steven. 1996. "Muslims, the State and the Public Sphere in Britain." In *Muslim Communities in the New Europe,* edited by Gerd Nonneman, Tim Niblock, and Bogdan Sjazkowski, 167–186. London: Ithaca Press.

Vertovec, Steven. 2007. *New Complexities of Cohesion in Britain: Super-diversity, Transnationalism and Civil-Integration.* Report written for the Commission on Integration and Cohesion (CIC). At http://www.compas.ox.ac.uk/fileadmin/files/Publications/Reports/Vertovec%20-%20new_complexities_of_cohesion_in_britain.pdf. Last accessed July 9, 2013.

Vertovec, Steven. 2011. "The Cultural Politics of Nation and Migration." *Annual Review of Anthropology* 40:241–256.

von Blumenthal, Julia. 2009. *Das Kopftuch in der Landesgesetzgebung. Governance im Bundesstaat zwischen Unitarisierung und Föderalisierung* [The headscarf in federal state law: Governance in the federal state between unification and federalization]. Baden-Baden: Nomos.

Weber, Eugen. 1976. *Peasants into Frenchmen: The Modernization of Rural France, 1870–1914.* Stanford, CA: Stanford University Press.

Weil, Patrick. 2008. "Why the French Laïcité Is Liberal." *Cardozo Law Review* 30(6):2699–2714.

Weill, Nicolas. 2006. "What's in a Scarf? The Debate on Laïcité in France." *French Politics, Culture and Society* 24(1):59–73.

Wetenschappelijke Raad voor het Regeringsbeleid (WRR). 2007. *Identificatie met Nederland.* Amsterdam: Amsterdam University Press. At http://www.wrr.nl/fileadmin/nl/publicaties/PDF-Rapporten/Identificatie_met_Nederland.pdf. Last accessed October 7, 2007.

Wiltse, Evren Çelik. 2008. "The Gordian Knot of Turkish Politics: Regulating Headscarf Use in Public." *South European Society and Politics* 13(2):195–215.

Wimmer, Andreas. 2013. *Ethnic Boundary Making: Institutions, Power, Networks.* New York: Oxford University Press.

Wimmer, Andreas, and Nina Glick Schiller. 2002. "Methodological Nationalism and Beyond: Nation-State Building, Migration and the Social Sciences." *Global Networks,* 2(4):301–334.

Winter, Brownwyn. 2008. *Hijab and the Republic: Uncovering the French Headscarf Debate.* Syracuse, NY: Syracuse University Press.

Wise, Amanda, and Selvaraj Velayutham, eds. 2009. *Everyday Multiculturalism.* Houndsmills, UK: Palgrave Macmillan.

Wodak, Ruth, Rudolf de Cillia, and Martin Reisigl. 2009. *The Discursive Construction of National Identities.* Edinburgh: Edinburgh University Press.

Wouters, Cas. 1987. "Developments in the Behavioural Codes Between the Sexes: The Formalization of Informalization in the Netherlands, 1930–85." *Theory, Culture and Society* 4:405–427.

Yavuz, Hakan. 2009. *Secularism and Muslim Democracy in Turkey.* Cambridge, UK: Cambridge University Press.

Yavuz, Hakan. 2013. *Toward an Islamic Enlightenment: The Gülen Movement.* New York: Oxford University Press.

Yavuz, M. Hakan, and John L. Esposito, eds. 2003. *Turkish Islam and the Secular State: The Global Impact of Fethullah Gülen's Nur Movement.* New York: Syracuse University Press.

Ye'or, Bat. 2005. *Eurabia: The Euro-Arab Axis.* Madison, NJ: Farleigh Dickinson University Press.

Yükleyen, Ahmet. 2011. "State Policies and Islam in Europe: Milli Gorüs in Germany and the Netherlands." Workshop on Religion and Immigrant Integration in European Union Countries, University of Toronto, November 11.

Yükleyen, Ahmet, and Gökçe Yurdakul. 2011. "Islamic Activism and Immigrant Integration: Turkish Organizations in Germany." *Immigrants and Minorities* 29(1):64–85.

Yurdakul, Gökçe. 2006. "Secular Versus Islamist: The Headscarf Debate in Germany." In *Politics of Visibility: Young Muslims in European Public Spaces,* edited by Gerdien Jonker and Valérie Amiraux, 151–168. Bielefeld: Transcript Verlag.

Yurdakul, Gökçe. 2009. *From Guest Workers into Muslims: Turkish Immigrant Associations in Germany.* Newcastle, UK: Cambridge Scholars Press.

Yurdakul, Gökçe. 2010. "Governance Feminismus und Rassismus: wie führende Vertreterinnen von Immigranten die antimuslimische Diskussion in Westeuropa und Nordamerika befördern" [Governance feminism and racism: How immigrant women leaders promote anti-Muslim debates in Western Europe and North America]. In *Staatsbürgerschaft, Migration und Minderheiten. Inklusion und Ausgrenzungsstrategien im Vergleich* [Citizenship, migration and minorities: Inclusion and exclusion strategies in comparison], edited by Gökçe Yurdakul and Y. Michal Bodemann, 111–125. Wiesbaden: VS Verlag für Sozialwissenschaften.

Yurdakul, Gökçe, and Y. Michal Bodemann. 2006. "'We Don't Want to Be the Jews of Tomorrow': Jews and Turks in Germany After 9/11." *German Politics and Society* 24(2):44–67.

Yurdakul, Gökçe, and Anna Korteweg. 2013. "Gender Equality and Immigrant Integration: Honour Killing and Forced Marriage Debates in the Netherlands, Germany and Britain." *Women's Studies International Forum* 41(3):204–214.

Yuval-Davis, Nira. 1997. "Citizenship and Difference." In *Gender and Nation,* 68–88. London: Sage.

Yuval-Davis, Nira. 2006. "Intersectionality and Feminist Politics." *European Journal of Women's Studies* 13(3):193–209.

Yuval-Davis, Nira. 2011. *The Politics of Belonging: Intersectional Contestations.* London: Sage.

Yuval-Davis, Nira, Floya Anthias, and Eleonore Kofman. 2005. "Secure Borders and Safe Haven and the Gendered Politics of Belonging: Beyond Social Cohesion." *Ethnic and Racial Studies* 28(3):513–535.

Zhou, Min. 1997. "Segmented Assimilation: Issues, Controversies and Recent Research for the New Second Generation." *International Migration Review* 31(4):975–1008.

Zırh, Besim Can. 2012. "Yerelden Merkeze Erdoğan İktidarının 10. Yılında Türkiye'de Cemevleri Sorunu" [From the periphery to the center: The issue with *Cemevi* in the 10th anniversary of the Erdoğan government in Turkey]. *Birikim* 284:48–55.

Zolberg, Aristide, and Long Litt Woon. 1999. "Why Islam Is Like Spanish: Cultural Incorporation in Europe and the United States." *Politics and Society* 27(1):5–38.

Index

abstract individualism, 19–20, 22
Acar, Mustafa, 85–86
Action Committee of Muslim Women
(*Aktionsbündnis Muslimische Frauen*)
[Germany], 173
"active pluralism," 102, 109, 112
Adalet Partisi (Justice Party) [Turkey], 66
Afghanistan war (2001), 25
agency: Dutch Muslim women on wearing
headscarf as issue of, 110–112; headscarf
debate over Muslim women and their, 10,
34–35, 37
Ahmadiyya Muslim Jamaat (Germany), 153
Akgün, Lale, 157, 164
Akin, Fatih, 139
Ak Party (*Adalet ve Kalkinma Partisi*)
[Turkey]: balancing religious and
democratic messages, 68–70, 84; CHP's
call for removal from government of,
84–85, 95; Democratization Package of,
63, 64, 68–69, 86–87, 93, 94–95; failed
attempt to ban abortions by, 88; four
headscarf-wearing women legislators
for, 95; lack of pro-secular and religious
women solidarity within, 88; *Milli Görüş*
movement roots of, 68; position on the
headscarf issue by, 73–74; pro-religious
national narrative emerging through,
61; responses to Gezi protests by, 63;
social exclusion of headscarf-wearing

wives of, 80–81; Turkish news media
supporting, 76; women critical of the,
93–94; Women's Branch (*Ak Parti Kadın
Kolları*) of the, 90. *See also* Turkish
political parties
Albayrak, Nebahat, 106
Alemdaroğlu, Kemal, 80, 81
Alevis minority (Turkey), 64, 94
Alex W., 164–165
Algerian upheavals (1990s), 25
Alliot-Marie, Michèle, 45
Al Nisa (Dutch Muslim women organization),
129–131, 135
Amara, Fadela, 35
Amir-Moazami, Schirin, 141
Amirpur, Katajun, 171, 172
Anticapitalist Muslims (Turkey), 95
apartheid, 134
Arat, Necla, 83
Armenian minority (Turkey), 64
Arınç, Bülent, 84
Atatürk, Kemal, 57, 65, 76
"At Home in Europe: Muslims in Berlin"
(Mühe), 168
Atif, Fatima, 53–54
Auschwitz concentration camp, 177
Azough, Naïma, 106, 135

Baby Loup (Paris banlieu daycare), 53–54
Balkenende, Jan Peter, 126

237

viewing headscarf wearing women with patriotic French slogans on cheeks, 176; multiple articles on the Muslim headscarf issue (2003–2004), 38; as politically moderate, 18, 22; position in headscarf debate by, 22; on prominent women's support of headscarf ban, 35; reporting on Bouzar's argument for headscarf role in redefining Muslim identity, 32; supporting burka and niqub ban, 44. *See also* French newspapers

Moors, Annelies, 8, 100, 122, 185

Motherland Party (*Anavatan Partisi*) [Turkey], 72

Moussaïd, Ilham, 135; candidacy interpreted as freedom of expression, 53–54; examining the political candidacy of, 19, 50–51; *Le Monde* article on impact of candidacy of, 52; as representative of veiled women both laïc and feminist, 51–53, 56

Moussaoui, Mr., 44

Mühe, Nina, 168–169, 174

multiculturalism: Breivik's murder of seventy-seven Norwegians (2011) to fight, 119; British "mature multiculturalism" approach to, 178, 179; Canada's national narrative centering on, 180–182; comparing German and Dutch approaches to, 11–12; French state's task of guaranteeing "equal protection" against demands of, 20; German *Multikulti*, 146, 148; "the headscarf affair" as representative of dilemma of, 187; informing Dutch national belonging narrative, 19; not part of German policy, 140. *See also* difference; diversity

Mumcu, Uğur, 77

Muslim Canadian Congress, 181

"Muslimification of Muslims" (Amirpur), 171

Muslim-majority countries, 2–3

Muslim Voices (*Muslimische Stimmen*) [Germany], 156, 168, 172

Muslim women: active political participation in the Netherlands by, 106–107; art and humor used in dissent by Dutch, 129–135; *Behind the Walls: Women in Muslim Countries* study on, 90; examining headscarf debate role of, 7; French burka ban

and unintended stigmatization of, 48–50; French debate on burka as expression of oppression of, 21–22, 33–38, 45–48; German headscarf debate and pro-secular and feminist positions taken by, 160–164, 168–174; German "neighborhood mothers" (*Stadtteilmütter*), 177; headscarf ban argument on the dignity of, 37; how the media presents headscarf-wearing, 176–177; immigrant women as conduits of children's integration, 37; *Le Monde* article on Nadia, a veiled woman, 33–34; nonwearers among, 8, 9; NPNS charged with "educating" on not wearing burka or niqab, 42; sexual aggression against those living in the French *banlieues*, 35, 36; Turkish feminine national narrative on the new Republic, 89–95; veil as expression of oppression of, 21–22, 33–38, 45–48; Wilders on headscarf as sign of oppression of, 119–120. *See also* feminism; headscarves; Islam

Muslim Youth in Germany (*Muslimische Jugend in Deutschland*), 168

Myard, Jacques, 26

Nachtsheim, Katharina, 155

Nahles, Andrea, 148

national belonging: as being about demarcating difference, 3–4; comparative analysis of headscarf debates in context of, 2–3; each nations' unique and distinct sense of, 5–6; how "regular" people discuss, 7; messiness nature of, 4; national narratives and conflicts of, 3–7; questions focusing on, 2–3; rethinking transnationalism and, 184–187; social norms, values, and practices identified by, 4–5. *See also* belonging; citizenship; conflicts of belonging; *under names of specific countries*

national narratives: conflicts of belonging and changing, 4–7; how media images share and reinforce identity and, 6; made explicit when threatened, 175; multiculturalism at center of Canada's, 180–182; Muslim and non-Muslim politician roles in producing and changing, 12–13;